CONCISE
ENCYCLOPEDIA
OF HERALDRY

CONCISE ENCYCLOPEDIA OF HERALDRY

GUY CADOGAN ROTHERY

SENATE

Concise Encyclopedia of Heraldry

First published in 1915 as ABC of Heraldry by Stanley Paul & Co.

This edition published in 1994 by Senate, an imprint of Studio
Editions Ltd, Princess House, 50 Eastcastle Street, London
W1N 7AP, England

Copyright © this edition Studio Editions Ltd 1994

Reprinted 1995

ISBN 1 85958 049 1

Printed and bound in Guernsey by The Guernsey Press Co. Ltd

CONTENTS

CHAPTER   PAGE

INTRODUCTION vii

I. THE ORDINARIES 1

II. THE SUB-ORDINARIES 10

III. THE CROSS AND ITS VARIATIONS . . . 17

IV. ANIMALS: I. FOUR-FOOTED BEASTS . . . 35

V. ANIMALS: II. BIRDS 47

VI. FISH, AMPHIBIA, OPHIDIA AND INSECTS . . 57

VII. FABULOUS CREATURES 64

VIII. THE HUMAN FORM AND ITS PARTS . . . 78

IX. CELESTIAL CHARGES 91

X. COMMON CHARGES 99

XI. PLANTS AND FLOWERS 120

XII. MARSHALLING 136

XIII. DIFFERENCING AND MARKS OF CADENCY . . 147

XIV. CANTING ARMS 159

XV. THE FLEUR-DE-LIS AND ITS VARIATIONS . . 165

XVI. THE ROSE 179

XVII. THE IRISH HARP IN HERALDRY . . . 191

v

vi

CHAPTER		PAGE
XVIII.	FEATHERS AND HORNS	198
XIX.	SHIELDS AND THEIR OUTER ORNAMENTS .	205
XX.	CRESTS, HELMS AND BADGES . . .	213
XXI.	CROWNS, CORONETS AND CAPS . . .	231
XXII.	SUPPORTERS	242
XXIII.	COCKADES AND LIVERIES: THEIR USE AND ABUSE	259
XXIV.	ROYAL ARMS OF ENGLAND AND OF THE UNITED KINGDOM	270
XXV.	ARMS OF THE OVERSEAS DOMINIONS AND COLONIES	282
XXVI.	STANDARDS, BANNERS AND FLAGS . . .	289
XXVII.	BRITISH FLAGS	294
XXVIII.	FLAGS OF VARIOUS NATIONS	300
XXIX.	HERALDS' COLLEGE	312
XXX.	HERALDRY IN THE APPLIED ARTS . . .	316
XXXI.	GLOSSARY	322
	INDEX	341

INTRODUCTION

ALTHOUGH the origin of heraldry cannot be traced with certainty, yet it is clear that the adoption of tribal, national and personal badges began in prehistoric times ; at all events we find traces of such a custom even in the rude remains of forgotten races. Hence some writers trace the beginning of heraldry very far back indeed. No doubt this may be justified if we look for the germs of the art, which certainly adds enormously to the interest of our study. In Greek sculpture, in the paintings and incised designs traced on ancient pottery, we find a number of well-defined symbols constantly associated with mythical or historical heroes, as well as with races of people. Often these symbols are borne on shields, adorn helmets or standards, just in the style so common in our own middle ages, in China and Japan, and, indeed, even among semi-barbarian and savage tribes. All the gods had their special attributive symbols, and these were so far hereditary that they were adopted by their demi-god terrestrial "sons" and "daughters." Much the same condition of things prevailed in connection with Roman and Etruscan social conditions. This adoption of symbols was also carried very far by the Assyrians, Hittites and other Asiatic peoples. In Egypt, not only were there symbols for individual rulers, but family badges common to the several dynasties, and the kingly and priestly sons of the great gods also bore the divine symbols. Moreover, each territorial division had its elaborate symbol, usually combining naturalistic plant and animal forms with purely conventional designs, while the lotus stood as the peculiar attribute of Northern Egypt, and the papyrus of the Southern regions, the union of the two parts of the fertilising Nile being represented by the intertwining of the stems of these plants in intricate knots. Symbolism, being co-eval with the first glimmerings of human intelligence, is a thing of natural evolution, erratic in its modes of growth, and in its essentials independent of time or clime. However, the heralds, having made symbols their chief props, it is necessary to attempt more or less systematic tracings of the Protean manifestations peculiar to particular emblems. This aspect of the subject will be dealt with more fittingly when the different heraldic charges are under discussion.

SHIELD FROM GREEK VASE.

For our immediate purpose, it must be remembered that heraldry strictly so-called only became a science when laws were laid down for its guidance, and when the various symbols adopted were recognised as hereditary. It seems certain that this did not come about until the eleventh century, when nobles fought in armour, and each led his particular body of retainers into the field. In this quite restricted sense, the Emperor Frederick Barbarossa is believed to be the real father of the art. Even long after his day nobles were allowed to do much as they listed in the matter of adopting and varying coat armour. In England, although two heralds, Norroy and Surroy, were appointed by Edward I and Clarencieux by Henry IV in 1411, it was not until the reign of Henry V that proclamation was made forbidding any one to assume armorial bearings without permission from the King or his heralds. It was the Earl Marshal's Court which upheld this law, though the King himself was the final authority. However, it was not until some centuries later that Heralds' Visitations to enforce its rulings were instituted. During these visitations the heralds went round from town to town, summoning all knights, esquires and gentlemen to appear and register their arms, all marriages, births, deaths, and other family events. These visitations took place at irregular intervals, eaeh circuit lasting for about eighteen months to two years. The records of these journeys are mines of information, though perhaps not so interesting as the older Rolls of Arms, giving metrical or prose descriptions of bearings of knights at various periods. The paintings on some of these Rolls demonstrate the great flexibility of practice in those days, together with the growing tendency to crystallise vague guiding principles into exact rules.

Henry V was a great patron of heraldry ; he instituted the office of Garter King of Arms, and as his pursuivant, Blue Mantle. It was also during his reign that coat armour became regularly hereditary, and descended from father to son, the eldest alone wearing the shield as his father did before him ; the younger ones having to make some difference, such as adding a border, or using other marks of cadency. The oldest coats-of-arms are generally very plain, and have few charges besides the Ordinaries. With time, owing to this practice of the younger branches of a family accumulating charges, altering the outlines of others, changing their colour, and assuming ornamented borders, while simple knights often accepted the privilege of placing on their shields some charge from the armorials of their overlords, the great feudal chiefs, heraldry became more complicated.

Sir James Lawrence, speaking of heraldry and nobility, in his " Nobility of the British Gentry," thus explains the original use of, and the different methods of obtaining, armorial bearings : " Any individual who distinguished himself may be said to ennoble himself. A prince judging an individual worthy of notice gave him patent letters of nobility. In these letters were emblazoned the arms that were to distinguish his shield. By this shield he was to be known, or *nobilis*. A plebeian had no blazonry on his shield, because he was *ignobilis*, or unworthy of notice. Hence arms are the criterion of nobility. Whoever has a shield of arms is a nobleman. In every country in Europe, without exception, a grant of arms, or letters patent of nobility, is conferred on all the descendants." Thus it will be seen that the essential part of heraldry to chivalry was the hereditary character of coat armour. It may be as well to explain that this appellation of a coat-of-arms originated from the practice of embroidering the family insignia on the surcoat, a garment worn over the armour or shirt of mail. These surcoats in later times were used only by heralds, by whom they are still worn, when on official duties, and by pages and menials of princely or noble houses. But arms were not only seen on the surcoat. They appeared on the caparisons of a knight's horse, on his shield and other accoutrements, were embroidered on the wall hangings of the castle hall, and lent greater authority to his engraved seal.

SEAL AND COUNTER SEAL, GEOFFROI DE CHATEAUBRIAND, BRITTANY, 1217.

From the arms of the head of the State to arms of concession, there are altogether ten degrees : First, arms of dominion, or national armorial bearings borne by sovereigns. Secondly, we have arms of pretension, or armorial bearings adopted by sovereigns of kingdoms or provinces over which they are actually reigning. (If a man marries an heiress, he is entitled to wear her arms in an escutcheon of pretence placed over his own, but this properly belongs to the eighth degree.) Thirdly, arms of community, such as the arms of bishops' sees, of towns, universities, colleges and corporate bodies.

Fourthly, arms of patronage, which are arms of community worn by the occupants of various offices of responsibility and dignity. Fifthly, arms of succession ; arms borne by the inheritors of fiefs, manors, either by will or donation. Sixthly, arms of assumption, when a victor adopts the whole or part of the insignia of the vanquished. A sub-division of arms of assumption, also known as arms of pretension, are those borne by a non-ruling claimant to territorial dignities. Seventhly, paternal arms ; the arms descending from father to son. Eighthly, arms of alliance ; arms borne in a shield of pretence by the husband of an heiress and then quartered by the descendants in order to show their descent. Ninthly, arms of adoption, borne by strangers in blood in accordance with the wishes laid down by will or other legal mode of donation, or arms borne by an adopted child of the original bearer ; but before adoption express permission must be obtained from the sovereign. And, tenthly, arms of concession ; armorial bearings ; parts of armorial bearings ; or special charges given by a sovereign to a subject. These last arms or charges are also commonly known as augmentations.

During the Heralds' Visitations two chief claims to the right to bear arms were recognised : (1) the claim to ownership of certain bearings by repute, (2) the right to bear by a direct grant. Evidence as to ownership by repute was either aural, as most of it was in the celebrated case of Sir Richard le Scrope against Sir Robert Grosvenor before the High Court of Chivalry, which was commenced in August 1385, with revised judgment delivered by King Richard II in 1390 ; or according to evidence afforded by seals, banners or monuments ; or that afforded by the Rolls. These last are a series of most interesting documents, in the form of long rolls of parchment, giving blazonings of arms borne by different individuals at certain events (such as the metrical description in Norman-French of the siege of Carlaverock, a Scottish border stronghold taken by Edward I in 1300, with an account of the arms of the great nobles and knights present). There are many of these Rolls, but none older than a little before the middle of the thirteenth century.

Grants of arms were made by the King or his deputy, the Earl Marshal, or his deputies, the Heralds, and were recorded on formal parchment documents. It is probable that up to the reign of Richard II the great territorial lords still preserved their feudal privilege of bestowing armorial bearings on their vassals and friends. In modern practice all arms are, or should be, borne by grace of a Grant or a Confirmation, issued by the College of Arms in England, the Lyon Office in Scotland, or Ulster King of Arms in Ireland, with the direct sanction of the Crown. Unless there is direct and clear evidence of a coat-of-arms having descended from father to son since a grant was made, or an entry recorded in one of the Visitations, persons before using arms are supposed to present a properly authenticated pedigree to the heralds, and then obtain a confirmation to their right to wear the coat-of-arms they claim. Persons receiving certain high honours, or offices of honour, from the Crown, must have arms, and then, if they and their immediate ascendants, have not borne arms, a search, involving genealogical work, is made to connect the person with some recorded coat. If no clear connection can be established, then a grant is made. But anybody who desires can make an application for a grant of arms, and if certain conditions are fulfilled a grant will be issued. In making these new grants, it has been too often the habit to bestow on an applicant, if not the identical coat of an old family of the same name, then some " colourable imitation thereof," even though the applicant cannot prove alliance. All new grants ought to be thoroughly distinctive to avoid misconceptions. This point will be clearly understood on referring to Chapter XIII on " Differences and Marks of Cadency," where the early principles of recording heraldically blood and feudal relationships are shown.

There are three principal divisions of coat armour—the field (or ground), the tinctures (metals, colours, and furs) and the charges or symbols.

The field is the ground of the shield or banner, and for the better description or blazoning of armorial bearings the shield has been divided into several parts.

It must first be explained that in describing armorial bearings, it is always assumed that they are on a shield or surcoat borne by the owner, and the description is from the wearer's point of view. Thus what the ordinary spectator regards as the left side of a shield is known to the herald as the dexter side, while the right becomes the heraldic sinister. This must always be kept in mind when blazoning is in question. We may now pass on to the divisions of the shield. These are : (B) Middle Chief, or middle of the upper part ; (A) Dexter Chief (left upper part) ; (C) Sinister Chief (right upper part) ; (E) Fess Point, or middle of the shield ; (D) Honour Point, between the Fess Point and the Middle Chief ; (H) Middle Base, or lower point of field ; (G) Dexter Base (left lower part) ; (I) Sinister Base (right lower part). With the complications introduced into feudal heraldry during the fifteenth century and

POINTS OF THE
SHIELD.

onwards, such minutæ as these became very necessary in order to avoid confusion, but they also tended to overlay the science with many fanciful notions as to the most honoured parts of a field, notions which most assuredly did not exist to worry knights in the days when heraldry was most simple, beautiful and important.

The surface of the shield may be divided by a horizontal, perpendicular, or diagonal line ; or by a combination of these lines. A field thus divided is said to be " per " or " party per," with the descriptive epithet following. A field divided by a horizontal line is said to be " per fess " ; by a vertical line, " per pale " ; by a diagonal line, " per bend " or " per bend sinister," as the case may be ; by an upright line and a horizontal line, " per cross " or " quarterly " ; by the right and left diagonal lines, " per saltire " ; if the lower parts of the right and left bends are brought to the honour point, the shield is divided " per chevron," which the French heralds term "mantelé." A field divided in three parts by two horizontal lines is " tierced per fess " ; if the lines are perpendicular the field is " tierced per pale." A field may be (though this is rare in practice) divided per fess and bend, or per pale and bend. A field divided per fess, per pale, per bends dexter and sinister is said to be " gyrony." A field may be borne " paly," divided by a number of perpendicular lines ; " barry," divided by a number of horizontal lines ; " lozengy " or " fusily," divided by a number of lines from left to right crossing others from right to left ; " paly-bendy," perpendicular lines crossed by diagonal lines ; or " barry-bendy," if

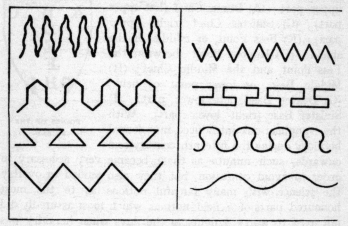

LINES OF DIVISION : RAYONNY ; URDY ; DOVETAILED ; DANCETE ;
INDENTED ; POTENTÉ ; NEBULÉ ; WAVY.

divided by horizontal and diagonal lines ; if divided by horizontal lines crossed by perpendicular lines it is said to be " chequy " or " checky "; if by a series of wedges, it is " pily," or, as some rather unnecessarily term it, " pily counter-pily." It should be noted that if the space between two horizontal lines (forming a fess) is divided into squares, alternately of metal and colour, it is said to be compony or gobony ; if there are two such rows, it is said to be counter-compony ; if three or more, then it is chequy. All these terms will be better understood after a perusal of the next two chapters.

The divisional lines described above may be either straight or variously shaped ; such as an " embattled " line, also em-

battled grady, a " potenté " line (like the Greek key pattern),
" wavy " (or " undée "), " indented," " invected," " nebulé,"
(or cloud-like), " urdy," " danceté," " embattled," " raguly "
(which is a line with the
battlements at a slant),
"dove-tailed," " en-
grailed " or " bevilled."
Such lines of demarcation
are also used in drawing
certain classes of charges.

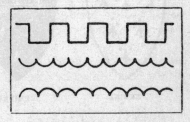

LINES OF DIVISION : EMBATTLED ;
ENGRAILED ; INVECTED.

The tinctures comprise
two metals, nine colours
(five of which are in
general use), and three furs, with their variations. The terms
employed to describe them in formal heraldic language are
old French. Some heralds (of the seventeenth century),
in order to give additional importance to the science, as
they thought, invented the plan of emblazoning the arms
of peers and peeresses with the names of precious stones,
and those of sovereigns and princes with the names of planets
and other heavenly bodies instead of using the ordinary terms
for tinctures. In drawings or engravings these colours are
represented by dots and differently arranged lines, an invention ascribed by some to Colombière, and by other authorities
to Silvestro di Pietrasancta, who both flourished during the
seventeenth century. When the colours are not represented
by lines, numerals or symbols are adopted instead.

TINCTURES

1. Gold   .   Or, represented by dots. . . .
                 Topaz.
                 Sol, represented by o.

2. Silver   .   Argent, represented by a plain surface.
                 Crystal.
                 Luna, represented by ☽.

3. Red   .   Gules, represented by perpendicular lines.
                 Ruby.
                 Mars, represented by ♂.

ERMINE.

ERMINES.

PEAN.

ERMINE.

VAIR.

POTENT COUNTER
POTENT.

VAIR.

COUNTER VAIR.

POTENT.

COUNTER POTENT.

FURS.

xvi

4. Blue . Azure, represented by horizontal lines.
   Sapphire.
   Jupiter, represented by ♃.

5. Black . Sable, represented by perpendicular and horizontal lines crossing each other.
   Diamond.
   Saturn, represented by ♄.

6. Green . Vert or sinople, represented by lines from dexter chief to sinister base.
   Emerald.
   Venus, represented by ♀.

7. Purple . Purpure, represented by lines from sinister chief to dexter base.
   Amethyst.
   Mercury, represented by ☿.

There are four additional colours sometimes mentioned by heralds, which, however, are seldom used except for special charges, external accessories and for liveries. These colours are " sanguine " or " murrey "—a deep blood-red (sardonyx, Dragon's Tail), represented by lines from dexter chief to sinister base ; and " tenné " or " orange " (hyacinth, Dragon's Head), represented by lines from sinister to dexter base, crossed by horizontal lines ; and flesh colour, sometimes called " carnation." Bleue celeste, a light sky blue ; an ashen grey and brown are also, though rarely, seen.

The furs are " ermine," white with black spots, and its four modifications—" ermines," black with silver spots ; " erminetes," black with white spots ; " erminois," black with gold spots ; and " pean," gold with black spots. The ermine spot varies a good deal, but the most usual form is like an inverted clove, with three sepals showing, and three dots, one and two, above. " Vair " is represented by blue and white shields, or glasses, in horizontal rows, the bases of the white resting on the base of the blue. This fur has also one modification, which is termed " counter-vair," in which the glasses of one colour are placed base to base. " Vair " is always emblazoned argent and azure, and counter vair, or and azure. If other tinctures are used, they must be specified. "Potent " is represented by crutch-shaped charges; it is emblazoned argent and azure, the base of one colour being placed on the base of one of metal; and its modifications " counter-potent," sometimes termed " vairy-cuppy," which is of the same tinctures as " potent," but the crutch-shaped charges of one colour have their bases placed against the bases of one of the same colour; and " potent, counter-potent " in which the arrangement is different. Here again, if other colours are used, the tinctures must be specially named.

In describing a shield, the tincture of the field should be first mentioned. A shield may be parti-coloured, as we have seen when describing the divisions. For instance, a shield divided down the middle by a perpendicular line, the left side green (vert), and the right red (gules), would be described thus : Party per pale gules and vert. It is a strict general rule that metal must not be placed on metal, or colour on colour. That is to say, if the field is of gold or silver, the charges thereon must be of colour or fur. However, many exceptions are allowed. Thus a parti-tinctured shield, where both metal and colour are used, or a fur-covered field, may bear charges of either metal or colour. On the other hand, if the parti field is half metal and half colour, it is usual to " counter-change "

ST. BARTHOLOMEW'S HOSPITAL, LONDON.

the charges. Thus the arms of St. Bartholomew's Hospital are : per pale argent and sable a fess counter-changed, which are the arms also assigned to Geoffrey Chaucer, the father of English poetry, with the tinctures altered to argent and gules. Rodenstein, a German feudal leader of the early fourteenth century, bore : per pale or and gules, a fess counterchanged. Then again, the accessories of a charge are not subject to such a rule. For instance, a silver or gold lion, or other animal, may have tongue and claws of red or blue, if the field be blue or red, while if the field is gold or silver, the coloured beast may have tongue and claws of silver or gold. Crowns, coronets, chains attached to animals are also free from the general law. So are marks of cadency. Occasionally arms violating this rule are found. These are what Continental heralds call " armes à enquirire," arms to be inquired about, as being exceptional. Such are the arms of the Kingdom of Jerusalem, first bestowed on Geoffrey de Bouillon : argent, a cross potent between four crosses, all or.[1]

While discussing this point something may be said of diapering, though this will be described more at length at a later stage. Diapering is a method of decorating plain surfaces by tracing thereon a faint design of a running floral or geometrical pattern. These patterns are often quite complicated, but they must be subordinate to the general design, as they are non-essential and merely ornamental. They are of importance just here, because often enough this diapering of thin outline running patterns may be carried out in silver upon gold, or gold upon silver, even red on blue, or blue on red, and so on. As a matter of fact this is not an infraction of the general rule, because the diaper had no heraldic value, and being non-essential is regarded as non-existent except from the purely decorative point of view.

Gold may be represented by yellow, and silver by white, but even when this is so, they are regarded as metals.

The sixteenth and seventeenth century heralds appear to have paid some attention to the symbolical attributes of colour in designing arms, and no doubt this was to a certain extent a ruling motive of the eleventh to thirteenth century man in selecting so largely the royal gold, the martial red, and the celestial blue.

---

[1] Some writers state that the five crosses represented the wounds of Christ, and that they were originally emblazoned gules, which gave a better colour symbolism. The crosses were subsequently changed to gold so as to make the bearings a striking contrast to any other royal or feudal shield.

" In a symbol there is concealment and yet revelation . . . there is ever, more or less distinctly and directly, some embodiment and revelation of the Infinite ; the Infinite is made to blend itself with the Finite, to stand, visible, and as it were, attainable there."—THOMAS CARLYLE, " Sartor Resartus."

CHAPTER I

THE ORDINARIES

A CERTAIN class of what may justly be called the fundamentals of heraldic ornament appear to be little else than structural parts of the shield, slightly developed for decorative and distinctive purposes.

These include at least eight of those bands—horizontal, perpendicular, diagonal and their combinations—which have been called the Ordinaries, or the Honourable Ordinaries, and are generally held, by the most competent of the old heraldic authorities, to be ten in number.

It is quite true that even in remote times some of these had assumed a distinctly symbolic form, as we shall see, but their origin seems unquestionably to belong to the reign of structural members, developed and embellished. Now, at the dawn of heraldic science, as these ordinaries already existed on the escutcheons of the principal nobles, and indeed on nearly all of the earlier coats-of-arms, the heralds, who were appointed for the purpose of introducing a little order and method in the science, classed them as the first and highest order of heraldic charges. It is hardly astonishing to find that nearly every one of these ten different charges has a special meaning or legend attached to it.

One of the greatest contrasts between the earlier and probably the best period of the art—say from the eleventh

century to the thirteenth century—and the growing alliance
between ill-regulated invention and extravagant formalism
which began with the sixteenth and lasted to the middle of
the nineteenth century, is the simplicity of the primitive
specimens, compared with the overcrowded, out-of-balance
compositions of the decadence. Naturally enough, the en-
lightened attach a particular value to the escutcheon according to its simplicity, as the escutcheon of the younger branches
of a family often had new ad-
ditions to distinguish them
from the elder.

ROCHESTER

In later times, however, with
us, as also on the Continent,
the escutcheon was valued by
the number of charges, in
many cases the ordinaries as
well as the field being heavily
charged. In English heraldry
it was always allowable to
emblazon the honourable ordinaries with almost any common or minor charge, but the
practice is not so much re-
sorted to as on the Continent.
Throgmorton bears : gules, on
a chevron argent, three bars gemells sable ; and Trenowith,
Cornwall, argent, on a fess sable, three chevronels couched
sinister silver. The Count of Neuburg bore : or, on a pale
gules three chevrons argent. Many of the ordinaries are
borne " over all," that is to say, they are placed across the
charged field. If the charge happens to be an animal, it is
said to be " debruised." If one ordinary is borne across
another, then the term " surmounted " is used.

The principal ordinary is the " chief " ; it occupies the
upper part of the shield and should fill a third of the surface
of the field. In many old writers this upper part of the
shield is alluded to as the " Sovereign."

Each ordinary has a certain number of diminutives, or

modifications of the parent charge. In the case of the "chief," its diminutive is the "fillet," one-fourth of the chief, and is always placed in the lower portion of the "chief." A chief may be borne on a field with any other ordinary except the fess or its diminutive, the bar. In practice it is usual to allow rather less than a third of the field for the chief, to distinguish the bearing more readily from a field divided per fess, which cuts the shield horizontally in two. Most of the other ordinaries, though supposedly occupying a third of the field, are slightly under their allowance.

The "pale," second in importance, is a band, occupying one-third of the shield, from top to bottom. Its diminutives are the "palet," half the size of the pale, and the "endorse," which is half the size of the palet.[1] The word endorse comes from the French *endorse*, to place back to back. A pale when emblazoned between two endorses is said to be "endorsed" or "indorsed." A pale between its two endorses is sometimes said to be "cotised," but erroneously, as will be seen on perusal of the following paragraph. A curious variation of the pale is seen in the arms of d'Aussez, Normandy : argent, on a chief azure three martlets of the first, a saw blade in pale, the teeth to the sinister. That is to say, a pale with the sinister side invected. From France also we have a modification of the palet, De Briez bearing : or three palets couped and fitchy at foot gules. This gives us three stakes.

The "bend" represents a band, one-third of the shield, crossing from the dexter chief to the sinister base. The bend has three diminutives ; they are the "bendlet" (sometimes called a "garter"), the "cotice," and the "ribbon." A shield divided into several parts by lines "in bend" is said to be "coticed." When a bend is charged with symbols, these take the diagonal trend of the ordinary—they are placed on the slant.

---

[1] In every case the first diminutive ought to be one-half of its parent charge ; the second one-half of the first ; the third one-half of the second. This rule does not apply to the chief, the saltire, or the quarter.

4

The "bend sinister" is the bend, or bend dexter, reversed,
coming from the sinister chief to the dexter base. The
"scarpe" and the "baton" are its diminutives. The baton,
variously called "baston" and "batoon," is the charge used
by heralds as a mark of bastardy.[1] It is sometimes borne
"couped," when its extremities do not touch the sides of
the shield. This was a special privilege, and at one time

rarely conceded, except to the illegitimate
offspring of royalty. Another mode of
lessening the disgrace of this charge was to
have it reversed, a privilege conferred only
in extraordinary cases. After the bravery
displayed on the battlefield against the
English by John the Bastard of Orleans,
Charles VII allowed him to turn his baton
from sinister to dexter. A like boon was
granted to the Earl of Murray by his sister,

BEND.

Mary Queen of Scots. More on this subject will be found
in the chapter on "Differences and Marks of Cadency."
Gelre gives the arms of Raman von Konigstein as : per
bend or and sable, the upper half of a bend sinister argent.

The "fess" is a horizontal band in the middle of the
shield, and occupies one-third of its surface. It was supposed to represent the waistband, one of the symbols of
knighthood or high military command. The officers' and
non-commissioned officers' scarves, still worn in our army, are
relics of this ancient scarf of authority. But as a matter of
fact the fess is one of the constructural members of the shield.
The "bar," the "closet," and the "barrulet," this last always
borne in couples, are the diminutives of this charge.

The "chevron" is formed by two bands rising from the
sides of the shield and meeting in a point in the centre. It is
one of the charges formerly given to younger members of
families, and is highly prized. In English heraldry the lower

[1] The term "bastard bar" has been popularly, but erroneously,
given to this symbol; the bar is a diminutive of the "fess," and
therefore the term "bar" cannot be applied to the diminutive of the
"bend sinister."

lines of the chevron commence just above its dexter and
sinister base, and the apex ends about the honour point.
In Continental practice, this ordinary commences from a
lower point and rises higher, so becoming more acute.
Roughly it may be said to be composed of the lower halves
of the bend and the bend sinister conjoined in chief. A
chevron is sometimes borne " rompu en pointe," that is
broken at the apex ; or " coupé," cut off from the sides of the
shield. The diminutives are the " chevronel " and the
" couple-close," which last is always borne in couples, and
often one on each side of the chevron, when the chevron is
said to be " couple-closed." When the field is covered with
couple-closes it is said to be chevronée. Sometimes a chevron

CHEVRON, WITH SINISTER   CHEVRON, PATÉE AT
CANTON.   POINT.

is borne reversed, as in the arms of the town of Newport :
azure a chevron reversed, or. A chevron and a chevron
reversed, interlaced, form a curious kind of saltire, probably
due to the amalgamation of two coats. It is seen in the
shield of Lagrenée : gules, a chevron or interlaced with a
chevron reversed argent. Many heralds hold that the chevron represents the principal rafters of a gable roof, to which
the term is still applied in the French language, and hence it
is an appropriate charge for the founders of a family ; another
theory is that it symbolically represents a park gate. Really
it belongs to the class of structural strengthenings, and
symbolically it appears to form a section of the extremely
ancient and widespread wavy line (found in Rome and
Greece, in Asia, Africa and America) representing water.
Indeed, it is notable that the pale, the fess, the bend and the

chevron, either argent, azure or sable, often appear on the shields of towns noted for their rivers, or on those of men who have won fame by their connection with rivers or the sea.

The following bearings of the chevron and its diminutives are of special interest. Among the feudal coats we find : Berkeley : gules, a chevron argent ; Clare : or, three chevronels gules ; Fitzwalter : or, a fess between two chevrons gules. Tourney bore : or, a chevron couched dexter gules ; whilst Bightine bore : purpure, a chevron couched sinister, or ; Holbeame : argent, a chevron inarched sable ; that is, supported by an arch. Robert Fitz-Hugh, Bishop of London, 1431–1436, bore : argent, three chevronels braced (or interlaced) in base or ; a chief of gold ; De la Rochefoucauld : barry argent and azure, over all three chevronels or, the top one couped at the summit. Von Viseleben had their shield chevronée reversed argent and gules.

The " cross " is a combination of the pale and the fess ; it is a favourite and much-valued charge. The ornamentation of heraldic crosses is so extraordinarily varied that this " honourable ordinary " is deserving of, and considered in, a chapter by itself.

The " saltire " is formed by bend dexter and bend sinister conjoined, and is also dealt with at length in the chapter on " Crosses."

ARGENT, A CHEVRON SURMOUNTED BY A PILE, BOTH SABLE, PIERCED OF THE FIELD.

The " pile " is in the form of a wedge, the point downwards. Its proper size is one-third of the shield in its upper part, but if it is charged its broadest end fills up two-thirds of the shield. A pile may be borne " transposed," that is to say, with the point uppermost. It may also come at a slant from the dexter or sinister chief, or dexter or sinister base. Sometimes two, or three, piles may be borne ; then their points do not reach the base of the shield. If there are three piles, they are now usually blazoned as " in point," that is to say, there is a thin wedge from the centre chief, and other wedges slanting from the dexter and sinister chiefs, their points almost meeting. A very broad pile used, especially in Continental practice, to take a coat-of-arms in marshalling, is called by the French a " chausse," and if reversed a " chape," while a reduced chape is a " chaperonne." Shields so divided are said to be " chaussé," " chapé " and " chaperonné."

The tenth and last Honourable Ordinary is the " quarter," which occupies the upper dexter portion of the shield, consisting of one-fourth of its surface. It has one diminutive, the " canton," occupying one-eighth of the shield.

All the above charges may be " voided," a term applied to a charge when it has its centre removed, showing the field through it. The " voiding " may be of any shape ; a cross is voided " per cross," " per pale," or " per fess " ; but in such a case the shape of the voiding must be specially mentioned, otherwise it would mean that the charge was " voided " of its own shape. Mr. Mark A. Lower, the author of " Curiosities of Heraldry," says that this custom of voiding was adopted because the bearers had lost their patrimonies, and retained only the " shadow " of their ancient greatness. But there appears to be no evidence of this. As a rule voiding is either the result of charging one ordinary with another of its kind, either for the purpose of differencing, or for recording alliances ; or the adoption of an embroidered ornament. We constantly find modifications of this kind being introduced by painters or sculptors more intent in securing effective results than observing technical rules.

The terms " in pale," " in bend," etc., when applied to common charges, denote that they are borne disposed in the form of the ordinary mentioned. We have already seen that a shield is said to be " paly," " bendy," etc., when it is divided by several lines in the form of the ordinary mentioned, the number of divisions being also specified with the tinctures ; the first division being of the first-named, the second of the second, and so on alternately. As also already mentioned a shield may be divided " per pale," " per bend," etc., when it is of two different tinctures and divided in the shape of the ordinary. The term " tierced " is applied to a shield which is divided into three parts ; it may be either " tierced in fess," " in pale," " in bend," " in bend sinister," or " in pall " (also called " en pairle "), according to the form of

THREE SHOVELS EN PAIRLE.

BOULOGNE-SUR-SEINE : PARTY
PER BEND SINISTER.

the three parts. German and French partition lines are occasionally extraordinarily complicated, forming odd geometrical patterns. For instance, we may have " party per pale potenté and per bend engrailed."

When any ordinary is pierced by a square hole it is said to be " square-pierced " ; but if, in the case of a cross, the whole of the intersecting portion is removed it is termed a cross " quarterly-pierced." Ordinaries may be simply " pierced," *i.e.*, pierced with a round hole, and also " lozenge-pierced." As with the chevron all ordinaries are often borne " couped," that is to say, they have their extremities cut off, and so do not touch the sides of the

MANCHESTER : BENDLETS
ENHANCED.

shield ; some of them may also be " broken," or " rompu," when the ends instead of being cut off with a smooth edge are torn off and present a ragged edge. A fess, a pale and a bend may be borne " engoulé," that is to say, ending in the mouth of man or beast, placed at the edge of the shield, but within the field. Three of these charges, a fess, a bend and a chevron, together with their diminutive, may be borne " enhanced," that is, higher than the fess point, their proper place. This is the case with the three golden bendlets of Manchester, borne enhanced on a red field. They may also be borne " debased," that is lower than their proper position. On the feudal coat of Fitzwalter, described above, the chevron is borne both enhanced and debased.

CHAPTER II

THE SUB-ORDINARIES

THE Sub-Ordinaries, charges of lesser degree and supposedly of less antiquity than the honourable ordinaries, are sometimes stated to be twelve in number and sometimes more, the principal authorities disagreeing as to how many and what charges should be included under this denomination. Many of these—the fret and the border, for instance—partake, like the ordinaries, of a structural character—strengthenings of the shield ; but others are more markedly distinctive or symbolical in origin.

The " gyron " (from *gyrus*, a circle) is a term applied to a shield when it is quartered and divided per cross and per saltire, each division being alternately of metal and of colour. An ordinary gyron is called " gyron of eight," but it may be a gyron of only six, or of ten or twelve.   Somewhat akin to

GYRON.

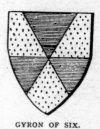

GYRON OF SIX.

this is that very curious device known as a " whirlpool," " gurge " or " gorge," a blue spiral ribbon, starting from the fess point and circling round until it covers the silver field. Quite an old type was represented by a series of diminishing rings, one within the other.   A gurge is always argent and azure, unless other tinctures are specially mentioned. Both the gyron and the gurge are met with among quite primitive symbols in most parts of the world, and generally seem to have reference to elemental phenomena, seasonal changes, movement, whirlpools.

The "fret" is a combination of the baton and the cotise, interlaced by a lozenge. If the shield is covered with lattice-work it is termed "fretty," or "fretty cloué" when instead

FRET WITH PELLETS
AT EACH POINT.

FRET, FLORY AT
EACH POINT.

FRET WITH FOUNTAINS
IN CLAIR-VOIES.

of being interlaced the dexter lattice is placed over the sinister bars and nailed. Certain charges, such as swords and lances, may be borne in trellis. For instance, the ancient Provençal family of De Villeneuve bear: gules, six golden lances in trellis, semée of inescutcheons, or. The terms "treille" and "trellis" are also used. The interspaces are sometimes termed clair-voies.

FRET.

FRET COUPED.

CHEQUY GULES AND AR-
GENT, AN INESCUTCHEON
ARGENT.

The "inescutcheon" is a small shield borne as a charge. It is usually placed in the fess-point, but must not be confounded with a shield of pretence. Three or more inescutcheons may be borne. Both the Scottish Hays and the Norman de Villiers bear three inescutcheons of gules on a field of silver.

The " border " or " bordure " is a broad band encircling the shield ; it is borne both plain and charged, and has been made of great use in distinguishing cadency and in differencing arms, as will be shown in Chapter XIII. Some heralds have enumerated the border with the honourable ordinaries. Its diminutives are two. The " orle," which, unlike the " border," does not touch the edges of the shield, is also described as an " inescutcheon voided " or a " false inescutcheon." The idea thus expressed is that the orle is really an inescutcheon with the centre removed. In Continental

BORDER.　　　　　ORLE.　　　　DOUBLE TRESSURE
　　　　　　　　　　　　　　　　FLORY COUNTER FLORY.

practice it is sometimes as though the charge consisted of two shields superimposed on a third. The second diminutive is the " tressure," which is a thin orle and is almost invariably borne " flory," that is to say, adorned by six fleurs-delis. In the " tressure flory " the fleur-de-lis all point outwards, but if three point outwards and three inwards, then the charge is called a " tressure-flory counter-flory." This last is sometimes borne double, one tressure within another, as in the instance of the Scottish arms : or, a lion rampant within a double tressure flory counter flory, gules. This form of the tressure in Scotland is most highly esteemed, it being a royal charge, and was only granted to private individuals by a royal warrant, and then only in cases where the recipient had performed some great deed for the good of his sovereign or country. It was also granted to the families directly descended from the female members of the royal family. The tressure flory, however, was a common mark of difference.

The "pall" or "pallium," an ecclesiastical vestment and ornament, is a combination of the upper part of the saltire, and the lower part of the pale. It appears in the arms of the sees of Canterbury, Armagh and Dublin, and formerly in those of York. A pall couped, with the ends pointed, is called a "shakefork." Charges may be borne "in pall." For instance Bismarck bears: azure, three oak leaves argent in pall, conjoined to a trefoil in fess point or.

PALL.

The "flanches" are the dexter and sinister portions of the shield, when they are cut off from the rest by curved lines; they are always borne in pairs, and the fact of their sometimes being charged has made some authorities class them as honourable ordinaries. The diminutive of the flanche is the "flasque," or "voider," also always borne in pairs. Many of the early Greek shields were pierced flanche-wise, that is to say, had curved pieces cut out of their sides.

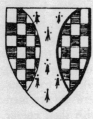

FLANCHES.

The "lozenge" has four sides, the upper and lower points acute, and the side ones obtuse. Its diminutives are the

LOZENGE.

FUSIL.

LOZENGY.

"rustre," or lozenge with a round hole through the centre (when the hole is square it is termed "square-pierced");

the " fusil," which has its upper and lower angles much more acute than the lozenge, and is always borne erect ; and the " mascle," a lozenge showing only a narrow rim, through which the field is seen. The " mascle " probably was intended to represent a link of chain armour. A field may be borne lozengy, fusily or masculy, that is, covered with lozenges, fusils or mascles. The Duke of Teck bears : lozengy or and sable. The Duke of Suabia bore : argent a fess fusily (or three fusils in fess), gules.

Among some of the most ancient charges are the " roundels," small circular charges, which are sometimes classed as sub-ordinaries. Roundels are called " bezants " when of or ; tinc-tured argent, " plates " ; gules, " torteaux " ; azure, " hurts " ; sable, " ogress," or " gunstone," or " pellets " ; vert, " pom-mes," or " pomeis " ; purpure, " golpes " or " wounds " ; sanguine, " guzes " ; tenné, " oranges." The plate is some-times borne barry of seven argent and azure, when it is called a " fountain." These names are of comparatively recent origin, as formerly the heralds acknowledged bezants (from the golden Byzantines coins, familiar to the Crusading armies), plates (from the Spanish word for silver, *plata*), and torteaux,

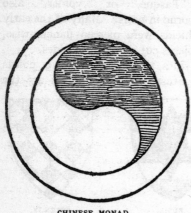

which were always men-tioned with their colour. These circular plates and small globes are among the earliest and most widespread symbols, representing the moon as a rule. When adorned with a whirl, or, as in that very ancient Eastern emblem, a circle enclos-ing two tadpole - like figures, they stand for the diurnal journey of the sun—night and day

CHINESE MONAD.

—the conflict between good and evil, the eternity of life. In China this is generally a venerated symbol, in which the figures are painted white and black, representing respectively the active or male principle, and the passive or female principle. This last symbol is greatly honoured in many Asiatic countries, and may be found in certain of the heraldic badges of Japanese feudal houses. The fountain also partakes of this early universal symbolism, standing for the fertilising water of the earth. In heraldry bezants and plates have been largely employed to symbolise both travel and commerce. On the other hand, they are often martial in character, as in the case of the three silver cannon-balls on the black fess, granted by Charles II to Admiral Sir William Penn, father of William Penn the Quaker settler of Pennsylvania, on the capture of Jamaica. All roundels may be charged. We have seen the plate with its three bars wavy of blue converted into a fountain. Another notable instance is the chief golden pill of the Florentine Medici adorned with the fleur-de-lis granted by Francis I.

An " annulet," or plain ring, really a separate charge, suggestive of the circle of eternity, but heraldically more directly connected with the tournament tilting-ring, has been described as a " false roundel," that is, a pierced or voided roundel.

The " mullet " and " star " have sometimes been classed among the sub-ordinaries. The mullet is a charge representing a spur-rowel, has five points and may be pierced. The star has six points or more ; they are always wavy, but, if it has more than six points, only every other one should be represented as wavy. The mullet and star were respectively military and ecclesiastical charges.

Billets are small long rectangular figures, variously supposed to represent parchment rolls, plates of metal or billets of wood. They may be of any colour, are sometimes (though rarely) charged, and are frequently borne powdered over the field, when the shield is said to be " billettée." They are frequently found on grants made to lawyers and learned clerks.

Flames of fire, when borne alone, may be counted as sub-ordinaries. They are borne as symbols of bravery and valour of the original bearer, ever impatient to lift his eyes and thoughts upwards ; always thinking of and aspiring to perform, and no doubt sometimes having accomplished, brave deeds. The charge is often seen on the Continent. Firebombs, fire-buckets, fire-beacons, and torches in flames are of more frequent occurrence, but these cannot be classed as sub-ordinaries ; they belong to the vast number of common charges.

CHAPTER III

THE CROSS AND ITS VARIATIONS

THIS device, which is one of the most highly esteemed of the Ordinaries, as well as a much varied charge, owes its place in heraldry as the accepted symbol of Christianity. But it is a very ancient religious symbol, being found in early Egyptian art, chiefly under the form of the cross patée (cross with expanded limbs), representing the four " gateways " or quarters of the world, and the tau or T cross, apparently a combination of the pillar (tree, emblem of fertility) and the lintel (the cover of heavens), the whole representing strength. This tau cross with the addition of an ovoid loop at the top, becomes the ankh, or symbol of life. In the ancient art of Asia the cross generally appears in the shape of the Swastika, or cross cramponée, with the extremities bent to right or left, representing at once the " gateways "—East, West, North and South—and the diurnal journey of the sun.

SWASTIKA OR CROSS CRAMPONÉE.

In Christian art the cross represents the Passion of Christ, and also His Church. In decorative design the principal forms are the Latin *crux immissa*, with a long lower limb; the Greek, with all four limbs of equal length; St. Andrew's, or cross in the form of a letter X (*crux decussata*); and the tau (*crux commissa*). The crucifix is the Latin cross bearing the effigy of the Savour nailed thereon. The Passion or Calvary cross is a Latin cross, bearing the crown of thorns, label, nails, and having the lance with reed and sponge placed at the back. A Latin cross elevated on three steps is said to be "graded," the steps representing Faith, Hope and Charity. Frequently the cross is represented as diffusing light, either in the form of a glory or rays from the point of intersection of the four limbs, or from the entire cross. In the crucifix the Head is frequently surrounded by a glory, while light radiates from the wounds.

In heraldry the cross is a combination of the pale and fess, the extremities touching the edge of the shield. It is of the Greek form, the four limbs being of equal width, and should occupy a fifth of the shield, or if charged one-third. The Latin cross is rarely used except as a badge or crest. These two are different forms of the ordinary. But there are very many variations of these, some of which may be classed as their diminutives, though most of the crosses mentioned below are generally treated as common charges. The following list has been made as complete as possible.

A cross flory is perhaps one of the most frequent charges ; it is ornamented at the extremities of its limbs by fleurs-de-lis ; it is a device of one of the French monarchs, who adorned plain crosses with the national emblems, and bestowed these honourable augmentations on favourites or great captains. Some writers give a cross fleury. It is a Greek cross couped

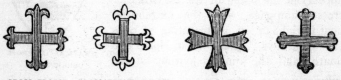

CROSS FLORY.   CROSS FLEURS-DE-LIS.   CROSS PATONCE.   CROSS BOTONY.

and ornamented, with fleur-de-lis, whilst in the cross flory the fleur-de-lis forms part of the cross. The cross patonce is very much like the cross flory, and undoubtedly owes its existence to an accidental alteration made by some careless painter of armorial bearings ; its terminations expand into three points, but do not display a distinct representation of the fleur-de-lis as the parent charge does. The cross botonée, botony, or by some styled Bourbonée, is another modification of the cross flory ; only its limbs are terminated by trefoils or triple buds. It is seen, with a glory at the intersections, among the badges on the Bayeux tapestry. Besides these there is a cross triparted fleury. Edmondson says it is " composed for four fleurs-de-lis, conjoined and united in the centre fess point." The bourdonée has its four limbs

PATÉE FLEURY.   PATÉE CONCAVE.   PATÉE INVECTED.

terminated by spherical excrescences, ornamented with fleurs-de-lis.

The cross patée, the distinguishing badge of the Knight Templars, is a cross whose four limbs expand at the extremities, and whose outer edges are flat. The cross is a favourite as an ornamental emblem on crowns and other regalia, and also as the badge of many orders of knighthood. There are

PATÉE, FITCHY AT   CROSS FORMÉE OR PATÉE
EACH POINT.   THROUGHOUT.

many modifications of this form. It is sometimes ornamented with a pearl on each flat end, when it is termed a cross patée-pomettée ; and sometimes with a fleur-de-lis, when it is termed patée-fleury. Then there is the cross patée-concave, with the extremity of each of its limbs curving slightly in-

wards; patée-convex, with the extremities rounded outwards; patée-crenellée, with the extremities ornamented
with embattlements; patée with an engrail at each point,
with a slight indentation at the point or extremity of each
limb; patée-fitchée at each point, or a cross patée with a
spike terminating each limb; and patée voided in the foot
in the shape of a V reversed. But the most strange shape
given to this cross is termed a cross patée conjoined and
annulated in the dexter and sinister bases; it is really four
stripes formed into a square, the angles ornamented with
two wedge-like projections, and the lower conjunctions of
the stripes are pierced by circular holes. The cross patée

ought never to touch the edges of the
shield, but there is a modification of
this cross, whose outline
is rather more curved
and whose edges in-
variably touch the
shield; it is called a
cross formée. Guillim
specially mentions a
cross recercelée, which,

CROSS RECERCELÉE
VOIDED, OR ENTRAILED.

CROSS
RECERCELÉE.

however, appears to be nothing more than a cross formée-
voided.

The cross potent, of Jerusalem renown, had its four limbs
of equal dimensions, terminated by crutch-like ornaments.

There are variations. It is termed a cross
potent-crossed when each limb, in addition to
the crutch-like ornament, has a transverse bar.
It undergoes further changes under the name
of potent-rebated, when part of the crutch-
shaped object is removed from one side of each
limb; potent quadrate (or cross of St. Chad);

CROSS POTENT.

potent-double fitchée and rebated. Edmondson also mentions a cross potent fleury, fleurs-de-lis being placed at
each end, and some heralds a cross potent rebated in four
points.

The four limbs of the Maltese cross, celebrated as the

badge of the Knights of Malta, expand, and terminate in
eight points. These eight points were said to be symbolical
of the eight Beatitudes.

The cross-crosslet has its four limbs crossed near the ends
by thin bars. It is sometimes mounted on three steps, and

POTENT QUADRATE.	POTENT DOUBLE FITCHY AND REBATED.	POTENT FLEURS-DE-LIS.
MALTESE.	CROSS-CROSSLET.	CROSS CROSSLET PATÉE.
PATRIARCHAL CROSS.	CROSS OF LORRAINE.	

is then termed a cross-crosslet Calvary; it is also borne as a
cross-crosslet-patée.

The patriarchal cross has two, and sometimes three or four,
horizontal bars at the top; it is often formed into a patriarchal
cross-crosslet, and sometimes into a patriarchal cross-crosslet-
patée. The well-known " White cross of Lorraine " was a

patriarchal cross, but with the longer bar placed as near the base as the shorter one is near the top. It was adopted as the badge of the Holy League during the reign of Henry III of France. The very peculiar shape of this cross gave rise to the following unpleasant verses, which were sung by the opponents of the Holy League :

> "Mais, dite mois, que sinifie
> Que les Ligeurs ont double croix ? "
> "C'est q'en la Ligue on crucifie
> Jésus Christ encore une fois."

It is now used as the badge of the international organisation for the suppression of tuberculosis.

The opinions of the old heralds are very much divided about the definition of, or difference between, the cross pomel and the cross pomettée. Some have held that they are both the same. Guillim calls a cross with its ends ornamented with round balls a cross pomel ; Edmondson follows his example, and he calls a cross ornamented with double balls a cross pomettée.

POMEL.

The pointed cross has the extremities of its four limbs shaped into sharp points, and is termed by Edmondson urdée. Guillim mentions a star cross ; it differs from the cross fitchy at all points, in its limbs being straight instead of forming sharp points.

URDEE.

The cross nowy has round projections at the angles formed by the conjunction of the limbs.

A cross quadrate has its centre square instead of round.

CROSS NOWY.　　CROSS FUSIL.　　CROSS FUSIL REBATED.

The extremities of the cross urdee are ornamented by diamond-shaped objects ; Edmondson calls it cross fusil at each point, and he further terms it a cross fusil rebated, when the tips of the diamond-shaped charges are cut off.

The cross raguly has large dents in it, evenly cut, but slanting downwards, and opposite to this indentation is a similarly shaped projection, slanting upwards. The upper limb has one indentation on its dexter side, and one projection on its sinister side ; the lower limb one projection on its dexter, one indentation on its sinister side ; the dexter horizontal limb has one projection on its upper line, and one indentation on its lower line ; the sinister limb one indentation on its upper outline, and one projection on its lower line.

COLCHESTER : TWO STAVES RAGULY IN CROSS (OR CROSSWISE).

Long cross raguly and trunked, so called by Gerard Leigh, Boswell and Edmondson, is termed a cross portant by Holmes.

AVELLANCE.

The avellance cross is formed by a round ball at the conjunction of the four limbs ; each limb is somewhat bell-shaped with a ragged outline at the extremities of the three points. There is also a cross-double avellance.

The cross crescented has its four limbs ornamented by crescents.

The cross clechée is formed of spear-like ornaments. Edmondson, in his "Complete Body of Heraldry," gives the drawing of a cross termed "nowy, grady, conjoined, and fitchée in the foot" ; it is a cross whose four limbs are terminated by two steps, or degrees as they are generally termed in heraldry ; each transverse bar is further ornamented by an oval projection, and the lower limb, beneath the two degrees, is fitchy.

Cross nowed lozengy, is also mentioned by Edmondson.

The cross tron-ornée is a French charge ; it is a Greek

cross cut into five pieces, each part being placed in such a way as to leave a part of the field visible between.

The cross barbed has its limbs terminated by arrow-heads ; it is sometimes emblazoned cramponée and tournée, but Edmondson gives the last name to a totally different cross, one not unlike the cross fourchée.

A cross double parted or triparted, sometimes termed crosses of two or three endorses, is formed of either two or three horizontal and an equal number of perpendicular stripes, placed in the form of the cross ; sometimes the double-parted cross has the additional term fretty attached to it ; in which case the bars are interlaced with each other.

CROSS TRIPARTED.   TRIPARTED FLEURY.

Gerard Leigh mentions a curious cross which he terms a cross entrailed ; he says it should always be sable, and no thicker than the stroke of a pen ; the extremities of each limb are terminated by three loops.

The cross masculy-pometty is formed of four quadrangular links conjoined in the fess point, and each link at three of its angles bears a circular ball. Guillim says it is a French cross, and calls it a *croix clechée*. The famous Toulouse cross, of the Counts of Toulouse, was a cross " vidée, clechée et pomettée." The Pisan cross is similar, but not voided.

Both Guillim and Gibbon mention another French cross, termed a *croix de quatre pieces de vaire appointée* ; it is formed of four of those shield-like objects used in heraldry to represent the fur termed vair.

The cross moussue, or rounded, is a cross whose limbs, instead of being cut straight, are all rounded.

A cross pandell, or spindle, is formed with four elongated globes.

Degraded or degreed and conjoined is a cross mentioned by Edmondson.

A cross cornished and fleury, sometimes termed cornished, is a plain cross with its four limbs terminated like columns, and ornamented with fleurs-de-lis; there is another cross some-what resembling this one, termed a cross capital. There is yet another architectural

CROSS
CROSSLET
DEGREED.

cross, if one may use the term, which is ornamented with scrolls and is called a cross cotised.

The cross thunder, or thunderbolt, is formed of two heraldic thunderbolts placed crosswise, but with the wings left out.

Of crosses ornamented with letters of the alphabet we have two : the cross on each limb a Saxon B, and a long cross on a ball, the top ornamented with a P. Both of these were

FOURCHÉE.

probably adopted as rebuses on the names, or titles, of the original bearers.

The cross fer de fourchette is merely a Greek cross with curved iron rests, formerly used for resting firelocks, fixed to its ends. But fourchée is like a moline with the ends cut off. The cross couped with an annulet

at each end, is a plain cross ornamented with rings ; this cross has a modification termed a cross annulated and re-

CROSS MOLINE OR   CROSS MOLINE.   CROSS
MILLRINE.   ANCHORED.

bated ; and again a cross annuly and fretted with a ring, which latter has a small ring entwined with the annulets which terminate the four limbs. It will be noticed that many crosses owe their distinct classification, as separate crosses, merely to the ornaments which they bear at each extremity. The strangest of these is the cross gringollée, or guivrée, whose four limbs are each ornamented with two snakes' heads, one looking to the right and the other to the left.

Perhaps, however, one of the most singular shapes ever given to the cross is that represented by the lambeaux. It is an old device, and displays a curious combination of the

CROSS
LAMBEAUX.

Latin and patée crosses with the label. The upper portion of the cross is shaped like a cross patée, with its lower limb quite straight, until it terminates in a label of three points. One of the old heralds, Sylvanus Morgan, gives the following quaint account of it. It has, he says, " a great deal of mystery in relation to the top, whereon the first born Son of God did suffer, sending out three streams (of light ?) from His hands, feet, and sides." There is also a cross lambeaux in all four limbs, when a label of three points terminates each limb.

Some of the prettiest heraldic crosses are the floral ones ; they are generally of the Greek, though sometimes of the Latin shape. There are the oak crosses, formed of oak leaves and acorns ; the laurel cross ; and cross formed of ears of wheat and barley. Then we have crosses formed of roses, either red or white ; and lily crosses. Crosses are frequently angled with acorns, leaves, ears of corn, passion nails, and fleurs-de-lis. A cross fruitage is formed of cup-like pods, bursting and displaying a quantity of grapes ; the stems are joined together in the fess point by an annulet. The cross of triangles was probably intended to repre-

CROSS PATONCE,
ACORNED AT EACH
ANGLE.

sent a cross formed of thorns, broken off from the branch, and the spikes stuck into the bases of others, just as children are so fond of making wreaths and other ornaments with the thorns of roses and brambles. Roses and other charges when five in number are constantly borne either in cross or in saltire. The quatrefoil is mentioned by some heralds as a cross of leaves.

When the lower limb of any of these crosses is represented as having a spike, which is of constant occurrence in heraldry, it is termed a cross fitchy or fitchée.

These crosses were used by pilgrims while on their long journeys, when they could not avail themselves of village churches or market crosses;

they therefore stuck their little crosses in the ground as a preliminary to their

FITCHY.

CROSS CROSSLET FITCHY.

daily devotions; the soldiers of the Crusading armies are said to have made use of their swords for this purpose. Of this practice we have an instance in the brave Chevalier Bayard, who, when he received his death wound on the battlefield of Romagnans, and perceiving that no priest was forthcoming to perform the last offices, ordered his attendant to stick the pointed end of his long knightly sword into the turf, and thus improvise a small altar.

Crosses are either simply fitchy, when the lower limb is sharpened into a point, or fitchy in the foot, as a cross patée

CROSS CROSSLET FITCHY AT FOOT.   DOUBLE FITCHY AND REBATED.

fitchy in the foot, when the lower limb is of its proper shape, but with a spike affixed to it. A plain cross may be fitchy at all points, double fitchy at all points, and sometimes the last cross has the tips of the spikes cut off, and is then termed rebated. Besides these there is a cross used by French heralds termed a cross " fourchée a douze pointes," which is a cross fitchée at all points. Guillim also mentions that he saw in a French work a cross called " croix à seizes pointes," each limb being fitchy of four points.

Componée, or gobony, is a term applied to a cross, or any other ordinary, when it is formed of a row of small squares, alternately of colour and metal, the tinctures always being mentioned. Roundels are frequently borne in the form of the cross, each roundel touching the other, and these charges are emblazoned as a cross beyantée, platée, etc., according to their tinctures. There are also crosses fusily and lozengy, being composed respectively of acute and blunt lozenges. But the cross lozengy must not be confounded with the cross lozenge, which is a cross composed of four lozenges, placed with the four acute angles, meeting in the middle or fess point.

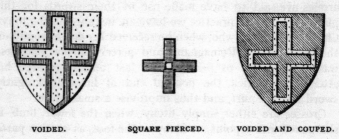

VOIDED.   SQUARE PIERCED.   VOIDED AND COUPED.

A cross masculy is formed of quadrangular links, the links formerly used in chain armour. A cross annuly, or a cross of annulets interlaced, is formed of circular links. Crosses may also be voided, that is to say, only the mere outline of he cross is drawn, showing the field through it ; the voiding may be in the shape of the pale, the fess, or in the shape of some other cross, but when merely emblazoned voided it is voided of its own shape. A circular hole is often made at the junction of the four limbs ; this is termed pierced, or, if the hole be square, square-pierced ; but if the whole of the intersecting part of the cross is removed, it is termed quarterly pierced. This last forms a field checky of nine pieces, and is called by French heralds equipollé.

A cross may be divided per pale, per fess, or per bend, each

half being of different tinctures ; it may also be quartered.
A cross divided per pale, per fess, and per saltire, is termed
a cross quarterly-quartered. Sir George Mackenzie gives
as the arms of Glendening of that ilk : per cross, argent, and
sable ; a cross parted per cross, indented, and counterchanged.

Fimbriated is a cross with a border of a different colour ;
for instance, the cross of St. George in the "Union Jack" is
a cross gule fimbriated argent. The badge
of the Knights of St. Iago of Spain is a
red cross patonce fitchy, fimbriated argent,
with a silver escallop shell. If the limbs
of a plain or long cross do not touch the
sides of the shield, it is termed indifferently
couped or humettée, if cut off with a smooth
edge ; but if with a jagged edge, erased or
rompu. The rounded or moussue cross is a
cross humettée, only instead of the ends being cut straight

BADGE OF
KNIGHTS OF
ST. IAGO.

they are rounded off. It must be remembered that these terms, couped and humettée,
can only refer to the plain or long crosses,
or to the saltire. The term crusily is applied
to a shield whose field is strewn with crosses.
The term cantonnée is used to describe a
cross placed between four crosses or four
other charges. Engoulé is a term employed
when the extremities of a cross, saltire, or

CROSSES OF
JERUSALEM,
CANTONNÉE.

other ordinary, enter the mouths of
lions or any other wild beast.

One cross may be charged with another
of the same or of a different form. [1]
Besides being charged with different

CROSS MOLINE IN PALE
AND PATÉE IN FESS.

[1] There is a general confusion with regard to
crosses *charged, voided,* and *fimbriated.* A cross
is always voided of the field. The border of a
cross fimbriated is very narrow ; much more
so than the edges of a *voided* cross. When a
cross is *charged with another* the charge is always
less than one-third of the size of the first, and, generally, both crosses
are of a different tincture to the field.

crosses Edmondson gives us a peculiar cross termed moline in pale and patée in fess, which is a mixture of the pattée and moline crosses. The Murrays of Ochtertyre have a cross surmounted by a saltire, both couped.

Waved, invected, engrailed, nebulé, are terms applied to crosses, and other ordinaries, of any shape according to their outline. Crosses are often represented as surrounded by a glory, or by rays of light radiating from the junction of the limbs, when they are termed rayonnant, or rayonnée, for the same reason as that given by Sylvanus Morgan for the lambeaux.

CROSS
RAYONNANT.

Edmondson says of the cross ermine, " This blazon, though used by several authors, is absurd ; and will lead the reader into a mistake if not cautiously attended unto. The blazon should be thus : Argent, four ermine spots in cross, their tips meeting in the centre point." But although this is true of the cross ermine, it is quite possible to see a plain cross or a cross patée ermine, or covered with many ermine spots; and such a blazon would be perfectly correct.

Crosses, indeed, are formed out of many extraordinary charges. For instance, keys may be borne in saltire, or saltire-wise (the celebrated cross-keys of the Roman See, being the badge of St. Peter) ; or as double claved ; in the latter case we have a cross formed of four double-warded keys, joined to a single ring in the fess point. When swords, lances, pilgrims' staves, branches of trees, thigh-bones or other charges are formed into a cross, they are generally emblazoned "in cross " or "crosswise."

CROSS DOUBLE
CLAVED.

One or two curious examples may be given here.

The arms of the family of Baynes (county Middlesex) are : sable, a shin-bone in fess surmounted by another in pale (thus forming a cross), argent ; on a canton of the last a vulture, proper.

The Newtons : sable, two shin-bones in saltire, argent.

The arms of the Coopers (county Hereford) are : vert, a fess embattled, or, between two pheons in chief, points downwards, and in base two human thigh-bones in saltire, argent.

The arms of the Williamses of Bodelwyddan, Wales, are : argent, two foxes saliant counter saliant in saltire, gule, the dexter surmounting the sinister ; and those of Des Fossez, a French family, are : gule, two lions, or, rampant adossé in saltire, that is to say, counter rampant.

Baron Bramwell had as crest two lion's jambs in saltire, or, supporting a sword in fess, proper.

The crucifix is a very rare charge in English heraldry ; it appears in the crest of the La Poer family : a stag's head, caboched, proper, attired or, between the horns a crucifix, proper. The arms of the bishopric of Waterford are : azure, a priest in full canonicals, with a glory round his head, seated, and holding a large crucifix, all proper.

The saltire, one of the ordinaries, is formed by two beams crossing each other diagonally, and, in heraldic parlance is a combination of the dexter and sinister bends. It is one of the prehistoric symbols, apparently standing for the cardinal points of the compass, those gateways for elemental forces, the portals of life and death. Many of the old heralds have written lengthily about its origin. Menestries is of opinion that it was anciently used by horsemen. According to him knights hung these wooden frames from their saddles, and used them to mount and dismount, when accoutred in their massive and heavy armour. Upton and Spelman believe that it was formed of two logs of wood, placed at the entries of parks or forests, which were called by the French, *saults*. Gerard Leigh says that it was used by soldiers for scaling walls. As a rule, however, it was generally adopted as a cross. Mr. A. Macgeorge in his work on flags suggests that the saltire was derived from the Greek letter X (Ch.) for Christus.

The saltire is also known as the Cross of St. Andrew, a tradition asserting that, in the year A.D. 67, St. Andrew suffered martyrdom on a cross of this shape. It has always been a favourite charge with the heralds, and is the national badge both of Scotland and Ireland. An old legend attributes the origin of this cross as the Scottish national badge to the fact of its having miraculously appeared to the King of the Picts (Lowlanders) on the eve of the battle in which his people gained a signal victory over the Northumbrians.

It is largely employed in Scottish heraldry, either borne singly, in pairs, by threes, or the shield covered with them ;

SALTIRE. SALTIRE BOTONY. SALTIRE CROSSLET.

SALTIRE CROSSLET FLEURY. SALTIRE CROSSLET PATÉE. SALTIRE MOLINE.

in the latter case the proper heraldic term is, a field semée of saltires. When more than one saltire is blazoned they are always couped, straight across, not diagonally, but as they are always borne thus, it is unnecessary to blazon them as couped. This rule, of course, does not apply in a case where a single saltire is borne couped, for in such a case it is absolutely necessary to mention it, otherwise it would be taken for granted that the ends of the saltire touch the edges of the shield.

The term salterwise is applied to two objects borne in the

form of the saltire ; unless otherwise blazoned the object
in sinister bend should always be uppermost ; five charges
placed two, one, two are blazoned in saltire ; a shield may
be party per saltire.

Saltires patée, pomettée, fleüry, potentée, and crossed,
assume the peculiar forms or ornaments of the crosses bearing
these different names.

Saltires may also be formed of the different lines of partition,
and Guillim mentions a saltire-raguly, which is the cross of
Burgundy.

A saltire of two tinctures divided into eight portions is
termed a saltire quarterly quartered.

Four chains are sometimes borne in saltire, each being
fixed to an annulet in the centre.

A saltire joined in the base has a horizontal band joining
the two lower limbs of the saltire. Robert de Bruce (temp.
Henry III) bore : or, a saltire gules and a chief of the second ;
while the most ancient branch of the Nevils bore (as early
as the reign of Edward II) : gules, a saltire argent.

The pall is formed by the upper portion of a saltire conjoined to the lower part of the pale, and in fact resembles
very closely the letter Y. It is a Roman Catholic ecclesiastical vestment. The Pope on raising a priest to the dignity
of archbishop always sends him a pall, and he is not, according
to the strict etiquette of the Church, qualified to perform
any archiepiscopal duties until he has been duly invested with
the pall. It was first used in 1152.

In heraldry it is seldom used, except for bishops' sees or
ecclesiastical communities. The arms of the archbishopric of
Canterbury are : azure, an episcopal staff in pale, or, ensigned
with a cross pattée, argent, surmounted by a pall of the
second, edged, and fringed, or charged with four crosses-
pattée fitchée, sable. The arms of the archbishopric of
Dublin are the same as those of Armagh, only the pall is
charged with five crosses instead of four.

The cross tau, or St. Anthony's Cross, closely resembles
the Greek letter tau, from which it derives its name. Besides
the plain cross tau there is one termed cross-tau ends con-

vexed, and graded ; it is mounted on three steps, and the two
ends of the horizontal bar are terminated by crescents.

CROSS TAU RAGULY.   CROSS TAU PATÉE.

The cross portrate is a French charge, and held an important
place in the list of their heraldic charges. It is a saltire
with the upper portion of the bend dexter cut off.

La Colombière, Edmondson and others mention a charge
which they call a cross potence, but which Holmes affirms
should be termed a Saxon F, which it certainly resembles.
Holmes also states that it forms the insignia of the bishopric
of Chemin, a province of Saxony.

CHAPTER IV

ANIMALS : I. FOUR-FOOTED BEASTS

IN the early days of heraldry, when each knight could decorate his shield with the emblems that pleased him best, many chose for the principal charges on their coats-of-arms some of those animals most renowned for bravery. Therefore the lion, the leopard, the eagle, the wild boar, and, at a much later date, dragons and griffins, were widely adopted as distinguishing badges. But as sovereign princes in nearly every case chose one of the warrior beasts, to avoid confusion, gradually extraordinary posture, contour and colouring crept into the art of blazoning.

The lion, chosen at an early date by the kings of England, was perhaps the animal most highly esteemed by heraldic authorities; it is, therefore, hardly astonishing to find that it has undergone many curious alterations. The lion is borne in fifteen postures :

(1) " Rampant," erect on its hind legs, going from sinister side to dexter, its head being in profile, and its tail erect and nearly touching its back. (2) " Rampant-guardant," erect on its hind legs, and full faced. (3) " Rampant-regardant," erect on its hind legs, its head in profile looking backwards. (4) " Passant," walking past in profile, its right front paw held up, and its tail reflexed over the back. (5) " Passant-guardant," walking past, full-faced, right leg lifted, and tail reflexed over back. (6) " Passant-regardant," in the same position as the last two, only with its head in profile looking backwards. (7) " Standant," with all four paws on the ground; it is generally emblazoned full-faced. (8) " Saliant," or in the act of springing forward; there is really but very

little difference between saliant and passant, but the former has its two front legs in the air. (9) "Sejeant," seated on its haunches, its head in profile, and front paws on the ground. (10) "Sejeant-affronté," sitting upright, full-faced, with its front legs held straight out on either side. (11) "Couchant,"

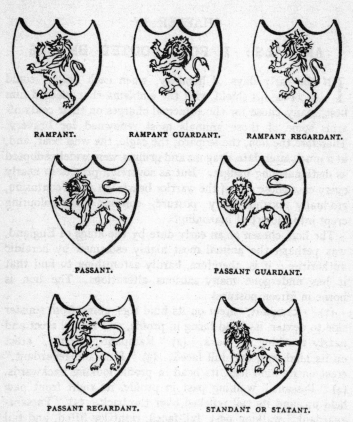

RAMPANT.   RAMPANT GUARDANT.   RAMPANT REGARDANT.

PASSANT.   PASSANT GUARDANT.

PASSANT REGARDANT.   STANDANT OR STATANT.

lying down, its head erect, and tail beneath it. (12) "Dormant," with its head resting on its front paws. (13) "Coward" or "cowé," the same posture as standant, its head held rather lower, and its tail between its legs. (14) "Rampant-combatant," two lions "rampant-passant" placed

face to face. (15) " Rampant-adossé," or " addorsed," two
lions "rampant-passant," placed back to back.

In accordance with fairly early practice a lion is always
given a tongue and claws of a different tincture to that of
its body. If a golden or silvern lion is placed on a blue,
black or green field the tongue and claws are red ; if on a
red field, they are blue. Sometimes, though this is rare, a
golden lion on a black field has a tongue and claws of silver.
On the other hand, the red lion has a blue tongue and claws
whenever possible, or failing that they are gold or silver ;
and the blue lion has red tongue and claws. Such lions,
and other beasts so treated, are said to be " langued and
armed " of the special tincture. Unless otherwise described,
the tails of lions are borne reflexed over their backs, and in
mediæval examples the tails are often nearly twice as long
as the whole body. This is the case in the very spiritedly
carved lions on the coat of Edmund of Langley, Earl of
Cambridge and Duke of York, fifth son of Edward III, as
seen carved on his tomb in the church of King's Langley,
Hertfordshire. But the tails may be " nowed " (tied in a
knot), " fourchée " (bifurcated towards the tip) or borne
double, as in the well-known Bohemian beast.

A lion may be borne dismembered, as in the coat of Maitland (or, a lion dismembered, gules)
when the head, four limbs and tail are
severed from the body, a thin line of the
field showing between. Akin to this is
the demi-lion, the upper part, which is
used not only as a crest, but also as a
charge, a striking and suggestive example being the demi-Scottish lion of
augmentation on the chief of Thomas
Howard, Duke of Norfolk (see Chapter

TRI-CORPATE.

XII). Shadows of lions have appeared on German shields,
a mere outline in a darker shade of the field being drawn.
Then there are bi- and tri-corpate lions. In the first
instance the two bodies are borne salient from dexter and
sinister, the first " contourné," so that they face each

other, the two necks being joined to a single full-faced head ; in the second, the bodies radiate " en pairle," to dexter chief, sinister chief and base, the necks meeting in a single head in fess point. On the Continent lions are seen wearing helmets and even, as in the case of the Brittany Hattes, with the head smothered in blue cloth, while the red lion of Reinach, which apparently had been dancing, for it is contourné, has its head covered by a tight-fitting blue sack. It is tempting to speculate whether one ought to read some political allusion in these quaint devices (as with the knotty club, and the smoothing plane which the Dukes of Burgundy and Bourbon added to their escutcheons, to make manifest their keen desire to be at each other's throats), or whether they should be regarded as merely grotesques. Such humorous renderings of heraldic compositions were common enough at tournaments, when knights desired to preserve their *incognito* while hinting at their personalities or their hidden motives. Some of these may (as the " tenants " or supporters undoubtedly were), have been permanently adopted by the knight or his squire. Many odd additions unquestionably are errors introduced by careless painters and ignorantly prepetuated, but others have real meaning. Thus it is with the blue cape semée with golden fleurs-de-lis, which we find on the rampant red lion within an orle of plates on a field gules, belonging to the Cardilacs. Vulson de la Colombière tells us this was a personal honour bestowed by the King of France for services rendered ; but whether the services were such as are performed *sous le manteau* tradition is silent.

With us it is common to see lions holding swords, lances, flags, human heads and other trifles between their paws. In French heraldry they may be seen having thrown aside the trappings of war, and, if not having converted swords into ploughshares, at all events taken up implements of husbandry. For we find that Athenor bore : azure, a lion rampant with human head, coiffed with a broad-brimmed and tall crowned hat, holding a hoe, or. Lions' heads (with the neck) and faces (without the neck, showing the mask only), also " gambs " or " jambs " (legs) and paws are borne, as

well as plain tails. An English bearing is that of Corke:
sable, three lions' tails, argent. When a number of small
lions are figured on a coat they are blazoned "lioncels."
In olden phraseology the word "leopard" was generally
applied to lions passant-guardant, though there was nothing
in the drawing to justify the name. Later the lion passant-
guardant came to be called a "lion-leopardé," but it was
merely a term applied to the beasts in a special attitude, and
had no other significance. This is important to remember
as in old writings the English cognisance is constantly referred
to as the golden leopards. As we shall see presently, these
kings of the beasts have also been converted into dragon-
lions and marine lions.

Among the famous lions of chivalry are the golden lions
passant-guardant of England; the red lion rampant of
Scotland; the silver lions passant of the native Princes of
North and South Wales; and the black lion rampant of the
Griffiths, Princes of Cardigan. Then there are the white
lion of the Earls of March; the gold lion statant with extended tail, the badge of the Percys; the Howards' gold
lion statant-guardant with extended tail, with a ducal coronet
of silver; the Lacy Earls of Lincoln purple lion rampant, and
others. Going abroad we find the valiant winged lion of
Venice, with its nimbus about its head, its paw on the table
of laws. This, of course, is the Biblical lion of St. Mark.
The lion of Flanders is black and rampant; that of Bohemia
was silver, and also rampant, with double tail proudly whisk-
ing at its back; that of Gelders was rampant or, crowned
gules; that of Leon, rampant and originally purple, though
it has long since become red; while the Luxemburg beast
is barry of gold and red.

Heraldic leopards belong to the early sixteenth century;
the spots are represented by a number of roundels, often of
varied tinctures, powdered over the body. The "leopard's
face" (a lion's face without the mane) is often met with. This
mask of the leopard is constantly blazoned as "jessant-de-
lis," that is shown with the tail of a fleur-de-lis coming out of
its mouth, and the lobes showing up behind. To make

matters worse the leopard's head "jessant-de-lis" is as likely as not to be borne reversed, that is upside down, as in the arms of the See of Hereford.

Heraldic tigers have the bodies of lions and the heads of wolves, and are usually spitting fire. It was supposed to be proper to depict them as statant, gazing into a mirror on the ground. This was in reference to the old traveller's tale that when a leopard was deprived of its whelps, it was well to place a mirror near the den, so that the mother might be attracted by her reflection, and stay either to admire herself or to puzzle out the ghostly presence of a possible rival. The striped tiger was introduced into heraldry by adventurous travellers and successful soldiers of the eighteenth and nineteenth centuries, who had won fame and fortune in India.

JESSANT-DE-LIS.

FOXES IN SALTIRE, OR RAMPANT COUNTER RAMPANT.

A lynx and a catamount, or wild cat, are much alike, spitting fire, and being adorned on head and limbs with tufts of fur.

Bears are also very old symbols, as witness the rampant bear and ragged staff of the Earls of Warwick, the beast having, it is alleged, been derived from Urso d'Abitot, one of the Conqueror's barons. The bear is also seen on the shield of Berne City, this being a canting coat. Polar bears are the result of eighteenth and nineteenth century exploring work.

Wolves naturally play a big part. They are shown "rampant," "passant," "courant," "vorant" (devouring prey), "ravisant" (carrying it off), and in many other positions; while their heads are favourite charges. It is significant that the ravisant wolf is often seen on Spanish shields. Wolves are borne as warlike or sporting symbols, but quite often as punning allusion to the wearers, the Wolves, Lovels, and so on, as will be seen more at length on referring to Chapter XIV.

The fox is another creature of the chase largely used, either whole, or his mask, or his brush. A fox rampant, with a hood on its back in which there is a goose, is to be seen on a German coat-of-arms, that of the Schaden von Leipolds. It is strongly reminiscent of the satirical Gothic church carvings.

Oxen are shown passant, though they are occasionally rampant. The ox's head and his scalp with horns are also borne. These may represent great landed interests, but more frequently they bear some canting allusion, as in the ox on the blue water on the shield of Oxford City. The winged, nimbus crowned bull of St. John is also among the heraldic charges, and his prototype may be found in the great symbolic winged bulls of Nineveh. A shaggy maned buffalo is seen on the shield of Manitoba.

Sheep also partake of mixed symbolism, now representing agricultural or commercial interest, and anon religious sentiment. In the former case we may have either the live sheep (sometimes bearing a sprig in its mouth, as in the case of Bolton, where the sheep has a sprig of the fructed cotton-

LEEDS : A FLEECE BANDED.

plant, to represent the woollen and cotton industries), or the fleece, that is, the undressed skin with head and hoofs. The golden fleece of classic tradition was the cherished emblem of a noble order of knighthood founded in connection with the Holy Roman Empire, and now bestowed both by the King of Spain and the Emperor of Austria. The " Paschal lamb " has a nimbus about its head, and often carries a cross or a banner with cross. It is borne both passant and couchant.

The beaver represents both the extinct European variety and the Canadian. We have : vert on a base barry of five argent and azure, two beavers rampant-combatant or, for Thomas Beveridge of Chester (1575) ; and argent, a cross gules between four beavers passant proper, for the Hudson Bay Company.

Akin to these is the otter. It is often shown as vorant fish, either the whole animal or its head being borne. On the ceiling of the cloister at Canterbury Cathedral is to be seen the coat of Proude of Canterbury : three otters in pale each devouring a fish. The Luttrells (for the otter is called a *loutre* in French) bear : argent, a fess between three otters sable. For crest, an otter devouring a fish.

Elephants and camels are not altogether recent importations from the East, though no doubt returned Nabobs and soldiers have been responsible for the introduction of many into our armorials ; but both these Eastern symbols of wealth and power were adopted by the Crusaders, who added them to the heraldic menagerie. As a matter of fact, the elephant was accepted by the Romans as a symbol of wealth and eastern dominion, as numismatic art and carvings testify.

Both the rhinoceros and the hippopotamus are found in heraldry, but the latter is a new comer, due to activities of one kind or another in Africa, while the kangaroo has come to us from Australia. The rhinoceros is of older date. We see one, used as the crest of the Apothecaries' Company, because its horn was one of the most highly prized of remedies in fifteenth and sixteenth century medical practice.

Antelopes have long tapering horns, long tufted tail, and tufted beard.

The " wild boar " was one of those charges early adopted as a symbol of bravery, and was given to, or adopted by, great warriors. A young wild boar is termed a " grice." The " pig " also makes its appearance on shields, but especially in Continental heraldry. The old Spanish heralds made

constant use of the unsightly pig in order to show the hatred
for the Jews and Moors, who abhorred the unclean animal.

The horse, as might be expected, is a valued charge. It is
sometimes borne completely furnished for war, when it is
called "caparisoned"; or else rearing on its hind legs, when
it is termed either "effaré" or "forcené." A "spancelled"
horse has two of its legs fettered by a log of wood. Among
the famous heraldic horses are the white horse of Kent, probably introduced on these shores by the Angles, for it is an
extremely ancient Germanic symbol of warfare and strength,
later to be represented on the shield of Westphalia and
Hanover. On the arms of Naples it was a black horse which
pranced, certainly an appropriate charge for the dashing
Prince Murat, who quartered them with the three naked legs
of Sicily, bearing over all the Imperial arms of France. Don-
keys and mules are also seen. Askew bears : argent a fess
between three asses passant sable ; and Assil : sable, an ass
argent.

After the horse, it is well to mention dogs. These are
chiefly represented by the talbot, a kind of mastiff ; the
alant or aland, a short-eared mastiff ; and the greyhound.
Talbots appear on the coat of the Talbots. An interesting
example of the use of greyhounds is to be seen in the arms of
the town of Marlborough. These are : per saltire, gules and
azure, in chief a bull passant argent, armed or, in fess two
cocks of the first, and in base three greyhounds in pale of the
last ; on a chief or, a pale gules, between two roses gules,
thereon a tower or. Supporters, two greyhounds ; crest, a
tower or. These arms are intensely interesting, as the
symbolism is unusually explicit, though in strict, if complicated
heraldic style. Marlborough is an ancient royal borough,
possessing a strong royal castle, represented here by the tower
and the roses. But the Mayor and Corporation had acquired
manorial privileges, including forest wardenship and rights
of sport, which were jealously cherished. In later days,
local sports took place, including coursing with greyhounds
and bull-baiting, and the presentation to the Mayor of two
cocks ; all this may be read in the shield. These sports

themselves were merely symbolical of the forestry and hunting privileges. Anciently the arms were : azure, a tower, triple towered, argent. The other emblems came later to record civic privileges.

The rabbit is termed a " conie," the badger a " brock " or a " gray " ; the hedgehog a " herison " ; then there are goats and goats' heads, asses and asses' heads. Hares are not unknown. Indeed, that of Cleland, saliant with a hunting-horn round its neck, is found on many a noble coat, or as a crest, owing to family alliances. Other musical hares are those of FitzErcald, co. Derby : argent, three hares sejant gules, playing upon bagpipes, or. Hopwell bore the same arms, only both hares and bagpipes were red. Sir William Mauleverer (temp. Edward III) bore : argent, three leverers gules.

The stag is said to be at " gaze " when it is standing still, " trippant " when passing, " courant " or " at speed " when running. When its antlers are of a different tincture to that of the animal it is said to be " attired," just the same as the lion, or other savage beast, is said to be " armed " when its claws, teeth, or beak are of a different tincture. The antlers are sometimes borne alone, and are then known as " attires," while a branch is a " tyne." The male is called a " hart " and the female a " hind." A young stag is termed a " girl." Within the last three hundred years the reindeer and moose have been introduced from Canada, and the gnu, springbok and gemsbok from Africa.

STAG'S HEAD
CABOCHED.

" Caboched " is a term applied to the head of any animal when it is represented, either full-faced or without a neck. If the neck is shown with a clean cut, it is said to be " couped," but if with a jagged edge, then it is " erased " ; terms which apply to all members of human beings, the lower animals, plants, or inanimate objects, when respectively clean cut or torn off. Any beast of prey lying down with its head held up is said to be " couchant," but a stag or other beast of chase in this position is said to be " lodged " ; a wild beast eating its food is termed " vorant " ; " vulned " is a term applied to an animal, or part of an animal, dripping with blood ; an animal " courant " is running ; " saliant," it is about to spring forward ; " respecting " is applied to other animals, except lions and other beasts of prey, when they are placed face to face ; in this position beasts of prey are said to be " combatant." A tortoise walking is said to be " gradiant."

All beasts deprived of their tails are said to be " defamed " ; if the tails are borne between their legs they are termed " couée " or " coward." If an ordinary is borne over them, they are said to be " debruised." But all animals may be crowned, and they may also be " gorged," either with a wreath of leaves or flowers, a collar or a coronet about their necks. If flames issue from their mouths or nostrils, they are " incensed " or " inflamed." Beasts and birds are always supposed to face to the dexter, if otherwise they are said to be " contourné," or reversed.

GORGED WITH COLLAR
FLORY COUNTER FLORY.

While beasts and birds of prey are said to be " armed " when their teeth, tusks, beaks, claws and talons are of a different tincture to that of their bodies, under these conditions wild boars and elephants are more frequently said to be " tusked." Hoofed animals are said to be " hoofed " or " unguled " of any special tincture. A horse, unicorn or lion with a mane of a different tincture to the body is said to be " crined " of a special colour ; a term which also applies to the hair of the human head.

It is to be noted that while many beasts and birds were introduced into heraldry, either as representatives of those virtues specially admired in warriors, or as symbols of the pleasures and jealously guarded privileges of the chase, a goodly number appear to have been adopted mainly, if not solely, because their names suggested allusions to the patronymics or titles of their bearers. Numerous instances of this will be found in the chapter on " Canting or Punning Arms." This fact, however, should be kept in mind when certain quaint, and certainly not very worthy, members of the animal kingdom are found holding a conspicuous place on some storied or perhaps little known shield.

CHAPTER V

ANIMALS : II. BIRDS

THE eagle is not only the king of all fowl, but the animal next in order of importance to the lion. It may be blazoned " displayed," with its wings spread out ; or " close," with its wings shut ; or " volant," flying. Eagles have a long ancestry as symbols of divine power and warfare. While in Egypt the hawk and the vulture were the chief sacred birds, in Asia it was the eagle. With the Greeks it was the support and the representative of Zeus, and carried his thunderbolt. With the Romans it was the bird of Jupiter. Borrowing the idea from Asia, the eagle was adopted as the Imperial symbol, linking the ruler with the divine, and,

EAGLE FROM CHARLEMAGNE'S SWORD.

after death, carrying his spirit to heaven. The eagle itself renewed its youth by flying into the sun, thus passing through the ordeal of fire. With the Greeks and Romans the symbolic eagle was a slightly conventionalised naturalistic representation of the real bird, with prominent hooked beak, formidable talons, large eye and fine plumage ; its wings were half open or spread out in flight. This naturalistic type has persisted in Italy from the earliest days down to our own time. It

47

was the type adopted by Napoleon I and by his nephew, Napoleon III. The naturalistic character is carried still further in the American national eagle, which is essentially a bird of prey, with its neck depressed, the head pushed forward, the beak open, the wings outspread, and the whole attitude showing readiness for a pounce. It grasps thunderbolts in

EAGLE FROM TRAJAN'S COLUMN, ROME.

the form of forked lightning, in its talons. The Teutonic eagle, on the other hand, is purely a creature of convention. It is attenuated, angular and rugged in outline, with long neck, prominent open beak, lolling tongue, large eyes, plumed legs, with great talons; its wings are ragged, the flight feathers appearing singly, not massed together, and its tail is a long projection, decorated with foliated scroll-work, often quite

BEDFORD: AN
EAGLE WITH
WINGS ABAISÉ.

architectural in character. A modified form of this may be seen in the north choir-aisle of Westminster Abbey, on a shield of Emperor Frederick II (*temp.* Henry III).

Displayed eagles have their wings open and elevated, sometimes the tips being carried on a level with the head and then ending horizontally, the pinions being carried erect, the wings spread fan-wise, with the feathers projecting above the head. The term "abaisé" is applied when the wings are spread, but the feathers point downwards. The Apostolic eagle has a nimbus round its head, and is the symbol of St. John.

The double-headed eagle of the Holy Roman Empire is sometimes crowned, sometimes bears the nimbus. This

DOUBLE-HEADED HITTITE EAGLE FROM CAPPADOCIA.

double-headed eagle is now used by the Emperors of Austria and of Russia. The dual heads represent dominion over east and west. Prototypes of the double-headed eagles are found in the ancient rock carvings of Cappadocia, where we see double-headed eagles supporting divinities, and in one case clutching a hare in its talons. These were adopted by the Seleuke Turcomans, and through them migrated to Eastern Europe.

DOUBLE-HEADED
HITTITE EAGLE.

A coat-of-arms is often borne on the breast of an eagle (as in the case of Prussia, Austria, Russia and the United States of America), or as we may see it nearer home, in the case of the town of Bedford, occasionally the shield being pendent from a belt held in the beak. Sometimes the outspread wings are also covered with armorial shields, as in the case of Russia and Austria. In early heraldry the eagle was often blazoned as an " erne " or an " alerion." Later the term alerion was applied to small beakless and talonless eagles. The arms of the Duchy of Lorraine are : or, on a bend gules, three alerions abaisé, argent. Legend says that the alerions came to Lorraine through Geoffrey of Bouillon, who when before Jerusalem shot an arrow which slew three strange beakless and feetless birds, which he straightway adopted as his personal cognisance. It is possible that they were indeed arms of assumption, some strange Eastern symbolism taken from the shield of a vanquished leader. Among our famous eagles is the green bird with red beak and talons on the gold shield

EGYPTIAN SACRED VULTURE WITH PLUME SCEPTRES.

of the redoubtable and influential Monthermer. On a Roll of Arms of Henry III, John de Beauchamp is said to bear : sable, an eagle argent armed or. One of the strangest looking of these fowls was on the feudal coat of the Margraf of Moravia : azure, an eagle displayed chequy argent and gules, crowned or. De Ganays, of Burgundy, who derive from a lawyer stock, bear emblematically : or, an eagle disarmed sable ; for the talons and beak properly belong to the warrior.

In the early days of chivalry hawking was one of the principal pastimes of nobility, and therefore both the hawks and the objects used in hawking were often chosen by those who had special rights of hunting over large extents of forest. Hawks often appear as " belled," " jessed " and " varvelled." The " bell," which is constantly used as a separate charge, is round with a long slit in it ; a piece of metal at the top is pierced by a hole, through which the " jess," or leather thong, is passed ; and so fastened to the leg of the hawk.

" Varvels " are rings attached to the leather thongs. Hawking has contributed two other names to heraldry : the hawk's " lure " or two wings joined with a thong, to which is tied a ring ; and " nowed," a term used when the thongs are knotted.

Swans, being royal birds of the chase, and also having a long and illustrious record in the legendary tales of most nations, more especially those of the North, where they appear as carriers of human souls to Thor's Valhalla, play an important part in heraldry. The swan is essentially a bird of chivalry, of queens, and knighterrantry. It is generally white or silver, with black beak and red legs, and is then blazoned " proper." In our history the most famous swan is the white one, gorged with a golden coronet, with chain attached, passing over its back, which belonged to the de Bohuns. They derived it from the Mandevilles, Earls of Essex, who got it from their forebears, the Fitzswans, whose progenitor came over from Normandy with Duke William in 1066. So that this is the real Norseman's mystic messenger from the outer

ARMS OF THE GUILD OF
MUSICIANS, LONDON.

world. The de Bohuns transmitted their swan to the Lancastrian branch of the Plantagenets, the Staffords and many other noble houses. Swan (*obit.* 1487) bore : azure, a fess between three swans argent. Black swans of Australia, with their red beaks and legs, are now occasionally seen. A " swan's neck " includes both head and neck.

Another equally long-pedigreed feathered messenger from the regions of shadow was the raven, usually styled a " corbie." These solemn sable birds, meeting in conclave and often acting in concert after such " conferences," have always been held in awe. In certain parts of India they are the preferred refuges of human souls, while to several American Indian tribes, west of the Rockies, the Great Raven, creator of the world, was their progenitor. Our mid-German Arian ancestors venerated the birds, so did the Danes, as certainly did the Celts of the western parts of our land. A raven standard

CITY OF CANTERBURY.

was borne by the Danes who invaded our shores in 787, and fell to Alfred at the battle of Westbury some hundred years later. It was always prominent in battle, and a bringer of omens. While a raven helped the Roman Valerius against the Gauls, causing him, so legend says, to assume the name of Corvus (though that was probably a reminiscence of totemism), a flock of them accompanied Owain Urien to the wars, and in later times they flew about Wales, declaring that Gwffydd ap Rhys ap Tudor would ultimately prevail and become Prince of Wales. To this day, the vanished King Arthur circles about our islands and Brittany in the form of a gigantic raven, awaiting the opportune time to reappear as ruler of the United Brittanies. With such a record of warfaring and wisdom, the raven was always much favoured by heralds, and is specially prominent as a crest. Griffith ap Rhys ap Uryan had for badge a black raven on a white quatrefoil, shipped and leaved gold. Thomas de Corbet (*temp.* Henry III), following the example of Valerius, took unto himself : or, two corbies, sable.

Swallows, with their long bifurcated tails and long wings, are messengers from afar off, who have been largely used. The martin, a smaller bird, usually borne " closed," is called a " martlet." This last has gradually been deprived of its beak and legs. Arundell of Wardour bore : sable, six swallows (3, 2, 1) argent.

The ostrich came to us early from the East, being brought back by the Crusaders. It was regarded as a symbol of endurance and martial ardour, partly no doubt owing to its swiftness of foot and combativeness at certain seasons, but more particularly because of its hardiness and power of long abstinence, combined with healthy digestive powers. This latter peculiarity gave rise to the legend that it could live on iron, hence the practice of heralds of showing it bearing a Passion nail (emblem of the Church Militant), a horseshoe (itself an old symbol of religion, but more particularly assumed as a reminder of knightly prowess on horseback), or a key (a symbol at once of religious and temporal power). How it became intimately connected with England will be discussed in another chapter, when dealing with the plumes of the Princes of Wales. Allied to the Eastern ostrich are the later introduced emu and apterix of Australia.

After the eagle and hawk the birds most commonly used in heraldry are the pelican, the peacock and the cock. The pelican is generally borne with its wings open and placed back to back ; or in her nest feeding her young with her own blood, flowing from a self-inflicted wound on her breast, when she is said to be " in her piety." It is a religious emblem. We also have storks, the bringers of children ; and cranes. The latter are nearly always depicted as standing on one leg,

PELICAN IN HER PIETY.

holding a stone in the other. This stone, travellers said, was held so that if the bird should nap, it would fall and waken the sentinel. Nevertheless, the crane is regarded as the symbol of vigilance. Doves, originally the birds of Aphrodite and Venus, took men's souls to heaven, hence their association with the symbolism of the Holy Spirit. Columball (*temp*. Richard II) bore : sable, three doves argent, beaked and membered gules, holding in their beaks sprigs of olives proper. Obviously allusive alike to the name of the bearer and the Biblical lesson. They are, indeed, mostly found in heraldry as an emblem of love and of religious ardour.

On the other hand, the owl, bird of Pallas Athene, and originally bird of death, is associated with worldly wisdom, and was largely allotted as a symbol for clerkly armouries.

The cock, owing to its pugnacity, was always regarded as

COCK CROWNED HEAD, ROMAN
COIN MINTED IN GAUL.

COCK HELMET, COIN MINTED
BY GAULS.

bird of battle, and in war time a white cock with red comb was sacrificed to Mars. On the other hand, it was sacred to Attis, the god of spring and fertility of the Eastern Mediterranean, thus bringing it, with the hen, into the circle of universal symbolism, as the hatchers of the great World Egg. Its wakefulness and matutinal clarion calls, associated with the repentance of St. Peter, made it a favourite Christian symbol, constantly placed on church steeple to call humanity to their duties. In heraldry it appears under its dual nature—a symbol of soldierly courage and of religious aspirations. It appears to have been associated with the religious cult of the Gauls, for Cæsar tells us that they fought under a cock standard. The bird appears on Gallo-Roman sculpture, and the Romans

GNOSTIC COCK-SNAKE GOD

placed a curious representation of a cock war helmet on coins minted in Gaul. We find it used in national symbolism of the early Bourbons, and it was definitely adopted as the French avian emblem under Louis Philippe. A good representation of the coq Gaulois is given in the plates, which shows the badge worn on the shako of an officer of the Civic Guards under that monarch. The cock, when its comb, gills, claws, and beak are of a different tincture from the body itself, is said to be " crested," " jelloped," and " armed." Birds possessing no talons are said to be " beaked " and " membered " when their beaks and legs are of a different tincture.

The peacock is generally borne " in its pride," that is to say, full-faced and with tail outspread. It held a high place in Eastern symbolism, as witness the peacock throne of Persia ; the peacock plumes of the Chinese mandarins ; and the peacock fans—wafters away of evil spirits—carried by the attendants of Eastern potentates. It was the bird of rainbow-throned Juno, consort of Jove ; and the rainbow hues of its gorgeous tail brought it within the Christian symbolism of the Resurrection.

Among game birds we have the partridge, the pheasant and the heath cock or moor hen. Partridge bears : gules, on a fess argent between three lions rampant, or, as many partridges proper ; while Saxby, of Kent, has the far prettier shield : vert, a garb between three partridges or ; Faisant : azure, three pheasants or, beaked and membered gules ; Mores : argent, a heath cock (or moor hen) proper, comb and gills gules.

Parrots appear under the name of " popinjays." These steeds of the Hindu cupid, or god of love, were used in heraldry as early as the reign of Henry III. In later centuries they were sometimes employed to commemorate administrative or commercial success in tropical countries. Marmaduk de Twenge (temp. Henry III) bore : argent, a fess between three popinjays vert ; and Richard FitzMarmaduk, of the same period : gules, a fess between three popinjays argent, a baton azure over all. Cornish chough is the name of a small bird of the crow tribe, with bluish black plumage, and red beak and legs. It was long a mark of Cornish origin.

Cormorants appear as symbols of sea-power, as in the arms of Liverpool: argent, a cormorant, sable armed gule, holding in its beak a sprig of laver seaweed, vert. One of the supporters of the national arms of Chile is a condor. David of Llwch prettily bears: azure, three seagulls argent; and Mewey, co. Devon: gules, three seamews argent, beaked and legged or.

LIVERPOOL.

A bird when raising its wings preparatory to flying is said to be "rising"; if flying "volant"; and when a bird of prey is represented as devouring its food it is said to be "preying." Sometimes a feather has its quill of a different tincture to itself, in which case it is emblazoned as "quilled" of such a tincture. A bird with wings closed is said to be "close" or "trussed."

PEACOCK IN HIS PRIDE.

CHAPTER VI

FISH, AMPHIBIA, OPHIDIA AND INSECTS

FISH are emblazoned in four principal positions : as "hauriant," in a perpendicular position, the head upwards ; " urinant," also perpendicular, but with the head downwards, as though diving ; " naiant," or swimming horizontally ; and as " embowed," or bent. The dolphin, a very favourite device, is always borne " embowed."

The dolphin was early employed by Asiatics and Greeks as a symbol of maritime power, and by the latter also as emblematic of youth. It was not only placed on the shield of Ulysses in token of his voyages, but was sacred to Apollo. It took the bodies of shipwrecked lovers of music and the gods safely to land, or conveyed their souls to the Fortunate Isles. The Egyptians paid worship to fish and used them as symbols. With them fish were guardians of souls. Two of them, Abtu and Ant, swam before Ra's boat during his nightly voyages through the Underworld of Tuat. In Christian iconogprahy it represents the Resurrection, for the dolphin is beautiful in death, rapidly changing into the colours of the rainbow, that sign of hope. Dolphins are conventionalised figures of a large-headed, finned, cetaceous mammal. On Greek coins and vases they appear as somewhat elongated fish, with beak-like snouts, crested fins at the back of their heads, bifurcated tails, the body slightly bowed, forming a depressed arch from tail to head. A splendid example of two such dolphins may be seen in white on a black circular shield adorning a Greek vase preserved at the British Museum. In symbolism and heraldry they represent sea-power and travel, and so may be seen alike on the shields of sailors, merchants

57

and seaports. They are usually shown " embowed naiant," presenting an undulating outline, the body arched, the snout curved and the tail flat ; the dorsal fin prominent and spiky, being carried from the head almost to the tail ; the pectoral fins small ; the tail bifurcated or triparted. But for crests the favourite attitude is the diving one. They are sometimes borne in saltire and also endorsed. In Continental heraldry the dolphin is often shown " hauriant " as well as bent into a semicircle. It generally appears in this form, as on the quartered coat and as the badge of the former heirs-apparent to the Crown of France, who, from the reign of Charles V to the day of the unhappy son of Louis XVI, derived their title Dauphin, and their insignia of a blue dolphin with red eyes and fins on a gold field, from the ancient county of Viennois, later known as Dauphiné, from the title of Dauphin assumed by its rulers. Both the title and arms are mysterious, for the title was only assumed in 1100 by Guigue IV, and the dolphin did not appear until many years after. It has therefore been conjectured that the arms are allusive to the title, which itself is supposed to have been derived from the Celtic *dal*, (district) *na*, (of the) and *pen* or *pin* (point, hill, head, chief, leader) ; thus the embowed fish stood for district head leader. Twice failure occurred in the male line, though the title and arms were continued. Then Humbert III, last of the third line, sold his county to Philip of France, and the rich district became attached to the throne, and the title passed to the heirs thereof. Dolphins have also long been associated with the county of Devonshire. A dolphin is the crest of the Courtenays, Earls of Devon, and appears on the seal of Catherine of York, wife of Edward IV. It is used as a kind of supporter on the side of the shield. The Courtenays apparently derived it from De Abincis, hereditary sheriffs of Devon, whose heiress the first of the Courtenays to come to England married. A dolphin curled round an anchor or a trident is a venerable symbol, found on Greek vases ; both designs have been incorporated among heraldic emblems, chiefly as crests.

Another, and larger, denizen of the outer deep is the whale, which appears on the arms of Whalley Abbey, that once great establishment on the banks of the Calder, Lancashire ; gules, three whales hauriant, or, in each mouth a crosier of the last.

It is not only the whale which is in the habit of swallowing things. The town of King's Lynn bears : azure, three conger eels' heads erased hauriant, or, in the mouth of each a cross-crosslet fitchy, of the last.

Glasgow affords us a fine example of that curiously world-

CITY OF GLASGOW.

wide legend of a fish restoring a long-lost ring. The arms of the city of Glasgow show on a silver field a green oak-tree growing from a green mount. At the base of the stem, but in front of it, is a salmon on its back, shown in its proper colours, and having a gold signet-ring in its mouth. On the top of the tree is a robin redbreast ; on the left of the tree is an ancient silver handbell. The crest is a half-length figure of a bishop, wearing his vestments and mitre. The right hand is raised in the act of benediction, the left hand holds a crosier over his shoulder, all being painted in their natural colours. The supporters are two salmon, each holding in its mouth a gold-signet ring. Some argue that we have here purely spiritual symbolism—the oak is the tree of life ; the bird of the Holy Spirit ; the bell of the Church ; the fish of our Saviour ; and the ring the emblem of the marriage of the Church to Christ. Others have a more circumstantial tale to tell. They say the bishop is the good St. Kentigern, patron of Glasgow, who founded the city in 500 A.D. Kentigern means " Chief Lord " ; this was softened into Mungo, " Dear Friend," when he became a missionary and performed many miracles. He breathed on a frozen hazel-branch and kindled it into flames ; he restored life to the dead robin of the hermit of St. Serf ; brought a handbell from Rome which wrought wonders ; and by his intervention the lost ring of the frail queen Rederech, which had been cast into the Clyde in sign of marital displeasure, was restored by a salmon, thus bringing about reconciliation.

Now it must be remembered that the story of throwing a ring into the sea and its subsequent recovery by means of a fish which had swallowed it, and all the important events that followed therefrom, is pretty well as old as the hills, and met with in many unexpected places. Herodotus tells us the tale of Polycrates. In the Koran there is a story of how Satan by sundry wiles secured Solomon's signet and by virtue thereof sat on his throne for forty days, then, getting tired, how he threw the ring into the sea. It was swallowed by a fish which was captured by the wandering and disconsolate Solomon, who, finding the ring in the fish's belly, thereby was able to regain his kingdom. That is very much the same story as told to us by the Glasgow shield. Then in Germany we find a certain von Findelstein, of Bavaria, bearing : gules, an arm proceeding from the clouds, habited azure, the hand grasping a fish with a golden ring in its mouth. Hamilton of Hogg, bears : gules, a salmon's head couped fesswise with a ring in its mouth, between three cinquefoils, all argent. Other instances could be cited both at home and abroad.

Many fish are borne for the sake of a punning allusion to

family names. For instance, pike, of old called lucies, are
borne by the Lucies; Heringham has three herrings hauriant;
Heringot, Kent, (*temp.* Henry III,) bore a border of herrings;
while Heringod, of Icklesham, Sussex, bore: azure, semée
of cross-crosslets, six herrings naiant in pale, or; and Heringod, of Elmstead, as seen sculptured on a cloister ceiling of
Canterbury Cathedral, bore: azure, three herrings hauriant
between six crosslets fitchy, or. Troutbeck of Troutbeck,
Westmorland, a family of feudal descent, bore: azure, three
trout fretted, tête à queue, azure (thus forming a ring).
For crest, a head resting on a wreath of trout. In a Roll of
Arms in the Harleian Collection, British Museum, the three
fish of Troutbeck are shown two in saltire, heads abased, the
third hauriant. Both of these compositions are curious.

Sometimes three fish bodies are borne en pairle, with a
single head in the fess
point. Bream are gener-
ally borne semi-hauriant;
that is, naiant in bend.
Thus De Mare, Abbot
of Peterborough, bore:

KINGSTON-ON-THAMES.   YARMOUTH.

azure, three bream bendwise, two and one, or. The Counts
of Bar, intimately connected with our Plantagenets, bore
two barbel hauriant embowed and addorsed in a field
crusily. But by no means all fish are borne for the sake of
the pun. Many are allusive to important water rights. Thus
Kingston-on-Thames now bears: azure, three salmon naiant
in pale, or, in base a Saxon K, of the last, but formerly

bore : azure, three salmon hauriant in fess, argent; thus
reminding us that of old the Thames was a great salmon
river. Great Yarmouth formerly bore : azure, three herrings
naiant, in pale argent. For centuries past this coat has
been dimidiated with the royal arms of England, the lion
coat appearing on the dexter side. The result is that we
have a shield per pale gules and azure charged with three
half lions gold, with herrings tails, argent. Many other
towns, such as Poole and Brighton, bear dolphins on their
shields.

The arms of Iceland are a golden stockfish (a codfish spread
open, deprived of its head and dried) on a blue shield. In
Germany we find skeletons of fish emblazoned. Eels are also
common charges. In Spain, as we shall see, they were
sometimes shown in cauldrons. Crabs and crayfish are shown,
and so are many shell-fish. The most celebrated of these
are the escallop shells, usually associated with St. James of
Compostella and pilgrimage, hence with Crusading, travel
beyond the seas, and later with commerce. Alstanton bears :
azure, three sea-urchins, needles erect, argent.

Coming to another branch of natural history we find many
snakes and serpents. When erect and wavy they are said
to be " ondoyant in pale " ; when wriggling across the
shield they are " gliding." They are often borne " nowed "
and are even found knotted round a human throat. Among
the celebrated heraldic snakes is that of Milan, ondoyant
in pale and vorant a child, carnation, on a field or. It is supposed to record the prowess of the first Duke of Milan in
slaying a monster which levied a tribute of human sacrifices
on the Milanese. But the snake is not always an exemplifi-
cation of evil, though we do see it on heraldic shields representing Satan in the Garden of Eden. It was, however,
also one of the creatures sacred to the sun, as in Egypt and
India, and stood as a symbol of sun and sun gods ; for
instance, Apollo, father of medicine and music. Snakes
therefore, are emblems of wisdom and are to be seen wreathed
about hand mirrors (the mirror is a sun symbol), about the
caduceus and distilling into cups. In this light they are

connected both with justice and medicine ; this doubtless also accounts for the Wise bearing : sable, three chevrons between as many adders argent. Others, like the asps of the Aspe family, and the vert, three asps in pale or, of Aspendall, are obviously of punning intent. Ednowain ap Bradwen, Merionethshire, bore : gules, three snakes nowed in triangle argent.

Crocodiles are comparatively modern. A good example is the supporter granted to Speke of Nile exploration fame.

Insects are also seen. These include scorpions, ants, butterflies, bees and grasshoppers. Bees are very ancient emblems, favourites as badges with royal personages as exemplifying an industrious community clustering round their sovereign. They were used by the Romans and by the French kings, but more notably by Napoleon I and his nephew. Bees also represent commerce. Probably the same root notion of association in industry caused the ant and ermite to make their appearance in heraldry. Certainly that appears to be the reason for their presence on the shield of the Benedictine Abbey of Pershore : sable, on a chevron between three ant-hills or, each charged with four ants proper, as many holly-leaves azure. The grasshopper appears in connection with knightly heraldry, and also with the symbols of commerce. A notable example in the latter sense is the golden grasshopper of Sir Thomas Gresham, Lord Mayor of London, Merchant Venturer and Grocer, in the crowded days of Queen Elizabeth.

CHAPTER VII

FABULOUS CREATURES

THERE are many fabulous creatures used in heraldry, a number originating in the dateless symbolism of our remote ancestors, others introduced through the fantasy of romance-loving man, and yet more owing to the freaks of heralds and herald painters. In the main, however, fabulous monsters, especially the humanised beasts, belong to an early stage of mental development, a stage when man looked upon himself as part of natural surroundings, subject to mysterious outside forces but dimly recognised. To him animals and trees were dwellings of kin souls. Hence the worship of animals as manifestations of superhuman forces, as in the ferocious lion, the cunning tiger, the powerful whirl-wind dashing bull. Hence the picturing of the winged, human-headed bulls of Nineveh, the harpies, human-headed lions, the mermen and mermaids. Then came the bird-, beast-, and reptile-headed men and women, which, through totemism or other form of ritual, linked the whole animated world together, as we see in the long gallery of Egyptian deities. So men were shown springing out of the animals, as in the centaur ; then men stood on them ; and finally seated themselves on thrones representing animals, as with the peacock throne of Persia, dwindling down into our own lion-armed crowning chair. As I have pointed out elsewhere : " The science of paleontology has justified many of the queerest monster creations of early artists. There is the grebe-like *hesperonis regalis* of the Rockies, 6 feet high, with long jaws full of teeth ; other birds with prolonged vertebræ, suggestive of snake-like tails, and paws of reptiles with strong claws." (" Armorial Insignia of the Princes of Wales.")

Foremost among those monsters which particularly interest us are the dragons, a formidable army, springing from the mysterious East, the Nilithic swamps and the morasses of Northern Europe as well as of our own islands. For there are many types. Judaic dragons were amphibious, created with the fishes (Genesis 1); in Isaiah we are told of ." the dragon that lieth in the sea "; and in Ezekiel of the " great dragon that lieth in the midst of the rivers," which was Tiamat, the prodigiously huge four-legged, scaly-bodied she-dragon of Chaldea and Babylon, whom Bel, god of Nippon,

CITY OF LONDON. DRAGON
SUPPORTERS.

lord of the Underworld, overcame, and whom Marduk, the winged solar-god slew, splitting her in half to make the sky and the earth.

In the Far East the dragon is usually serpentine in form, with four legs, rugged head with spiked ears and is an aerial, but wingless brute. The Chinese Imperial dragon is golden, but silver or white on the standard, with blue scales, has five claws and is represented as attacking the sun, having long feelers projecting from its jaws circling round the golden or scarlet disc. As a symbol of delegated power appertaining to high officials, its colour and number of talons varied according to rank. The Japanese dragon rises from the sea and has only three claws to each of its feet. In the Near East the dragon is an aerial-amphibian, with long reptilian, scaly body, four short paws with formidable talons and saurian head with spiked ears, fangs and forked tongue, bat-like wings, and generally belches forth fire. It is this type that we see in Christian iconography trodden under foot by the Archangel Michael, St. George or other hero, and is represented in the badge of the Knights of the Garter. Something similar, though often having only two legs, was the common dragon of the Norsemen and Celtic people. It may be seen in the Bayeux tapestry, both among the Norman knights and Harold's followers. But there were dragons here before the Normans or even the Saxons came, for Geoffrey of Monmouth in his " Chronicle " tells us of the British Uther seeing a dragon-shaped comet in the sky, adopted a golden dragon as his war standard, and henceforth was known as Uther Pendragon. This legendary Pendragon was sire to the shadowy King Arthur. But Pendragon appears to have been a warrior title, for the Saxon chronicles tell us of Cedric's victory over Naud and his Pendragon, at a place which some have identified as Dragon's Hill, Berkshire.

After the Conquest the dragon was well to the fore. Richard I had a dragon standard when he went Crusading, and Henry III had a golden dragon, with wagging tongue and eyes of sapphire, borne before him at Westminster, and possibly at the disastrous battle of Lewes. Edward I marched into Wales under a golden dragon standard, and Edward III had it at Crecy. Edward IV had as a badge a black dragon segreant, with gold claws, which he had adopted when he became Earl of Ulster, deriving it through the Mortimers from the de Burghs, the first Earls of Ulster. Then came the Tudor rulers from Henry VII to Elizabeth, with their ruddy-gold, or gold and red squat dragons. It must be said that the Welsh dragon of war was red, but the righteous dragon was of ruddy gold. In Tudor days the under part was red, the upper gold.

At a fairly early date the heraldic dragon as depicted on coat armour was of a lionine type, having squat scaly body,

long legs with claws, barbed saurian tail, rugged head with
horny projections, barbed tongue, and great bat wings.   It

DRAGON.   GRIFFIN.
UNICORN.   HARPY.

is borne " volant," " segreant " (rampant), as in the Tudor
and the City of London supporters, passant, as in the Welsh
badge, and is used as a charge, a crest or badge and for

supporters. The serpentine form as a crest is shown on the helm of Roger, Earl of Winchester (1195–1265) (page 217). A dragon with a human head is blazoned as "monstreu." Dragons' heads and wings are met as charges and as crests. Field-Marshal Lord Beresford, for his victory at Albuera in 1811, received for crest : out of a mural crown, a dragon's head, pierced by a lance, which it holds between its teeth ; typifying the tenacious bravery of both vanquished and victors.

Winged serpents are also borne in heraldry, and apparently owe their parentage to the symbolism of ancient Egypt, where we find two opposing armies of winged ophidians, the evil ones warring against Osiris (the sun god) during his nightly passage through the Underworld, and the beneficent guardians of the noon-day sun, frequently seen wreathed about the solar disc. Both types may be represented in intricate knots (like the attenuated ribbon dragon with bird's neck and beak of the Celts), knots of all kinds standing for mystic " words of power." These are the " amphiptere " of French blazonry.

Wyverns, so constantly blazoned, are really the early type of serpentine dragon, having only two legs and a long tail, generally " nowed." It is the type of dragon still used in Continental heraldry.

The hydra, the many-headed serpent of classic legend, whom Hercules slew, is occasionally borne. A notable example is afforded by the arms granted to Ossip Ivanovich, who saved the life of the Emperor Alexander II in 1865. He bore : or, issuant from the sinister flank an arm proper, vested azure, the hand seizing a hydra sable, winged gules ; on a chief of the third a ship fully rigged bearing the Imperial standard, all proper.

Local monsters are to be seen in the shields of some towns and territorial magnates, as in the case of Tarascon, with its fierce tarask, a kind of dragon-basilisk.

Griffins, or gryphons, were known both to the Greeks and the Romans, as their sculptures and coins testify. No doubt they came from the East, perhaps by way of Egypt. They have the forequarters of dragons, the hindquarters of lions, eagles' heads with prominent pointed ears, and small bat wings. These ears are of great importance in distinguishing

GRECIAN GRIFFIN.

the griffin, for it is said to have been one of the fiercest, most active, and quickest of animals. They are emblems of vigilance, so the pointed eared head as crest or charge is a favourite. Gerard Leigh, a herald of the time of Queen Elizabeth, speaking of griffins, in a manner clearly showing he believed that they had a real existence, says, " I think they are of great hugeness, for I have a claw of one of their paws which should show them to be as big as two lions." Lady Mary Wortley Montagu in one of her chatty letters, dated from Ratisbon (in 1716), mentions having been shown in a Roman Catholic church a huge claw set in gold, which

HAWK-HEADED HORUS.

was said to be a griffin's claw. " I could not," says Lady Mary, " forbear asking the reverend priest that showed it, whether the griffin was a saint ? The question almost put him beside his gravity, but he answered they only kept it as a curiosity."

A cockatrice is a wyvern with a cock's head, but barbed tongue.

A harpy has the head and bust of a woman and the body of an eagle, and like so many other of these monsters may be traced through classical art to Eastern imagery.

Sphinxes, with their lionine bodies and women's busts and heads, belong to the mysticism of Egypt, and, though known to the Romans, only appear to have entered the realms of heraldry towards the end of the eighteenth century, when the land of the Nile began to be a field for European enterprise. It is one of the war badges of several of our regiments. Sir John Moore, the hero of Corunna, in honour of his earlier services in Egypt, bore : argent, on a fess engrailed azure, three mullets of the field, in chief a sphinx proper, all within a border engrailed.

Unicorns also reached the Greeks and Romans from the East, for they thought the beasts were to be found in India, though some kinds of African quadrupeds are far more likely to have given the idea. Indeed, a perfect representation of the unicorn is to be seen on a Roman-Egyptian papyrus in our national collection at the British Museum. It is there shown seated in a chair playing a losing game of draughts with a smirking lion. Unicorns of this description are also to be found in far older hieroglyphic inscriptions in the land of Osiris. It is amusing to find this antagonism between the two beasts shown in this way, for the legend of their enmity is one of the firm beliefs of old-time writers. This was unfortunate, for while the lion was regarded as the symbol of martial valour, the unicorn stood for purity, the protector of virtue. Its horn was regarded as a sovereign cure for many dire diseases, a grand antidote against all poisons. Many royal and other collections in mediæval days and somewhat later contained fragments of unicorn horns. In an inventory of royal jewels made for Queen Elizabeth we find mentioned, " Imprimis, a piece of unicorn's horn," and some time later a German traveller, one Hentzner, saw at Windsor Castle " a horn of about eight spans and a half in length, valued at about £10,000." These and other such horns are well authenticated, and presumably were the teeth of narwhals. The heraldic unicorn has the body of a horse, the legs of a stag, the tail of a lion, a fine mane, and a single horn springing from its forehead. It is almost invariably white or silver, but it is usually armed and unguled of gold. Such is the famous unicorn supporter of the royal arms of the United Kingdom, brought to us from Scotland by James I. This unicorn is gorged with a royal crown, with a chain attached and reflexed over its back. The unicorn is used as a charge, a crest and a supporter. Both the Chinese and the Japanese have a unicorn, which has the body and hoofs of a deer, the tail of an ox, and a horn on its forehead. So it is not unlike our own, only rather heavier in build. Curiously enough its companion is also a lion, the so-called " dog of Buddha," which has tufts of curling hair round the neck and on the limbs. This rather assimilates it to the Assyrian lion, with its elaborately plaited mane and solemn mien, so different to attitude and expression as characteristic of our own " leopards."

The heraldic antelope must be mentioned here, for it is like nothing seen in nature, with its body of a stag, but fantastic head, a great horn growing upon the tip of its nose, and its grotesque tufts of hair down its neck, back, on its chest, thighs and tip of its tail. There is, however, a later antelope, with two horns, and altogether more natural, introduced by modern African adventurers of all sorts.

Henry Fitzroy, Duke of Richmond, natural son of Henry VIII, derived the yale as one of his supporters from his mother. It is described as "a yale argent bezanty, horned, hoofed and gorged with a crown and chained or," and is an heraldic antelope with the horns of a ram and the tail of a dog.

Salamanders are short-tailed, horny skinned lizards, having four fairly long legs, and are usually shown gambolling amidst flames and breathing fire. Legend said that the salamander was of so cold a nature that it could extinguish flames, and appears in earlier symbolism to have been adopted as an emblem of religious ardour and of faith overcoming trials ; later as representing perseverance overcoming worldly troubles of all kinds. It is probably from a mixture of the two ideas that the salamander was adopted as the badge of Comtes d'Angoulême, from whom it descended to Francis I, who has left splendid examples of his royally crowned cognisance, carved, painted and traced in needlework at the Château de

IRONMONGERS' COMPANY, LONDON. SALAMANDER CREST AND SUPPORTERS.

Blois. It was under one of these that the following lines were inscribed :

"Ursus atrox, Aquilæque leves, et Tortilis anguis
Cesserunt flammæ cain Salamander tuæ."

This, of course, refers to the French king's victories over the Swiss, Germans and Milanese, who are represented by their national emblems of the bear, the eagle and the serpent. As in the case of the badge of François, salamanders may be blazoned gorged with a crown or coronet, with chain attached, and reflexed over the back.

Another creature associated with flames is the phœnix,

or mystic golden sun eagle. It was known to and honoured by the Egyptians as a religious emblem representing the continuity of life. They held that when the phœnix grew old it flew into the sun or into a fire, immolating itself. A worm sprang out of its ashes, and out of the worm was hatched a full-fledged young phœnix. This parable of the efficacy of self-sacrifice was seized upon by the early Christians, and the phœnix rising from the flames may be found in the Catacombs of Rome, representing belief in the doctrine of resurrection. It was in this sense that it was welcomed in armoury, where it is represented as an eagle displayed rising from flames, the head turned skywards. The usual tinctures for the eagle are sable or gold. In China and Japan the phœnix is the badge of the Empresses.

A pegasus is a winged horse, generally represented as " volant " and " animé " (with an eye of a different tincture to the body itself). It is the winged steed of Apollo, so largely connected with intellectual arts. Thus Rusticuli, of Italy, bear : or, on a mount of Parnassus vert, with springs of water, azure, a pegasus of the third. Our Michael Drayton had the better shield : azure, gutty d'argent, a pegasus of the second. The pegasus borne as the arms of the Inner Temple is said to be a mere imposition. One of the badges of the Knights Templar was a horse on which two knights were mounted, in allusion to their vow of poverty. Probably unwilling to take such a vow the lawyers transformed the two poor warriors into two wings. Sir John Jervis (Lord St. Vincent), for his victory off Cape St. Vincent, was assigned the following crest when raised to the peerage : a pegasus springing from a naval crown, its wings charged with a fleur-de-lis.

Centaurs belong to classic legend, wherein they found their way from the dark regions beyond the Caucasus, those lands where man seemed to form one with his steed. The centaur has a horse's body, but from the shoulders up the bust, arms and head of a man. It was an emblem of courage, tempered with wisdom. When a centaur bears bows and arrows it is blazoned as a " sagitarius," and appears quite early as one of the signs of the zodiac. A " sagitarius " was possibly adopted as a badge by our King Stephen.

The manticora and the chimera both belong to this class. A manticora, also known as a lampago, or a man tiger, has the body of an heraldic tiger with the head of an old man adorned with long spiral horns. A manticora of purple was the badge of Lord Fitzwalter (*temp.* Henry VII or earlier). Probably his son, described as " Master Ratleefe " (Ratcliffe) in the " Book of Standards " of the Heralds' College, had one not only with human head, but feet as well, crowned with a cap of dignity, with a chain of gold round its neck and a sun pendent therefrom beneath a padlock. A chimera has the body of a goat, the face of a man, mane and legs of a lion, and tail of a dragon. Luckily she is only encountered as a crest.

Almost all animals have been represented at one time or another in heraldry with fishes' tails, when they are said to be " marined." First among these is man, together with his helpmate. Mermen or tritons are seen represented in the earliest Greek and Roman sculptures. They have the upper part of the body human, ending either in a single fish tail, or each leg from the thigh down is separately " marined." They usually carry tridents and conch-shell trumpets, and may be wreathed about the head with seaweed. River tritons usually carry vases and have wreaths of bulrushes. They are among the symbols of sea power, and are often associated with the arms of seaports and sailors. An interesting example of how this could come about, although it is extremely bad heraldry, is afforded by the insignia of Sir Isaac Heard, Garter-King-at-Arms, who flourished at the end of the eighteenth century, and who had been a sailor in his early manhood. He bore : argent, a triton proper, crowned or, a trident in his dexter hand, his sinister hand grasping the mast of a ship issuing from the sea in base ; on a chief azure, the arctic star of the first, between two water bowgets of the second. The elucidation of this complicated composition is that Heard was saved from drowning after shipwreck.

Mermaids, the melosines of the French, are much more interesting. Appropriately enough the goddesses of both Phœnicia and Babylonia were mermaids. The heraldic mermaids have long hair, partly covering the shoulders and breasts, and may have single or double tails. They usually

BRISTOL MERCHANT ADVENTURERS.   SUPPORTERS, A MERMAID AND A WINGED SATYR.   BARRY WAVY OF 5 ARGENT AND AZURE, ON A BEND OR A DRAGON PASSANT IN BEND VERT, ON A CHIEF GULES, A LION PASSANT GUARDANT GOLD BETWEEN TWO BEZANTS.

carry a comb in one hand and a mirror in the other, but a German crowned example is armless, with two fish wings, each charged with three barbels embowed. A mermaid holding a dagger is the crest of Harry, co. Cornwall. This forms a very favourite composition, both as a charge and as a crest, and was used to represent sea-service, exploration and over-seas commerce.

Some other of the marined animals deserve special attention.

Sea-horses in the earliest heraldic examples closely resemble the queer fish known by that name (the *hippocampus*), but classic art had furnished quite another type, the forequarters of a horse, with mane and hoofs, and the hindquarters replaced by a fish's tail. Neptune and Boreas were often shown riding these steeds over crested waves. The common type of heraldic charge shows a horse with webbed feet, a scalloped fin down its back and a fish's tail.

Sea-lions, lions with fishes' tails, may often have been produced by heraldic manipulation of two different coats, as was shown in the preceding chapter when describing the dimidiated shield of Yarmouth. The dimidiated shield of Hastings in the same way gives us a lion-ship, for the arms of Hastings are azure, an ancient galley between two lions passant guardant in pale, or; which was dimidiated with England, so that the charge is converted into a half-lion with a ship for hindquarters. But the sea-lion was known to the ancients. With us it is one of the symbols of sea dominion and has been largely employed as a crest or supporter, to commemorate naval victories. For instance, the Earls of Thanet and Viscounts Falmouth bore a sea-horse as crest and had two sea-lions, argent, gutty de sang, as supporters, these having been granted to their ancestor, Admiral Boscawen. Viscount Bridport for his services as second admiral in command on June 1, 1794, was granted a sea-lion and an archer as his supporters.

Sea-dogs are male otters, which, as a matter of fact, often go out considerable distances in the sea. They, however, are depicted with webbed feet, fins down their backs and scaly bodies. They are seen on the arms of Fenner, Sussex: argent, a chevron engrailed gules, between three marine wolves or sea-dogs, sable, finned and dented of the second. Sea otters are the supporters of Lord Stourton.

A marine cock is borne by Geyss of Bavaria, and a sea-horse by Gundriphen of Suabia. Marined griffins and unicorns are also seen in German heraldry. Other marined animals are the sea-stag and the capricorn, the half-goat, half-fish zodiacal sign.

The vertical union of two animals, as the left-hand side of an eagle joined to the right hand half of a lion, occasionally seen on the Continent, is due to dimidiation. I know of no example of such mechanical hybridisation in our own heraldry.

By way of appropriate tail-piece it may be mentioned Lord Stawell has a satyr as one of his supporters, and that Satan, with horns, a cloven foot and barbed tail complete, sometimes occurs in Continental heraldry, which is not so astonishing when we remember that in France we find the patronymics Le Diable softened into Le Maudit, Le Mallin, and Le Mauvais, and in Germany Teufel into Manteufel.

**DRAGON ON SHIELD,
BAYEUX TAPESTRY.**

CHAPTER VIII

THE HUMAN FORM AND ITS PARTS

MAN appeared rather late in recognised heraldry, and then seemingly by accident. Certainly the knights of the eleventh and twelfth centuries did not place human figures on their shields or on their surcoats. But such figures, generally of a religious description, were occasionally represented on standards, and even more frequently effigies of the owners, or of some allegorical import, were seen on seals, those alike of knights, ecclesiastics, ladies of high estate and corporations. There are a good many indications that seals, both of ecclesiastics and corporate bodies (quite commonly

SCARBOROUGH CORPORA-
TION SEAL.

pictorially symbolical), were given an heraldic character by placing the compositions on shields. Many episcopal arms—those of the sees of Chichester and Waterford are good examples—and of towns, such as Bristol, Scarborough, Huntingdon (the latter with a pictorial design of a tree and bird, a huntsman blowing on a horn and two dogs coursing a stag), provide other instances. The Scarborough arms as registered at the College of Arms are without tinctures, but may be described thus : in base a wavy sea, thereon to dexter an ancient ship of one mast with rigging and castellated top, in prow and stern the heads of two men affronté, on sinister side an old castle, a tower thereon, with a Moor's head appearing over the battlements ; in honour point, between castle and ship,

78

a wavy star of eight points. Lichfield's bearings are even more extraordinary : on a shield is a landscape with several trees on a hill to the dexter, a view of the Cathedral on the sinister, and in base the bodies, heads and limbs of three naked men scattered over the field together with crowns, swords and banners. It was in this way that angels, saints, pilgrims, knightly patrons or mere civic officers (like that forest warden of Huntingdon), came to be added to the treasury of available charges. When the step was once taken, precedents enough could be found, for classic lore told us of the horrific head of Medusa on Achilles's shield, which he derived from the target of Pallas Athene (a reminiscence of the barbaric habit of warriors adorning themselves with the scalps of their victims).

From the ecclesiastical group the following among the most notable may be given. On the blue shield of the see of Chichester, Christ sits on a golden throne, with sword issuant from mouth, the right hand lifted in benediction. On the blue shield of the see of Waterford is a bishop in full canonicals holding a large crucifix in front of him. Moelor Crwm, of Wales, bore : argent on a chevron sable three angels kneeling, their hands on their breasts, wings displayed or. Beringer bore (*circa* 1413) : gules, an angel erect, hands conjoined on breast, wings displayed. Other angels appear, but they are more frequently seen as crests or supporters. The angel in elaborate armorial tabards, supporting the lilied shield of the French kings, is well known. We also have cherubs as charges, which could scarcely have been designed for the old schoolmasters, unless in a spirit of imposing abnegation. But we find Saint bearing three cherubs with differently coloured wings. By the way, the Gothic painter-decorators were quite fond of giving their angels (many of them forming corbels supporting armorial shields) red, blue, green, yellow and even party coloured wings, so that they have a gaudy parrot appearance. Saints themselves are often found—on shields. We have seen St. Mungo in connection with the arms of Glasgow. The insignia for the episcopal district of the Isles is : azure, on waves of the sea in base, St. Columba kneeling in a coracle, holding a dove, all proper, looking at a blazing star, or. For the see of Aberdeen we have : azure, in the porch of a church, St. Nicolas in pontificals, his right hand blessing three children in a cauldron, holding in his sinister hand a crosier, all proper. This bears allusion to the good saint's restoring life to the children boiled by Myra. Halifax bears the holy face of St. John the Baptist, thus : chequy or and azure, the head of St. John affronté, distilling three goutes of sang from neck, a nimbus about the head, or, in chief the word " Haley," in base the word " Fax," in Saxon letters countercharged of the field. The parish church was dedicated to St. John. In France St. Denis appears in coat armour.

Our first parents have not been forgotten. Adamoli, of Lombardy, bears : azure the Tree of Life, entwined with the Serpent and accosted by Adam and Eve, all proper (but not from the prude's point of view, for the man and the woman appear in a state of innocence). Sampson, of Verona, bore : gules, on a terrace, vert, Sampson (gilded, but *sans culottes* or clothes of any kind) bestriding a golden lion and tearing his jaws apart. Hercules is seen on Continental coats fighting with a lion, with a hydra, and rending a tree. Apollo, as god of the sun, of music and medicine, is frequently borne. On the arms of the Apothecaries' Company, London, he is blazoned as a Roman knight, bestriding a dragon, and wielding a bow and arrow. Atlas appears bearing the world on his back, Vulcan armed with his hammer, Mars in war panoply and Neptune with his trident and net. Bacchus may bear his grape-twined thyrsus ; but the German coat of Hopfer bears, punningly : or, the infant Bacchus, dancing, wreathed about his loins and head with hops, with a bunch of hops in his hand. Which calls to mind the quaint blazonry of the city of Dantzic : or, in a field gules two couples (*chacun sa chacune*, as we might say), dancing, proper ; in chief an eagle displayed, in base a cross, both sable. Sobieski's personal coat was : or, a queen, hair dishevelled or, habited gules, seated on a bear passant, sable, her arms extended in cross. Rather easier

to read is the rebus of Richard Barnes, Bishop of Carlisle,
1570 : azure, on a bend argent between two stars or, a bear
passant guardant powdered with golden stars, ready to
devour a naked boy ; on a chief silver three roses gules
radiant gold. Another version shows the naked boy full
faced and grasping in his hands the tongue of a bear. How
a youngster may be made to point a moral was shown by
an early Oswald, who bore: azure, a naked boy pointing to a
star in the dexter chief. A later worldly Oswald altered this
to : azure, a savage wreathed about the loins with bay-leaves,
having a sheath of arrows hanging by his side, bearing a
bow in his sinister hand, and pointing with the dexter to
a coronet placed in the dexter chief. Queen Mary bore as
one of her badges a figure of winged Time drawing Truth from
a well, with the motto " Veritas temperis filia." Fortune
(like Truth) appears as a nude female, erect on a wheel or
on a globe. Crehall has : argent, two bars azure, over all
on dexter side a naked man proper, hands over head holding
a pellet, on sinister an oak-tree eradicated vert ; Drummond :
or, three bars undy gules, over all a naked man naiant in
pale, grasping in dexter hand a sword, his sinister hand and
both feet in action, proper. But how he came to swim in
that sea of blood we know not.

A naked man of very doubtful antecedents appears on the
sable shield of the Scottish Dalzells. Originally he was
shown as standing full face, with arms extended in the form
of the cross. Then he was lifted aloft and dangled, still *sans
sark*, from a gallow tree. Since then he has been unhooked
and now appears, still full faced and unashamed, but with
his arms close to his thighs, as though at attention. He is
of carnation or " proper." To this shield Lord Carnwath
has added as supporters two armed men in ancient costume.
The legend runs that the original Dalzell recovered from the
gallows for King Kenneth II the corpse of a kinsman who
had been hung (and no doubt deservedly so) in a border raid.
But the whole affair is suspicious.

Tragedies of one kind or another, however, are not uncommon on armorial shields. We have already seen the

Milanese serpent devouring a boy. Grimsditch, of Chester (*temp*. Henry III), bore a griffin seizing a man in complete armour lying on his back; Warnchampe : vert, a wyvern passant volant argent, swallowing a child carnation. Barragan, of Navarre, bore : or, a naked corpse, proper, at foot of a tree, vert, a raven at head and one at feet, sable. Davies, a Welshman, bore : sable, a goat argent, attired or, standing on a child, proper, swaddled gules, and feeding from a tree vert.

Warriors are borne in many forms. If fully accounted in armour, he is blazoned a " chevalier," and may be borne on foot or mounted. Admiral Kempenfelt bore a chevalier with a sword above the head, and Horman bore a demi-man in armour. Blacker bore : argent, gutty de sang, a Danish warrior armed with battle-axe and sword in his hands all proper. They are more commonly seen as supporters, as in the case of Lord Carnwath with his primitive kilted Lowlanders, the Earl of Leven with his men-at-arms of Charles I's day, and many others, coming down to those with soldiers of modern times. Wood bore : azure, three wild men of the woods proper, holding in their dexter hands clubs argent, and in their sinister hands silver escutcheons, each charged with a cross gules. Chisholm, of Inverness-shire, who trace their ancestry from Harold, Thane of Caithness, Orkney and Shetland in the twelfth century, bear : azure, a boar's head erased, argent ; and for supporters two naked wild men, wreathed about their loins, carrying clubs, to represent the war-like clansmen. But for this branch of the subject readers should turn to Chapter XXII.

Comares, of Spain, bears : argent, a Moorish king passant, habited azure, with collar round his neck and chain attached, or ; evidently a prisoner. More peaceful are the arms of Lylde, otherwise Thomas de Insula, Bishop of Ely, 1341–61: gules, on three bezants the Kings of Cologne (the Magi of the Nativity). Middleton, of Belsay Castle, Northamptonshire, whose ancestor, (*temp*. Edward III), acquired valuable estates by marriage, a fact recorded by the naked wild men, wreathed about the loins and head, holding a fructed oak-tree in his hand. Similar in spirit is the demi-huntsman winding a horn, the crest of Clerk of Perth. In the same class of landed interests is the German coat of Roten : azure, a woman in old national costume carrying a fish in each hand. In some instances the maiden's arms are replaced by fish, a quaint Teutonic reversion to the old Greek metamorphised girls.

We have seen that a demi-man may be borne. This is natural as a crest, but when it occurs as a charge on a shield it is no doubt usually the result of some form of dimidiation, or the introduction of a crest or badge. But it is quite possible that in some cases the symbolism may have been intentional, for under feudal tenure many subtenants held land subject to the provision in time of war of half an armed man. That is, he had to join with some other tenant in providing a man-at-arms.

When we come to heads (which, together with other parts of the body, were depicted on shields much earlier than man as a whole), whether borne " coupe " (cut off smoothly at the neck) or " eradicated " (torn off with a jagged edge) we are undoubtedly in a region of war badges, for they are associated with the Medusa mask (that face distorted by fury, the tresses of hair replaced by curled and hissing snakes attached to the scalp). The long contest during the middle ages between Christendom and Mohammedanism in Europe, Africa and the Near East was largely responsible for the adoption of heads of Saracens, Moors and Turks as war badges among the Hungarians, Italians and Spaniards, these gradually finding their way into the universals of heraldry. The Saracen's head is generally that of a black, with a wreath of twisted linen across his forehead. Such a head appears in the arms of Gladstone, the forehead wreathed with green leaves. Sardinia bears : argent, a cross gules, between four Moors' heads couped, sable, banded (that is, wreathed with the linen twist) of the first. This tells of the constant invasion of that island by followers of the Prophet. Corsica was also subject to these incursions, and its old arms were : argent, a Saracen's head, sable, banded across the eyes of the first ; but when

Paoli had almost won freedom for his native isle, he lifted the
bandage from the eyes to the forehead. It is Corsica's Saracen's head which is seen on the arms of the Earls of Minto,
as a memento of Sir Gilbert Elliot's unfortunate governorship
of that island. While Newton bore : sable, a Saracen's head
couped at neck, argent, with three lions' jambs in dexter,
sinister and base points or ; Best had : gules a Saracen's
head couped at neck proper, navally crowned or, between
eight lions' jambs, chevronwise in pairs inwards gold. These
look like British sailors' victories over Corsairs. But it is
necessary to be cautious in this matter for the families of both
Mores and Moores bear Moors' heads ; so did the Malatestas
and the Testis of Italy. Lloyd of Plymog bore : gules, a
chevron ermine, between three heads couped at neck, bearded
and crined sable. These arms, tradition asserts, were given
to Edryfed Vysham ap Kendrig, Lord of Bryffenigh, Denily,
by the Prince of North Wales (*temp*. John), for his victory
over the English under the Earl of Chester, when he slew
three of the chief leaders. Through marriage and descent
these three English heads have been carried on to many
a respectable family shield. Rochead, a Scot, with his argent,
a savage's head couped, distilling blood proper, between
three black combs, is somewhat enigmatical, but it looks like
the gratification of an itch for a bad joke.

Women's heads, with long flowing hair, occur. One of
the oldest and most important of the City Guilds, the
Mercers' Company, bears : azure, within an orle of clouds,
argent, the head of a virgin, vested argent, crowned with a
celestial crown or, and wreathed about the temples gules. This
represents the Virgin Mary, patron of the Guild and the
whole corporate body of Mercers. Reading bears : azure, the
head of a virgin ducally crowned, between four virgins'
heads (this forming a saltire) all proper, crined, or. Reading
was noted for its religious foundations, and probably the
heads represent the Virgin Mary and four local martyrs,
saintly patrons of conventual establishments. It is amusing
to find that when William Camden made a re-grant of these
arms in the days of Queen Elizabeth, he added to the

blazoning the letters " R " and " E," and in the spirit of
this rather ill-placed homage, the central head has sometimes
been regally crowned. Queen Catherine Parr's badge was a
dainty conception : a maiden's head issuing from a Tudor
rose. The Herberts of Pembrokeshire have as a crest a
Moorish girl's head, couped at the shoulders, hair dishevelled,
and rings in her ears. Vaughan, Breconshire, bears : azure,
three boys' heads couped argent, having snakes knotted
round their necks ; and one of the early Lords Willoughby
had a full-faced Moor's head, without neck, the tongue
hanging out, as his badge. Janer, of Spain, placed the head
of Janue on his shield. Jay bore : argent, three Midas's heads
(with donkey's ears) sable ; while the French Santeuils chose
the head of Argus, which was represented as a human head
covered from scalp to bust with wide-open eyes, perhaps a
tithe of that hundred which phonetics demanded. The
ermine, three princes' heads couped at breast, crowned and
mantled proper, of Enfant and Fauntleroy ; the gules, three
boys' heads couped argent, crined or, of Infant ; and the
gules, three maidens' heads argent, crined or, of Madeston
are quite understandable. Henry Man, Bishop of Sodor and
Man, 1546–56, adopted an extraordinary design for his
shield : azure, a masculyn (a large mascle), and within it
five youths' heads couped argent, crined or. Heads are
also borne on swords and lances, and the crest of Thomas de
Barwe (Barrow), Lord of the Manor of Newington Barrow
(Highbury), shows an eagle pecking at the eyes of a head.
This brings us to skulls, shown alone or as the famous " death's
head and cross-bones " (thigh-bones borne in saltire), which
appeared on the *Jolly Roger* or pirate's flag, and also as the
regimental badge of the 17th Lancers. Bolters bore : argent,
on a chevron gules, three human skulls silver ; and Damboys :
paly of six or and gules a jaw-bone in pale, azure.

Even skeletons are not unknown ; de la Sabloniere, of
Holland, bore : argent, two skeletons, sable, holding between
them a sieve, argent. Evidently they were supposed to be
sanding, in punning allusion to the bearers. In France,
Italy and Portugal the families of Costa, Costanza, Coste and

others having similar names placed ribs on their shields, just as our Baines have crossed thigh and shin bones.

Eyes are, of course, among primitive symbols. In Christian iconography when placed within a triangle or a triquestra an eye represented the Deity, and these devices are occasionally found in connection with ecclesiastical armoury. But human eyes are more common. They are sometimes shown weeping, as in the case of the French family of Denis.

Human hearts, of the purely conventional shape, are favourite charges. They are shown with flames springing from the artery and vein ; pierced by one, two or three arrows, by nails, by swords ; or borne on the points of swords or lances. While some are given wings which may silently recall earthly or other wordly desires, others on the contrary are placed within fetterlocks. One of the most famous of the heraldic hearts is that appearing on the coat of the Douglas family. These arms originally were : argent, on a chief azure, three mullets of the field ; but to this, about 1333, William, Lord Douglas, added a red heart, placing it on the silver field ; about fifty years later a golden crown was placed on the heart. Now this augmentation was to commemorate the entrusting by Robert Bruce to Sir James Douglas the duty of carrying his heart to be buried in the Holy Land. When the king was dead, Sir James set out with his precious burden, but fell fighting against the Moors in Spain, in 1330. Jacques Cœur, the generous French merchant and financial adviser to the king, who flourished about the middle of the fifteenth century, bore these canting arms : azure, on a fess or, between three hearts, or, as many escallop shells, gules, with the motto " A cœur vaillant rien d'impossible." The Amants, also of France, had another, more subtle, pictorial pun on their name : azure, a chevron between three hearts inflamed, gules. Cheylau's heart sent forth a pansy, which is delightful, while more politically inclined versions of the same idea are seen in the fleur-de-lis sprouting from hearts. Colleoni, of Italy, bear : per pale argent and gules, three hearts reversed and counterchanged ; that is to say, the hearts are upside down, one silver, the other red

and the third half red and half white. But this is a very
much softened version of the arms borne by that redoubtable
swashbuckling condottiere, Colleoni of Milan, and his immediate descendants, which was a startling example of *armes
parlantes*, conceived in a spirit worthy of brave old Cyrano de
Bergerac, that pioneer voyager to the land of the Moon.

Hands and arms are borne under many guises. The fist
may be closed ; the thumb and two first fingers raised in the
attitude of blessing ; or the open palm, styled " appaumé,"
may be shown. It may be couped at the wrist or erased with
jagged edge. The blessing hand is appropriately borne by
Benoit : azure, three hands blessing, argent ; and this same
hand is also seen as the crest of the Scottish Millars. The
red open hand, cut at the wrist, is the " Bloody Hand of
Ulster," really the red hand of
O'Neil, Earl of Tyrone. The legend
attaching to its adoption is that when
a fleet of marauding northerners were
intent on invading Erin, the original
O'Neil severed his hand with his
sword and flung it on shore, thus
taking possession, *manus militaris*,
before any of his companions could
do so. It is worth while comparing
this with the legend concerning the

CREST OF WINGED
HANDS.

two hands in the coat-of-arms of the city of Antwerp ;
gules, a castle of four towers, in chief a dexter and sinister
hand appaumé, couped at the wrist, all or. It is said
that when Julius Cæsar was invading Gaul a kind of penin-
sula in the Scheldt was fortified like a castle, and therein
dwelt a giant who levied toll on all who passed up and
down the river, cutting off the right hand of any who tried
to evade the tariff, and flinging the severed member into
the river. This castle was seized by Salvias Brabo, King
of Tangres, and lieutenant of Cæsar, who cut off the
tyrant's head and hands, consigning them to a watery
grave, an event commemorated by Jef Lombeaux's fine
fountain and statue before the Town Hall, and also by the

charges on the civic shield. As regards Tyrone's red hand, this became famous or otherwise, when it was adopted as the badge of the new hereditary order of knights, the baronets, an order instituted by James I with a view to raise money to colonise Ulster. Since then all baronets of Ireland and of the United Kingdom have borne on their paternal coats an inescutcheon argent, charged with a hand appaumé, couped at the wrist, gules.

Traditions relating to the symbolism of the hand are numerous. According to Mahomedans the open hand illustrates the five associated points of the true religion : profession of faith, prayer, almsgiving, fasting, and pilgrimage. More generally the five fingers are taken to represent power, knowledge, will, worthiness, duty ; or force, authority, love, obedience : but in all cases the necessity for united effort is enforced. The right hand, open or closed, has always stood for power and authority, for it was the sword and spear wielder, and when placed on a sceptre became a veritable sign manual of the ruler. So sometimes an eye is placed in the palm of an open hand, to show the vigilance of ruling power ; though when associated with the blessing hand it represents the Divine sanction of the act. It is this recognition of the authority of the right hand that led to the policy of severing that member from prisoners, whether of war or criminals. Of course, it is not all hands that have this exalted origin, for there are several coats belonging to the same order as that of Baron Castlemaine, whose family name is Handcock, and who bears : ermine, on a chief, sable, a dexter hand between two cocks argent, armed, crested and jelloped gules. Thus the Tremaynes have three hands ; some branches of the family three bent arms, joined at the shoulders and arranged en pairle, the palms of the hands open. Henry de Malmaine in the days of the Plantagenets bore : or, three sinister hands gules ; and the modern Maynards change the tincture of the field to argent. Hands are shown grasping many things, such as swords, lances, cups and so on. Two hands clasped and winged at the wrists make a charming emblem of ardent friendship.

Arms are borne " embowed," or bent, and may be naked,
" manched " or " habited." If clothed in armour they are
said to be " vambraced." A " cubit arm " is one cut off
above the wrist, but below the elbow. Sir John Care, an
old-time knight, bore as his badge a dexter arm issuing from
the clouds, habited gules, cuffed ermine, holding in the hand
blue columbines with green leaves. Sometimes chaplets are
held ; but more frequently one sees weapons of war ; and
quite as often the hand grasps a snake, a human throat, or
that of a beast.

In Continental heraldry we frequently see a dexter and
sinister arm issuing from the flanks of the shield, the hands
clasped in the fess point. This charge is known as " Foi."
Faith, or brotherly love, may be displayed in the form of a
fess, right across the field ; in bend, the arms coming from
dexter chief and sinister base ; or in chevron, the arms bent
and the hand clasped in the honour point. Crespin bore :
sable, two arms issuing from the flanks and embowed in fess
(to form a chevron), argent, hands conjoined in honour
point, between three crescents of the second. De la Foy
had two arms, en chevron, the hands grasping a heart ; while
Purefoy, Bishop of Hereford, 1554–7, bore : gules, two arms
issuing from flanks, hands conjoined in fess, argent, between
three hearts, or. Later Purefoys and Purfeys varied this by
bearing respectively : gules, three pairs of hands back to
back, argent ; gules, three pairs of hands couped and clasped,
argent ; sable, six armed hands clasped argent ; and sable,
three pairs of dexter hands couped or, suffled argent.

Legs are treated much in the same way as arms. They
may be naked, habited, or covered in chain mail or plate
armour. They are seen as charges and as crests, and appear
on the coats of Legges. Tramail, of Devon, bears : argent,
a fess between three feet gules. A curious coat is that of
the Italian Bones-Combas, wherein we see two legs issuing
from the flanks, the feet bathing in the sea in base. Then
we have the three naked bent legs, joined at the hips,
and arranged in a triangle, on the arms of Sicily, the three-
cornered Trinacria. This is an extremely ancient symbol of

the swift-travelling sun of old-world meteorology. In some of the earliest examples we see a figure of the sun placed at the conjuncture of the three legs. This same symbol is found on the shield of the Isle of Man, only here the legs are in armour, and armed with spurs. At first the armour was of the chain-mail order, then of plates. No doubt this modification of the Mediterranean symbol was introduced into Man by descendants of the Norman Kings of Sicily. The Courtins of France bore : three naked legs in triangle, conjoined at the thighs, together with a doe tripping, which appears something like tautology, unless it meant that the bearer was swift of foot in hunting.

This idea of swiftness is associated with the foot, which is sometimes borne with two wings issuing from the shinbone, or from the sandal of Mercury strapped thereon.

ARMS OF READING.

CHAPTER IX

CELESTIAL CHARGES

REPRESENTATIONS of heavenly bodies and phenomena were early used alike in universal symbolism and in heraldic art.

Heralds depict the sun as " rayonnant," " in splendour," and in this they followed very ancient precedents, for in most corners of the world we find the solar disc surrounded by lambent or darting rays. For the most part, these are so arranged as to convey a notion of forward or rotary motion. On the platter found by Edward Muller in the undated ruins of Rhodesia among the astronomical signs is a sun image, consisting of a circle surrounded by wedge-shaped rays, curving from right to left, thus giving it the appearance of a wheel or flower. In the ancient badge of Sicily we see a human-faced disc placed at the conjunction of three bent naked legs. This latter is a form of the cramponed cross, or fylfot, of which more has been noted in another chapter ; but it is to be said that both the cramponed cross and the three conjoined bent legs (sun symbols) are recognised charges in heraldry. Marduk, the Chaldean and Babylonian solar god, was represented by a winged disc. So was his Persian descendant, Mithra, *Soli invicto Mithræ*, worshipped practically throughout the Roman Empire. But long before that Ra and Amen Ra in Egypt were also solar gods, and were worshipped in their material phase represented by Aten, the solar disc. This, too, was often winged, or twined about by winged snakes. Aten is also represented as emitting beneficent rays, sometimes shown in the form of small triangular wedges strung together like the tail of a kite, but often even

more significantly represented as long beams terminating in
human hands, spread out in the act of blessing. This idea
of the arm and hand issuing forth from the heavens is also
the common property of heralds. The University of Paris
bears : azure, three fleurs-de-lis or, a hand and arm issuing
from clouds in chief holding a book. Much the same symbolism is adopted by our College of Physicians. But these
heavenly gifts may be crowns, swords or battle-axes as well
as books.

A sun in splendour in later heraldry often has a human
face, and the rays may be straight or wavy, of equal length
all round, forming a fringe to the circle, or of varying length,
so as to produce a fringe having the form of a diamond.
The sun in splendour, as we shall see, was a badge of the
House of Tudor, and was subsequently charged with a Tudor
rose. It is also connected with another flower, the sun-flower,
heliotrope or girasole, which always turns its full blossom
towards the luminary, generally placed in dexter chief. Suns
are occasionally charged, as with the rose ; they are also
shown as sable discs, and are then said to be " in eclipse."
The Oriental method of representing an eclipse is to show a
dragon endeavouring to swallow the disc, as in the Chinese
Imperial dragon, which has its two jaw feelers curved round
the golden or red sun. Delahay bore : argent, the sun in
splendour or ; and John de Fontibus, Bishop of Ely, 1280–5 :
azure, the sun and moon in chief and seven stars in base all
or. The town of Banbury : azure, a sun in splendour, or.
The feudal coat of the lordship of Cardross was : gules, an
eagle displayed or, looking towards the sun in its splendour
in dexter chief. A sky with a radiant golden sun was borne
by the French Solanges, and the Dutch Zon as armes parlantes. The German Counts Sonnenberg for the same reason
bear : azure, the sun or, in base a mountain gold ; and the
Scottish Hills have : azure, a sun rising from behind a hill or.

Sunrays themselves are borne, either as single charges or
in connection with clouds. One of Richard II's favourite
badges was a " cloudburst " (a sun behind clouds, sending
forth rays). Rauf de la Hay (*temp.* Henry III) bore: argent,

a sunray gules ; but as we have seen above this ultimately developed into a sun in splendour. Sir Francis de Aldom (*temp*. Edward II) : azure, a sunray or. Another interesting coat is described as : gules, a chief argent, on lower part a cloud with golden rays proceeding therefrom. The clouds are sometimes replaced by a chief nebulé.

A full moon is said to be " in her complement," and is generally represented as silver, with a human face, and surrounded by short rays. Day picturesquely bore : gules, two flanches ermine, on a chief azure, a sun between two moons or.

Both in symbolism and in heraldry the crescent is more commonly met with than the full moon. This is due, in the first instance, to the striking phenomena of the waning and waxing of that celestial body. All over the world the waxing moon was associated with fertility and prosperity. According to the ancient Indian legend, the moon was a receptacle of nectar, which the gods drained, when she dwindled and lost her beneficial influence. But the sun replenished her, and then in her march to fulness she brought plenty to all her followers. It was, therefore, the symbol of acceptable and efficacious sacrifice, and as such was the badge of Siva, " Lord of the Mountains." It was the symbol of certain elemental gods of the Egyptians and was also the attribute of Diana, as well as several deities of the Mediterranean basin. In Egyptian symbology the crescent moon is often shown as containing the disc within its horns—the present containing the promise of the future. In heraldry it is said to be a " crescent " when on its back, " increscent " when the horns are towards the dexter ; and " decrescent " when turned to the sinister. We find the increscent and decrescent endorsed ; the three endorsed ; or the three interlaced. Gimball, France, bears : azure, three crescents interlaced in triangle or ; which was the device of Henry II of France, in fond allusion to Diane de Poitiers. Lunel, also from across the Channel, has four crescents in cross. It was by accident that the crescent became the Mahomedan cognisance, for it was adopted only after the capture of Constantinople, where they found the Byzantine crescent so largely used. It had been adopted by the Byzantine Emperors because it was the long recognised symbol of Keröessa, "the horned"

HAWK GOD WITH THE SOLAR DISC WITHIN THE CRESCENT MOON.

daughter of the moon goodess Jö or Hera. It is possible that many of the crescents in our early heraldry may have been brought back by the Crusaders. The idea of the cross surmounting the crescent was neatly pictured by Cathcart, who bears : azure, three cross-crosslets fitchy rising from as many crescents argent. On the other hand it is very certain that it was used here symbolically quite early, either through Roman influence in Britain, or indirectly through the Germanic tribes. We find the crescent on the coins of our early Saxon kings, generally placed on the king's forehead, a circular disc being shown between the horns, as in the Egyptian examples. This appears to represent the Alpha and Omega, Day and Night, Eternity.

Stars, however, are more frequently seen associated with the crescent. Here, again, the Turkish analogy is a late accident, for they adopted their symbolism from other and older civilisations. On the Kokip Sesvators, or sacrificial stone of the North West Indian tribes of Canada (found near the Deer River), and supposed to have been used by the ancestors of the Toltecs, there is sculptured on the surface " half an inch deep, the crescent figure of the moon with a shining star over it." This same combination is seen on a Roman medal (figured by Vulson de Colombière) showing the deathly tribute of the Sabines to the betrayer of Rome. We find it used by our Plantagenet line of kings on their Great Seals, evidently as religious emblems, and by Richard I as a badge. On the quaint old seal of the town of Wareham we find a crescent with a star within its horns, between three fleurs-de-lis reversed. The town of Portsmouth bears : azure, an estoile issuing from a crescent argent. Stars, or " estoiles," are borne apart from the crescent. Stars appear on coins of Cunobeline, king of the Trinobantes, and we find them on the coins of our first Norman kings, either William I or William II. They are there placed within a circle or on a disc. In heraldry there is some confusion between the mullet and the estoile, but it may be assumed that the pierced charge is really a spur-rowel, while the same figure, with five, six, eight or more points, when borne wavy, or the points alternating wavy and straight, are stars. This waviness was adopted to represent the lambent aspect, or "twinkling" of the stars, an effect resulting from the refractive power of our atmosphere. It is a device which has given rise to some confusion, for often there is a great resemblance between the daisy-like flower (probably the rose) of our early seals and the equally ancient star. This mingling of characteristics, however, is not unusual in symbolism. Gale Pedrick in his " Monastic Seals of the Thirteenth Century " says : " Ethiluwald, Bishop of Dunwich (an extinct episcopate), who swayed the crozier A.D. 845–70, used a bronze matrix dstinguished by an ornamental star of eight points, alternately leaf-shaped and fleury, with his name and description." This seems akin to the Egyptians, who identified Isis (Sirius) the morning star, with the rising of the fertilising waters of the Nile. Their star of five points, however, seems to have represented the united powers of the planets Mars, Mercury, Jupiter, Saturn and Venus. Probably the pentacle had the same planetary significance. De Burbentane-Puget (Provence) bore : argent, a cow passant guardant gules, and between the horns a star or ; which seems quite suggestive of the horn-crowned Egyptian cow goddess Hathor. Gilbert Hansarde (*temp*. Henry III), bore : gules, three estoiles argent. An " illegitimate " but very beautiful coat is that of Conti, Florence : per pale azure and bleue celeste, an estoile counterchanged. Pale sky blue is very rare in heraldry, except when used for flags, but it is found in the arms of the Kingdom of Greece. Sir Francis Drake bore : sable, a fess wavy between two polar stars argent.

The star of Bethlehem is usually an estoile of many points with rays projecting from the lower part. The Beaux of Luxembourg bore : gules, a comet star of sixteen rays, argent. They claimed to be descendants of Balthasar, one of the three kings, or Magi, who saw the star over Bethlehem from the mountain of Beaulx in India ; whence they journeyed to the Holy City, and thence to Cologne.

Both Australia and New Zealand have adopted the constellation of the Southern Cross. In the fly of the Commonwealth flag the constellation is represented by four large stars of seven rays, and a smaller one of five rays, while there is a large seven-pointed star beneath the Jack. In the Commonwealth arms the cross is charged with four stars with eight points, while over the blue field of the second quarter of the quartered shield the constellation is represented by one silver star of eight points, two of seven, one of six and one of five points. Victoria bears : azure the Southern Cross, represented by three large and one small silver stars. On the New Zealand blazonry the constellation is represented by four silver stars surmounted by as many red stars, on a blue field. The United States of America bear : paly of thirteen gules and argent, on a chief azure forty-eight stars of five points argent. A " comet " or " blazing star " is usually " bearded " or " coudé," that is to say, represented with a trail of rays forming a slanting tail. De Blacas, of Provence, bears : argent a comet bearded of sixteen rays gules. But Vulson gives the following strange blazon for Rabot of the Dauphiné : argent, three piles flamboyant and two comets gules. These figures are diminutives of the pile, three of them being reversed.

Rainbows are represented by a bend bowed of azure, gules, gold and sometimes argent, the colours subdued and blending one with another. Pont, of Scotland, bears : argent, a rainbow in fess proper. Claret : azure, a rainbow in fess proper, between two estoiles in chief and the sun in base, or. Barons Pfuhl, however, have three rainbows in pale on a blue field.

Clouds have already been mentioned in connection with the sun and sunrays. They are, however, also borne as an orle or bordure, for instance in the arms of the Mercers' Company. Frequently they are shown as a bank out of which an arm or other charge may issue. The tinctures are argent and azure. Azure, three clouds radiated in base or, each surmounted by a triple crown gold, lined gules, are the arms of the Drapers' Guild, London. Leeson, Earls of Milltown, Ireland, bear : gules, a chief argent, in base thereof a cloud proper, issuant therefrom rays of light paleways or. Tempesta, of Italy : gules, eleven hailstones argent.

In ancient Egyptian carvings the welcome rain is represented by a figure much like our label with two points, one at each end, and streaming from the lower side a series of chevroné or, less frequently, wavy lines.

Thunderbolts are borne as ordinary charges and also held in the talons of birds or paws of beasts. They are in the form of short double-headed voluted staves, with forked and barbed lines issuing from them, often flaming at each end, and winged. They represent meteorites, conventionalised into double sceptres. These are the " bolts from the blue," the darts of outraged divinities which punished, yet brought blessings in their train. For while observation showed that both lightning and meteorites could kill, yet, being associated with vernal thunderstorms, brought revivifying rains. Meteorites have ever been considered sacred and lucky in all countries. There is the black Kaaba at Mecca; the thunderbolt of Indra at Sambundth. In Mexico the Aztecs had a god Tecpatl (Flint-stone) who fell from the sky and broke into 1,600 gods. The Greeks and Romans showed Jove and Jupiter hurling thunderbolts, and their eagles carried the dread sceptres in their claws, hence their appearance in the talons of the Imperial eagles of Rome and France, and of the American bird of prey. Tomyris bears : azure, a thunderbolt or, shafted, and winged argent. A similar charge is the crest of the Carnegies, Earls of Southesk.

CHAPTER X

COMMON CHARGES

A PART from the two classes of ordinaries discussed in the preceding chapters almost every conceivable object in the sky, on the earth and beneath the sea has been utilised at one time or another as a charge for an armorial shield.

Naturally, the earliest employed were either of a conventional order, developments of structural members of shields, ancient symbols, or those things particularly associated with warfare, or the possession of land and all that it entailed. Then,

MERCHANT'S MARK,
JOHN CARLTON,
NORWICH,
15TH CENTURY.

MERCHANT'S MARK,
ADAM DE MUNDHAM,
NORWICH,
16TH CENTURY.

MERCHANT'S MARK,
JOHN DE AUBRY,
NORWICH,
14TH CENTURY.

with the expansion of our own social system, came many new interests ; this is reflected in armoury by the introduction of objects connected with travel, with professions and trades, for merchants' marks early assumed heraldic form. While it would serve no useful purpose to give a list of every single charge ever emblazoned on a shield, the principal classes employed will be considered here, as far as possible in the order just given.

Of the developed structural part of the shield, escarbuncles, fers-de-moline and staples are of chief importance. The escarbuncle may be described as a central boss with eight radiating limbs, treated, as in the beautiful example in the Temple Church, as foliated branches, or as a series of decorated sceptres. Sometimes these members are united by one or more series of decorated transverse bars. This was obviously the appropriate kind of decorative ironwork for lending

FONTENAY-SOUS-BOIS, PARIS.
AN ESCARBUNCLE IN CHIEF.

strength to a shield, and something similar may often be seen on old wooden church doors. At first it was a mere ornament and had no armorial significance, for we see it, as in the Temple Church example, sprawling over the three dancetté bars of the coat. Later, however, it was treated as a charge, and called a carbuncle, or rich ruby, sending forth blinding rays. The most famous examples of this bearing are the following:

Counts of Cleve : gules, on an inescutcheon argent, an escarbuncle flory or ; which was changed later to : argent, an escarbuncle or, over all an inescutcheon sable. Counts of Anjou : gules, a chief argent, over all an escarbuncle or. Abbey of St. John, Colchester : gules, a cross within a border or, over all an escarbuncle of eight points sable.

Fers-de-moline, or millrines, are variously drawn, but consist essentially of two outwardly curving members, conjoined at the back. They are like the clamps sometimes used to anchor a beam in a wall. In the fanciful minds of the fifteenth-century heralds they are supposed to denote certain seigneural rights, the privilege of owning mills. Fers-de-molines are extensively used. Sir William Saunsum (*temp*. Edward II) bore : or, a fer-de-moline, sable ; and Sir Robert de Willoughby is described in the Roll of Arms of the same period as bearing ; gules, a fer-de-moline argent. Molyner, with allusive intent, bore : or, a fer-de-moline azure.

Staples of the ordinary form are borne. Stapleton has : argent, three staples sable. The arms of the Priory of

Dunstable, Bedfordshire, were: argent, on a pile sable a staple affixed to the centre, interlaced with a horse-shoe or. In other words, a horseshoe is fastened by a double nail to the pile.

Warfare supplies us with a multitude of charges.

Spears and lances appear at quite an early date. They are usually of the heavy type, with large head and sunk hand grip. Six of these appear to form a fretty field on the coat of de Villeneuve, as already mentioned. Saint Vincent, also of Provence, had two gold lances on a field of gules. But the most interesting specimen is that on the arms granted in 1546 to the father of William Shakespeare, of Stratford-on-Avon: or, on a bend sable a spear of the field, headed argent. Spear-heads also are borne. Pryce, of Wales, has: sable, three spear-heads argent. Lance-heads of the jousting weapon, with its four blunt points, are called coronels. In later time spears of another kind, such as those of the American Indian, the African warrior, the Zulu assagai, have appeared to record war services or administration in our colonies.

Swords are also of various types. The falchion was a blade shaped like an elongated triangle. Knightly swords are long, straight, with prominent cross-guard handles. Scimitars have broad curved blades, serrated at the back towards the top. Seaxes, the ancient Scandinavian sword, is also curved, and has a notch in the back of the blade. It may be seen in the arms used by the county authorities of Middlesex and Essex. Naval cutlasses, Scottish basket-handled claymores, modern cavalry sabres, skenes or daggers are also seen. They may be "hilted" of any tincture. Swords may be borne in their scabbards, when they are said to be "sheathed"; the metal end-piece of the scabbard is a "chape," "crampet" or "boterole," which may be differently tinctured and is sometimes borne as a separate charge. Dymock bears: sable, a sword erect in pale, hilt and pomel or (a badge of office as King's Champion). Gellibrand (temp. Henry VIII): argent, two swords sheathed in saltire, hilts and chapes or. Becheton: azure, three chapes or. In ecclesiastical heraldry it is the symbol of spiritual and temporal authority, but more generally an emblem of martyrdom, as borne by the see of London : gules, two swords in saltire, argent, hilted or, the points in chief, in allusion to St. Paul who suffered by decapitation. Battle-axes are among the weapons.

Bows are borne bent ("stringed") and unbent. They led up to the cross-bow, the musket and the rifle. Gun bears allusively, but perhaps also emblematically, having regard to the chief : gules, two muskets in saltire sable, within a border argent ; on a chief or, a lion passant guardant of the field.

Arrows appear singly, in " sheaf " (or bundles), and sometimes, though rarely, in quivers or cases. When the head or feathering is of a different tincture to the shaft, it is said to be " barbed " or " flighted " of the special colour or metal. The city of Sheffield bears : vert, three wheatsheaves or, on a chief azure eight golden arrows in saltire, banded silver ; and for crest, a lion rampant gorged with a collar azure, holding in its paws an escutcheon azure, charged with eight arrows as in the chief. These arrows, of course, recall the iron and steel industry and the former important local production of arrow-heads. Sometimes they are shown with blunted or cross-headed points, and are then known as " bird bolts." A peculiar form of the arrow-head is the " pheon." It is like a broad arrow, but with the inner sides of the barbs serrated. Gules, three arrows double pointed or, is borne by Hales. Or, a pheon azure, were the arms of Sydney, Earls of Leicester.

We have also slings and catapults, battering-rams, cannon, hand grenades, chain and bar shot as well as cannon-balls. The calthrop is a ball with four spikes, so that, however thrown, one would remain uppermost ; they were used to disorganise cavalry.

Warfare also provides us with helmets, shields, gauntlets (azure, three gauntlets or, as borne by Vane), men in armour, spurs, stirrups, bridles, horses in armour, and much besides. The Wardens of the Marshes bore crests or badges of winged spurs to show their readiness for action.

Annulets, or thick rings, seem to be borne both as pieces

of chain armour and also as the tilting-rings. In the former
aspect they are sometimes borne " conjunct " or " conjoined,"
when two are united at their edges, and " embraced," or " interlaced," one link fitting into another. Gules, four annulets
or, was borne by Sir Nicholas de
Cromwell in the days of Edward
II.

Buckles should also be mentioned
in this connection. They were
borne both alone and attached
to belts. Doubtless sometimes
they were merely emblematic, but
occasionally they were assumed to
commemorate prowess in the field.
This was the case in the well-
known Pelham buckle borne as

WINGED SPUR CREST.

a badge and on the shield : gules, two half belts palewise in
fess, the buckles in chief argent. These were assumed by
Sir John de Pelham to commemorate the part he took in
the capture of King John of France at Poitiers.

Horse trappings include the barnacle, bray or twitchers,
used for training (azure, three pairs of barnacles expanded
in pale, sable, is borne by Bray of Cornwall), hames (or collars),
and, of course, horseshoes. Another of these equine charges
is the celebrated fetterlock, not unlike a single manacle or
handcuff, a semi-circle closed by a chain and padlock. This
is constantly used as a charge, a crest and a badge alone
and in conjunction with some other object. It is one of
the Yorkist badges used by Henry VII, with whom it was
made to enclose a white falcon, though his successor opened
the lock. It occurs in a curious combination in the arms of
the town of Bewdley : argent, an anchor azure, ringed argent,
interlaced with a closed fetterlock of the second ; within
the fetterlock on the dexter side of the anchor shaft a blue
sword erect, on the sinister side a rose gules. Scaling-
ladders are also used.

Directly connected with the gentle art of killing fellow
creatures are two interesting pieces indispensable in vic-

tualling armies. The first of these is the water-bowget reminiscent of the Crusading days, and representing in a

highly conventionalised form the animal skins used in place of barrels to convey water and other liquids. These appear quite early on mediæval shields. A notable instance is that of William de Ross (*temp*. Henry III), who bore: gules, three water bowgets argent. Trusbutt, in the reign of Edward III, also had three of these charges. Curiously enough the other commissariat charge, a great cauldron, appears on the shield of Mountbourchier, as shown on the cloister ceiling of Canterbury Cathedral. Possibly there, as in the case of

BOROUGH OF CLERKENWELL. CREST: WATER-BOWGET SURMOUNTED BY BOW AND ARROW. WATER BOWGET IN FOURTH QUARTER.

the Italian Pignatello, the cooking-pot may be allusive, in

the sense of a pun on the names. But with the De Laras and other grandees of Spain it was allusive to feudal position as great princes and leaders of men. It was borne by them as a symbol of their right to levy armies, and some of them placed eels in their pots. In

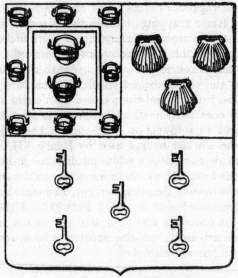

ARMS OF THE DE CONCHA-CHAVES OF SPAIN.

the same way both on the Continent and in England, nobles who raised troops often bore banners as charges or as crests. Sometimes these were badges of office, as with the Bannermans of Scotland. Banners are, of course, mainly allusive to war. But the gonfanon type, that is, a banner attached to a crossbar, which is slung horizontally across the staff, is ecclesiastical. Of old every ecclesiastical establishment and every parish had its banner, and on the Continent at least these were borne by the lay protectors, the avoués, or advocates of the foundations, who not infrequently added representations of these banners to their arms, either on the shield or attached to the helm or in the hands of the supporters.

An important group relates to buildings, the most prominent sub-sections consisting of towers and castles. A tower generally has one doorway, called a " port," which may be closed by a door or a gate, " portcullis." The top is always " crenelated," otherwise " embattled," but occasionally one, two or three small towers may spring from the top. The town of Newcastle bears : gules, three towers argent. The town of Morpeth bears : argent, three bars gules, within a border azure, charged with eight martlets or ; over all a tower triple-towered, of the field. Castles usually consist of a strip of crenelated wall between two towers ; an arched " port " in the centre, and one in each tower, and four oval windows. If there are three towers, the centre is the tallest. This is the type seen on the ancient seal of the town of Winchester : gules, five triple-towered castles in saltire argent, the middle castle between two lions of England confronté. That is to say, the dexter golden lion passant guardant is turned to the sinister. Edinburgh City bears : argent a triple tower sable, masoned silver, port, windows and flags gules. Dublin bears : azure, three castles argent, with signal flames issuing from the towers. Exeter has a curious castle : per pale gules and sable, a triangular triple-towered castle or. For crest the city of Cambridge has on a green mount a quadrangular castle, with four domed towers and two ports or, masoned sable. The

arms of the ancient castle town of Guildford deserve record.
On a black shield is a green mount supporting a silver castle
of two embattled towers, each having a spire surmounted
by a ball. From the battlement between the end towers
springs a triple-towered tower, charged with a small shield
bearing quarterly the arms of France modern (*i.e.*, blue with
three fleurs-de-lis, two above and one below) and England
(*i.e.*, red with three gold lions passant guardant, one above
the other). Under the battlements of the castle are two golden
roses ; in the centre of the black doorway are a key and portcullis in gold. On the mount before the doorway is a golden
lion couchant affronté. On each side of the castle is a silver
woolpack. Blue water occupies the lower part of the shield.
This appears to be an adoption of the ancient corporation
seal, and is fully descriptive of the physical and political
position of the town and of its commercial activity as an
olden wool centre. Towers and castles appear frequently on
personal arms. De la Tour d'Auvergne (whence sprang the
celebrated mid-seventeenth century Marshal de Turenne)
quite early bore : gules, a tower with portcullis close, argent.
In 1191, however, they bore : azure, a tower argent. In
1222 they powdered the field with fleurs-de-lis. De Castellane, of Provence, bore : gules, a castle of three towers or ;
which was allusive to his name and the office which gave
him his name. Another allusive use of this charge is in the
celebrated castles of the Kingdom of Castile, still to be seen
quartered with lions of Leon and the pomegranate of Granada
in the arms of Spain.

The term " masoned " is applied to the picking out of
the masonry courses in a tincture distinct from that of the
building. The city of Bath bears : per fess embattled azure
and gules, the base masoned sable, with crosses bottoné of
the last (really loopholes), in chief two bars wavy argent,
over all in pale a sword silver, pommelled gold. In the
arms of the city of Cambridge the embowed gold fess is
masoned sable and triple towered, and as it spans water with
three barges thereon, no doubt represents a bridge. Bridges
of two or more arches are occasionally found. Pount bore

(allusively): azure, a bridge of two arches argent. For the same reason Arches bore : gules, three arches, two single in chief, one double in base, argent, imposts or. Ruins appear on the shield of Bertie, quartered with battering-rams, which looks very warlike, but, as a matter of fact, the founder of the family was not only Captain of Castles in Sussex, but a contractor for their construction and repair. In the same spirit George Cubitt, Lord Ashcombe, the famous builder-contractor, emblazoned his shield, chequy or and gules, to represent brickwork, and had for supporters a mason and a carpenter. Mansard, Louis XIV's celebrated architect, had a silver pillar resting on a gold pedestal. Some charges, and many ordinaries, as well as partitions of the field, may be borne " crenellé," " embattled," or " crenelated."

Churches are emblazoned, but mostly in connection with ecclesiastical armoury. Of recent years lighthouses have been introduced into heraldry, chiefly as crests in connection with seaports, as at Broadstairs.

Castle gates, known as portcullis (from *porte coulis*, sliding door), or *herse*, is a frequent charge. It was one of the cherished badges of the House of Tudor, who derived it from their ancestors, the Beauforts. It is in the form of a grid, the cross bars being nailed at the junctions. Frequently chains are borne pendent on each side. The port of Harwich bore : gules, a portcullis or (now argent), cloué azure.

Keys may, not inappropriately, be mentioned here, for, though sometimes having a religious significance, they are for the most part connected with problems of defence. In the latter sense we find them significantly associated with castles on the armorial shields of Gibraltar and the town of Totnes. Gibraltar bears : gules, a triple-towered castle on a rock argent, the port opened, and pendent therefrom by a chain, a key with ward downwards or. Totnes bears : sable, a castle with central crenelated tower and two flanking domed turrets argent, masoned sable, the port open, between two silver keys, wards in chief and pointing outwards. The island of Mauritius, another strategical key, has for its fourth quarter azure, a key or. De Clermont-Tonnerre, France, Dukes and Counts of Clermont, Grand Masters and Constables of the Dauphiné, bore : gules, two keys argent in saltire. In Spain we find the Counts of Herrera de la Concha-Chaves, hereditary supervisors of Government buildings, having in base : or, five keys azure. Wood of Balbigno, Scotland, bears : azure, an oaktree growing out of mount in base or, pendent from a branch two keys gold, fastened by a strap gules. These keys are the badge of office as Thane of Fetter-cairn. Keys were used as badges of office, usually placed outside the shield, by Chamberlains at the French Court. From German sources we find quaint key combinations. Beheim bears : gules, a triangle or, thereon are threaded the rings of three golden keys, the barrels and wards pointed to dexter and sinister chief and the third borne in pale. Liedlow bears : azure, three keys argent, rings interlaced in chief point, the barrels and wards pointing to dexter and sinister chief and in base. In the religious sense keys were valued badges of the Moslems, for they bore allusion to the Kaaba and the Koran. They were largely used for decorative-symbolical purposes by the Moors in Spain. In Christian iconography a key is the emblem of St. Peter, and the Popes of Rome as successors of the Apostle assumed keys as their badge, using two crossed in saltire to represent their spiritual and temporal powers. Through Rome, singly and crossed in saltire, they are constantly seen in our own ecclesiastical heraldry.

Seafaring has enriched our armoury to a large extent, apart from the interesting family of fish, beasts and curious fowl already described. First of all we have the sea itself, which may be painted *au naturelle*, or " proper " as the heralds have it, or symbolically represented by blue and silver wavy bars. Then we have a ghostly fleet of strange craft. Fore-most among these is the lymphad, or ancient galley. It is usually depicted as a half-moon, with castellated poop and stern, with or without mast, and with one or more banks of sweeps, or oars. This form is seen on some of the early shields. It is frequently met with in Scottish heraldry, especially in connection with the coastal and island clans. It was the feudal ensign of the lordship of Lorne.

In heraldry ships almost invariably refer to sea dominion, warfare, exploring and commerce, but occasionally they have a religious reference, for in Christian iconography a ship represents the sheltering Church, which was derived from Noah's Ark, essentially the symbol of refuge. The Ark is seen as the crest of the London Shipwrights' Guild, with the dove alighting with its olive-branch. This ship of refuge, however, is a very old notion, found in many countries. In Egypt raft boats were sacred to Ra, who made his diurnal journey round the world in three boats. One was the "Boat of a Million Years," and as it passed through Tuat, or the Underworld, the souls of those who had passed the moat-test, were taken on board, and with Ra journeyed to the Elysian Fields. When Isis was seeking

SCHWANN, BARONETS. AZURE, A SWAN ROUSANT PROPER WITHIN AN ORLE OF LYMPHADS OR.

for the scattered members of slaughtered Osiris, she made a boat of papyrus, which was permitted to go unmolested by all the beasts and fishes. To commemorate this there was a feast of boats at Denderah, when thirty-four boats, lit by

365 lamps, were launched. In Japan there is a feast of boats, when small boys launch paper and straw boats with tapers alight. In New Granada the Spaniards found that the Casique El Dorado, glittering with precious metal, went on a raft on the boisterous water of a big lake to cast offerings therein. So the Doge of Venice sailed on his golden galley, throwing a golden ring into the waves in token of the marriage of the city to the sea.

A great number of our seaport towns have ancient ships on their shields, many of them having been transferred from symbolic but non-armorial seals, as in the case of Scarborough and Hythe, the latter having one man blowing on a horn, while two naked sailors are lying on the yard-arms, apparently furling sails, while fish swim in the sea. This crowded ship of Hythe is very close to the community emblem, which we find again in the city of Paris arms, which an old poem describes as manned by representative citizens. We find ancient ships on the seals and arms of the corporations of Winchelsea, Dunwich, Lymington, Aldborough, Ipswich, Yarmouth, Oxford, Newport, Truro, Bristol, and others. The curious lion-ships created by the dimidiation of the royal arms with those of the Cinque Ports and other seaside towns have already been mentioned. At Weymouth we have a Tudor man-of-war, a Great Harry. Since Manchester became a port, a three-masted trading vessel under full sail has been added on a chief; while at Govan we have a ship's hull on the building-stocks. Other types include men-of-war of different periods, rowing-boats and even coracles.

But sea power is represented variously. We have the anchor (which, however, is also frequently the symbol of Hope of Christian iconography). Anchors may have the flukes, the cross bar ("stock" or "timber") and the ring of tinctures varying from that of the shaft ("shank" or "beam"), and may be borne "cabled." When the cable is wound round the anchor it is said to be "foul," and this is the form in which it is used as a badge of the Admiralty. A curious use of the anchor has already been cited in the case of Bewdley. The anchor entwined by a dolphin is one of the sea-power and religious symbols of the classic ages, and was adopted by the early Christians as an emblem of Hope and Resurrection.

Oars are borne singly and crossed in saltire. Silver oars are badges used by the English Admiralty Courts, and many ancient sea-ports have silver oars borne before their mayors in addition to the civic mace, in token of their naval jurisdiction. Rudders are also used in a somewhat similar sense, again a symbolism which has come down to us from classic times, as may be seen on referring to old monuments and coins. The trident of Neptune is also a symbol of naval power, and is sometimes seen wreathed with a dolphin. On the exergus of the counter-seal of George IV, we see a rudder of the Roman type. On the Great Seal of William IV, the background represents the sea, with two lines of battleships, while on the exergus is a trident ensigned with a wreath of laurel, and on the counter-seal Neptune, bearing his trident, appears amid an allegorical group. The top part of a trident surrounded by laurel-branches appears on the exergus of Queen's Victoria's Great Seal.

Landscape shields, which are pictorial rather than heraldic, belong to the bad period, from the seventeenth century to the middle of the nineteenth. But conventionalised features of landscapes, to represent territorial dominion or origin, were introduced quite early. Mention has already been made of castles and beasts standing on mounts, even of a representation of Mount Parnassus. However, mountains alone are frequent charges. They form quite a feature of Scottish heraldry, representing the lordships of clan chieftains. In some cases the mountains are represented as crested with lurid flames, these being intended as war fire signals. But the flaming mountains are singularly like the conventionalised Japanese figures of smoking Mount Fujiyama, and many antiquaries have seen in the Scottish fire mountains survivals of clan badges telling of former vicinity to volcanoes, either local or Scandinavian. Mountains are also favourite charges on the Continent, both on municipal and knightly shields. In Italian and Provençal heraldry the mountains are usually drawn as high and steep. This is the characteristic of the sea-washed triple hill of Nice, straddled by the Lascaris eagle. De Meyronnet, of Provence, bears : azure, a mount issuing from the sea, and two crescents in chief argent. In English heraldry small hills, generally crowned by a group of trees, and known as " hursts," are more commonly met with. Our " parks " are really circular palings on a green terrace, and may enclose trees, harts or other animals. " Islands " are patches of green, circular in form, floating on the sea or on the field, and may grow trees. This type of island, crowned by palms, is seen on the shield granted to Christopher Columbus, but as a rule in Spanish, as in most other Continental countries, islands are represented by high, rocky hills, surrounded by the sea, as on the shields of the Pinzons, Columbus's one-time lieutenants. In modern practice more elaborate landscapes were admitted, as in the flower-bed mount of the Montefiores ; the ranges of small mountains, green hills of wheatfield of Alberta ; and the mountains and plain of Natal.

Of the component parts of landscapes, such as trees and wheatsheaves, much has to be said, and will be reserved for a separate chapter. Other charges connected with the countryside may be briefly reviewed. Sickles or reaping-hooks appear in British heraldry. A sickle was the famous badge of the Hungerfords, and was also the crest of the Dukes of Brunswick, who usually adorned the outer edge with a row of eyes from peacock feathers. Sicklemore bears : sable, three sickles interwoven, argent. Mayere, of Flanders, bore : gules, three sickles argent, handles gold, the points meeting in fess. Scythes also appear. Argent, a scythe sable, is borne by Snelson. They are also shown in the hands of men forming part of crests, or standing as supporters. Flails when borne are also usually held in men's hands. , Land suggests sport, which has endowed heraldry with many birds, beasts and fishes. Hawks' lures and bells, and bird bolts have already been mentioned. Hunting-horns are favourite charges. They are of the bullock-horn type, with mouth-piece, which may be of a special tincture, and is then said

to be "enguiché." We also have lobster-pots, nets, river
weirs and fish-hooks. Of quiet forms of sport the quaintest
are the chess-rooks, favourites in former days. Gules, three
chess-rooks argent, was borne by Richard de Walsingham in
the reign of Edward II. We also find dice and playing-
cards.

From the wardrobe quite a long list of charges has been
obtained. Perhaps the most striking and earliest of these
is the maunch or manche, an old-fashioned sleeve, with long
pendent cuff. Reinald de Mohun (*temp*. Henry III) bore :
gules, a maunch argent. But his successor in the days of
Edward III bore : gules, a maunch ermine ; and his descendant, the Earl of Somerset, bore : gules, a maunch ermine,
a hand proper issuing therefrom holding a fleur-de-lis or.
For very long, however, the maunch has been specially associated with Hastings, the head of whom in Edward III's time
bore : or, a maunch gules. At a later period the Lincoln-
shire branch of the family bore : argent, a maunch sable.
It has been conjectured that, at all events in the case of the
Hastings family, the maunch was originally a badge of office,
as we first hear of them as holding a post at Court corresponding to that of Master of the Household. Next we have the
surcoat, which is borne particoloured and also heraldically
emblazoned. We have already mentioned gauntlets and
helmets, but we also find gloves, caps, hats and shoes. Some
of these may have come in as badges. Most, however, owe
their presence to the ambitions of traders or trading corporations. Dame Berners in her "Boke of Saint
Albans" (1486) mentions a "cross-corded,"
which, she says, was first introduced, the
baronial bearer thereof having formerly been
a corder. However that may be, it is certain
that the trading guilds early obtained armorial insignia; even before that they

CROSS-CORDED.

adopted heraldically designed banners and common seals.
Among the charges thereon were generally found some
implement of trade. Thus our own trading guilds have
introduced hats and hatbands, gloves, plumbers' rules, stair-

rails, or banisters, butchers' cleavers and poleaxes, shoes, shuttles, basket-makers' tools and so on. Similar guilds on the Continent were following the same practice. There is ample evidence that office-bearers in these guilds, when they rose to wealth and influence, introduced some part of the guild arms into their own personal bearings. And certainly from the sixteenth century onwards we find successful professional men and traders recalling the sources of their prosperity by more or less appropriate heraldic charges. John Pep, Master of the Barber-Surgeons' Company, who was Groom of the Privy Chamber and King's Barber to Henry VIII, placed two silver combs on his shield. Thus we have the scales and swords of justice introduced by lawyers, the pastoral staff of ecclesiastics, the Aesculapian sceptre entwined with one or two snakes of the physicians, the fleams, or curiously razor-like lances of the surgeons, woolpacks and fleeces of woolmongers and a great many other charges of a like character. We have also the goats of the Skinners' Guilds, and the ermine of the Edinburgh Guild of Furriers.

In English heraldry mirrors are rarely seen except in the hands of mermaids, but when borne have a mystic meaning, for the mirror was always an object of awe, a symbol of revelation of secret things. In Japan it is emblematic of creation, representing the rising sun over the sea. Combs, also closely associated with mermaids, curiously enough are fairly common as charges. They are of the double-toothed variety.

Woolpacks are seen on the shields of Guildford, Godalming (in past days great wool-growing districts) and Rochdale, a centre of the wool-manufacturing industry. A woolpack also appears on the arms of Staple Inn, London, formerly one of the free markets where merchant-adventurers traded. Woolpacks are seen on the shields of Lords Tweedmouth and Holden, both heads of Yorkshire woollen manufacturing families.

Bury bears a shield which happily represents local industry while remaining heraldic in character : quarterly, argent and azure, a cross parted and fretted counterchanged, between,

WEAVERS' GUILD, EDINBURGH.

FURRIERS' GUILD, EDINBURGH.

SKINNERS' GUILDS, LONDON AND
EDINBURGH.

BRIDPORT.

in first quarter, an anvil sable, in the second a fleece of or, in the third two shuttles in saltire with threads pendent silver, and in the fourth three culms of the papyrus-plant proper. For crest, a bee between two fructed slips of the cotton-plant. Thus the iron, the woollen, the cotton and paper industries, as well as commerce generally, are represented. In the modern arms of Bolton-le-Moors a shuttle represents the weaving industry introduced into that town by Philippa of Hainault, Consort of Edward III, and a mule spinning spindle recalls that its inventor, Samuel Crompton, was born there. Shuttles are found in the arms of the Ibbetsons and the Kay-Shuttleworths, both of which families have won fame and fortune in the weaving trades. The ancient borough of Brid-port, bore : gules, a castle argent, the port close ; on each tower a fleur-de-lis or ; in chief a lion passant guardant and crowned of gold, in base barry wavy of eight argent and azure. Apparently, about the middle of the sixteenth century, the portcullis was drawn up, and in the open gateway three " coqs " or roper's hooks were introduced. They appeared there on the Visitation of William Henry, Clarencieux King of Arms, in 1565, and were approved and allowed on a subsequent Survey in 1623. Now, for long ages Bridport was renowned for its manufacture of ropes, and Henry VIII granted a monopoly to the town for the supply of cordage to the King's Navy.

GOLDSMITHS' GUILD, EDINBURGH.
COVERED CUPS.

Bottles and cups may have been introduced from trade sources occasionally, but they are of ancient use as badges of office. Take, for instance, the cups in the arms of the Butlers, who held the post of Chief Butlers to the King in Ireland. Cupbearers have always been important personages, and Kings not only had their Court butlers, but similar officials in different parts of their domains, while princes and feudal chiefs also appointed such officers. These cups are usually of the long-stemmed goblet pattern. Bottles are of two varieties, flagons, and leather receptacles, flat bottomed and ended, with semi-circular upper part, not unlike foot-warmers. Brewers and vintners introduced barrels.

BREWERS' GUILD, LONDON. BARRELS AND SHEATHS OF BARLEY.

We also find a variety of baskets, open and closed. Pentney Priory, Norfolk, bore : gules, three covered wicker baskets or. Middleton Abbey, Dorset : sable, three flat open baskets full of bread, argent. Winnowing-baskets, or vans, are seen as early as the reign of Edward II, when Sir Robert de Suens bore : " de azure a III vans de or " (Roll of Arms, *temp.* Edward II). Fish-baskets, not unlike lobster-pots, are another type, while the Basket Makers' Company, or Guild, place basket-maskers' tools on their shield and have an osier cradle for crest.

Books, open or closed, are often associated with seats of learning, as in the case of the Universities of Cambridge, Oxford, London, Paris and others, but also with trade, as in the case of the Stationers' Company and some personal arms.

Books and seats of learning naturally bring to mind scourges. They are not unknown to heraldry. Battuli of Bologna allusively (but let us hope not as a matter of official badge) bore : argent, a bend azure between two scourges, each of four cords ending in spiked balls, or. Croyland Abbey bore : quarterly first and fourth, gules, three knives erect in fess argent, handled or ; second and third, azure, three scourges erect in fess or, with three lashes each. Swift, of Scotland, bore : gules, three whips of three lashes each, argent. For crest the Lords Stourton have a demi-monk, habited in russet, wielding in his dexter hand a scourge of three knotted lashes. Knotted cords here have an unpleasant meaning, and so, to some extent, they have in that curious group of charges, the family badge knots, of which something is said in another chapter.

Music supplies us with many instruments, the harp, the military trumpet and bugle, Apollo's lyre (as seen in the crest of the Musicians' Company or Guild), the hunter's horn, drums, cymbals, hautboys, flutes, fiddles and that strange charge the clarion or rest. The upper part of this instrument is somewhat like a set of Pan's pipes, but has a curved horn-like handle. It has been described as a lance rest and various other things, but is clearly a form of musical instrument.

A group of pear-shaped charges with wavy tails are named "goutes." They are variously tinctured, and when of gold are called goutes auré or d'or ; of silver, d'eau ; of gules, de sang ; of azure, de larmes ; of black, de poix (or pitch) ; of green, d'huile. They are sometimes borne singly or in numbered groups, but usually powdered, or semée over the field. When a goute is drawn reversed, tail uppermost, it is termed an icicle.

A very doubtful group of charges are the mullets, which often look like stars, for they are more frequently borne unpierced than not. Yet the word mullet is derived from the French *molette*, and so they are usually taken to be spur-rowels. In early heraldry they were described indiscriminately as " estoilles " and " molettes." De Vere, Earl of Oxford (*temp*. Henry III), bore : quarterly or and gules, a mullet silver in the first quarter ; but in the reign of Edward III the contemporary de Vere was said to sport an "estoille." Nicholas de Moeles (*temp*. Henry III) bore allusively : " d'argent a deux barres de goules a trois molets en le chef de goules " (Roll of Arms). Sir William de Harpendene (*temp.* Edward II) bore : argent, a mullet pierced, gules.   In ordinary practice English mullets have five points and the French six points, but they may have many more.

CHAPTER XI

PLANTS AND FLOWERS

A WONDERFULLY lovely and varied garden has been planted by heralds of all nations during the long procession of years from the dawn of the twelfth century at least, for not only has the whole vegetable kingdom been put under contribution, but the nameless symbol makers of the remote past have also been drawn upon. Man became a worshipper of trees, seed plants, and flowers almost from the time he began to think, and remains so still. When we dip into art we find evidence of his linking the beautiful mystery of growing things bursting forth from the bosom of Mother Earth, with half-formed longings to peep into the unknown surrounding him, on all sides. This we shall see as we go along.

Trees are seen as single specimens or as groves, " hursts," which sometimes shelter men or hinds, but also from whence wild boar, lions and other destroying marauders emerge. Trees are borne " eradicated " (torn up by the roots), and " couped " (cut off smoothly), as stumps (generally with the reassuring presence of young sprouting twigs) and " fructed " (bearing fruit). Branches torn off are " snagged," and when roughly trimmed with projecting stumps along their whole length, they are " raguly " or " ragged." These " ragged " branches, or " staves," are often seen in cross, or saltire-wise, or as a component part of crests.

Pines and firs (this latter frequently found in Scottish shields) are very old symbols. A pine cone crowns the thyrse sceptre of Bacchus. It was the emblem of fertility and eternity with the Assyrians, and conveyed something of the

same kind to the Greeks.   Attis, the youthful son of Nana,
mother of the Phrygian gods, the vernal divinity, was closely
associated with the pine tree, under which he performed the
rite of self-mutilation, violets springing up from his spilt
blood.   Pine branches were used for marriage torches by
the Romans, and these branches are associated with marriage
ceremonies in Russia and Japan, but also, through their
sacrificial association, are appropriate to death and funerals,
as with the cypress and other varieties.   In China the fir,
with the plum tree and the bamboo, is the centre of " the
three friends," an emblem of longevity.   In most parts of
Europe firs and pine branches are associated with festivity.
De Chateaubriand, Brittany, originally bore: gules, semée
of gold pine cones (though subsequently the cones gave place
to fleurs-de-lis).   De Pins bore: gules, three pine cones or.
Chaton des Morandais, also of Brittany, bore: argent, a
pine tree vert, fructed with three cones or.   Pyne: argent,
on a mount in base, a pine tree fructed, all proper.   Mac-
Gregor bears: argent, a fir tree issuing out of a mount vert,
surmounted by a sword bendwise, ensigned by an Imperial
crown proper.   The latter charges are, of course, commemora-
tive augmentations.

Our oaks have almost as illustrious an ancestry.   They
were honoured among most nations, and with the Greeks
and Romans acorned oak branches were formed   into
crowns and awarded to victors.   Owing to the tree's suita-
bility for boat-building, it is particularly associated with
naval exploits.   Tree and branches when bearing the fruit
are said to be " acorned," or " englanté," a term applied to
any charge adorned with the fruit and cup.   These are borne
as well as the tree, slips and wreaths.   Forest bears: argent,
on a mount vert an oak tree, all proper.   Brayne: azure,
on a cross an oaken slip vert.   Milford: argent, three oak
leaves in pale vert.   Cambis (France): azure, an oak tree
issuing from a six-pointed hill, all or.   Oke: sable, on a fess
between six acorns or, three oak leaves vert.   Aikenhead
argent, three acorns slipped vert.

Palm trees, so prominent in ancient symbolical sculpture,

and introduced from Asia Minor among the Greeks and Romans, are rarely seen in old heraldry. Most of the palm trees were introduced after the era of exploration opened up by the Portuguese and Spaniards. They appear on the shield of Columbus, and have been adopted by men of recent centuries who have made their mark in tropical countries. A curious bearing is that of Vault : argent, an ape sejant on a heart and holding a palm branch proper ; which seems to tell a tale of success purchased at too high a price. Palm branches are more common, and are employed from two motives. The palm branch in religious symbology represents the martyr triumphant, and so we find it connected with ecclesiastical heraldry. On the other hand, it has a wider or at least more mundane reference to victory, and so is seen in connection with naval and military honours, as in the case of Nelson.

Olive branches, the symbol of fertility and prosperous peace, in early Mediterranean civilisations, are borne, sometimes derived from Biblical sources, the branches being carried in the beaks of doves. Olivier, county Bedford, bears : argent, on a mount vert an olive tree proper. Vanhatton : or, two olive branches vert. De Brebier, Anjou : argent, three olives slipped and leaved vert.

Orange trees are fairly common with us and on the Continent. Livingstone bears : azure, three oranges slipped proper, within an orle of thistles or. Sweetland : argent, on a mount vert, an orange tree fructed, proper ; on a chief embattled gules, three roses of the field barbed and seeded proper. De la Motte ; argent, on a mount vert, a lion rampant contourné gules, supporting an orange tree leaved and fructed proper.

Pomegranates are one of the " trees of life " as seen spread *en espaillé* in Assyrian carvings. The fruit is a symbol of fertility and prosperity. Heraldically it is especially associated with Spain, a pomegranate, open and seeded and slipped, appearing on the shield of Granada. It was brought over to England by Catherine of Arragon as her badge, and transmitted to both Mary and Elizabeth. Dr. Lupus, physician to Queen Elizabeth (*circa* 1591), bore: or, a pomegranate tree erased vert, fructed gold supported by a hart rampant proper, crowned and attired gold. Bilson, Bishop of Winchester (1597–1616), bore: gules, a demi-rose argent charged with another of the field (a reversal of the Tudor rose badge), conjoined in pale with a demi-pomegranate or, seeded gules, both slipped vert.

Vines in symbology are associated with the pomegranate, being "trees of life" both in pre-Christian and Christian iconography. It is a charming device when well drawn, spreading over the field. The town of Dijon bears: gules, a vine or, leaved vert. Levinz: argent, a vine leaved and fructed proper, over all on a bend sable, three escallope shells silver. Arabin: or, three vine leaves vert. Bradway: argent, a chevron between three bunches of grapes proper (but whether this means red or black we are left in doubt).

CLAMART, NEAR PARIS.   ROSES AND A WREATH OF VINE LEAVES AND GRAPES.

Apples and pears are naturally frequently blazoned on English and French coats. Estwire bears: argent, an apple tree vert, fructed proper. Appleton: argent, a fess sable between three apples gules, stalked vert. Both Periton and Walden, co. Worcester, bear: argent, a fess between three pears, sable. This is, indeed, the same coat as is borne by the town of Worcester accolé with its old bearings: quarterly, gules and sable, over all a triple-towered castle, port open, argent. The fructed shield displays insignia of augmentation, said to have been granted by Queen Elizabeth after a visit to the borough in token of her appreciation of the citizens' skill and diligence in the preparation of cider and perry.

Mulberries appear first in an allusive sense, for we find that Sir Hugh de Morians (*temp*. Edward II) bore : azure, three mulberry leaves or. A mulberry tree, and also a branch of mulberry with leaves and fruit, were badges of the Mowbrays, Dukes of Norfolk. Much later, and directly commercial in intent, Favenc (of London) bore : azure, a Spanish merchant brig under sail, proper ; on a chief invected argent two mulberry leaves, points upwards, on each two silkworms proper.

Cherry trees of heraldry are the wild cherry, the *crequier* of the French. They are drawn as somewhat stumpy, with a number of withy-like branches, bent outwards and inwards in the form of a crown. Such a tree is borne by the de Crequys of France. Estover bears : argent, a cherry tree fructed proper. Sergeaux : argent, a saltire sable between four cherries gules, slipped vert.

Almond slips have been mainly employed allusively. Thus the family of Almond bears : argent, an almond slip fructed proper ; while Jordan bears : sable, an eagle displayed between two bendlets argent ; on a chief or, three almond leaves vert.

Hazel nuts, termed either "avellanes" or "coquerelles," are sometimes borne as charges. A cross-avellane, formed of four nuts in their green coverings, stalks meeting in fess, is a very charming composition. Hazelrigg bears : argent, a chevron between three hazel leaves vert.

Fig trees and fig leaves are used, but I know of no instance of the fruit alone as a charge. Mirtle bears : per fess wavy gules and argent, in chief a lion passant guardant erminois, in base on a mount vert a fig tree proper. Greves : per chevron argent and gules three fig leaves countercharged. Figuerra (Spain) : or, five fig leaves in saltire vert. Castanea (Italy), whence sprang Pope Urban VII : bendy or and azure, a barrulet argent ; on chief gules, a chestnut, leaved and stalked or.

From the West Indies we have derived pineapples and sugar

canes ; and flowered slips of the tea shrub have come to us from China and Ceylon. A branch of the tea shrub and a slip of the coffee tree, both flowered and fructed, appear in connection with the heraldic distinctions of Sir Thomas Lipton.

Laurel, or bay, is sometimes seen as small trees or bushes, but more commonly as slips or wreaths. Bayford bears : argent, a chevron between three bay leaves vert. This is, of course, a punning coat ; but branches and chaplets of bay were granted to both military and naval victors, often associated with oak leaves and acorns.

Hawthorn is generally shown as " flowered " or " fleuri," silver or red. A hawthorn bush with a crown was one of the badges of Henry VII. Sylvester bears : argent, a hawthorn tree eradicated proper. Thornholme : argent, three thorn trees vert. Thornton : argent, a chevron between three hawthorn leaves vert. Bretland : argent, a hawthorn tree eradicated vert, flowered gules.

Holly is another favourite charge in different forms. Irvine bears : argent, three holly leaves proper. Owen, co. Pembroke, bears : gules, a boar argent, armed, bristled, collared and chained or, tied to a holly bush on a mount, all proper. Foulis : argent, a holly bush between three bay leaves slipped vert. Burnet, who were hereditary Foresters to the Crown, bore the feudal Irvine coat : argent, three holly leaves or, to which they added a hunting-horn in base sable, garnished gold, stringed gules.

Willows are represented by trees, slips and osier wands. Bennison bears : argent, a willow tree vert. Count de Salis : or, a salix proper. Willis, Dean of Worcester (*obit* 1596) : argent, a chevron gules between three willow trees proper. Skirlawe, Bishop of Lichfield, Bath, and Durham (1386–1400) : argent, six osier wands interlaced in saltire (poetically described " in true love ") vert. Osier wands slipped occur in connection with the Basket Makers' Company.

Alder and ash appear chiefly for punning effect. Alderberry bears : argent, three bunches of alderberries proper. Ashton argent, an ash tree proper, issuing from a tun.

Ashford, Kent : argent, three ashen keys between two couple closes sable ; and Ashford, Cornwall : argent, a chevron between three ashen keys vert. Ashen keys are branches laden with berries.

Maple slips of three leaves are the unofficial badges of Canada, and are also found in the arms of some of the Canadian provinces. Lord Mount Stephen bore : or, on a mount, in base a maple tree proper, in chief two fleurs-de-lis azure. Both these charges are in allusion to his successful career in his adopted country, the maple of the Dominion and the blue lis of the Province of Quebec. Baron Müller, the distinguished Australian botanist, was granted : or, two branches of eucalyptus accosted, stalks interlaced, vert.

Cotton trees and branches represent textile industry. Arkwright, co. Derby, of spinning-frame celebrity, bore : argent, on a mount vert a cotton tree fructed proper ; on a chief azure between two bezants an escutcheon silver, charged with a bee volant proper. A bee volant between two fructed cotton slips is the crest of the borough of Bury, well known as a cotton-spinning centre, and its paper industry is represented by three papyrus boles in one quarter of its shield. Huddersfield has the quaint and appropriate crest of a silver ram's head couped, bearing in its mouth a cotton slip vert, fructed.

Mention of leaves has been made in connection with specific plants. But Leveson bears merely leaves for the sake of punning. A curious use of leaves is found in Germany, where crests are often borne powdered with the tender green, sweet-smelling linden leaves, or these may be placed as an ornamental fringe round the crest. When any charge is thus decorated with leaves it is said to be " verdured " or " verdoyed."

A trefoil is a leaf with three pear-shaped lobes, and is generally borne " slipped," that is to say, with a stalk. It made its appearance quite early. A Roll of Arms of Edward II's reign states that Sir Edmond de Acre bore " goules a III foiles de or, III escalops de argent." At that date " leaves " apparently was sufficient to describe the trefoil.

The shamrock, badge of St. Patrick and of Ireland, is a modification of this charge. It should be given three heart-shaped lobes and the stalk drawn wavy.

Garbs (from the French " gerbe "), or wheatsheaves, are largely used, and are found in some of the most ancient records. One of the proudest of feudal shields was that of the Earl of Chester, and we find Ranulf de Blondeville using a seal with a shield decorated with three garbs. These were blazoned in the reign of Henry III as: azure, three garbs or. One and a half of these garbs not only appear on the coat of the city of Chester, dimidiated with " England," but the sheaves were also adopted by the Hattons, Vernons, Grosvenors, Cholmondeleys and many other families of the nobility and gentry within the County Palatine of Chester, either in token of blood relationship or of feudal allegiance. Garbs also appear on the arms of the Barons Sheffield, Earls of Mulgrave, from whom they were adopted by many Yorkshire families. Garbs are often " banded " with cords of a distinct tincture. Wheat is also borne in the ear, when it may be "bearded" of a special tincture. John Wheathampstead, Abbot of St. Albans (*obit* 1464), bore : gules, a chevron between three bunches of three wheat ears each or. On the quartered coat of the town of Luton (known for its wheat straw-plaiting industry) is a wheatsheaf ; and the crest is an arm, habited azure, issuing from the clouds, holding a bunch of wheat ears or. Occasionally sheaves or ears of other grain are borne, but if so the variety should be named.

Kitchen vegetables are not unrepresented. For instance, Beane bears : gules, three bean cods pendent or. Dammant : sable, a turnip leaved proper ; a chief or gutty de poix. De Chauvelin, of Burgundy : argent, a cabbage eradicated vert, encircled by a serpent or. Potatoes, so far as I know, are only represented in one example, on the coat of Neuilly-sur-Seine. This town bears : gules, an arched bridge, with a ship on the waves, all argent ; on a chief azure three potato flowers slipped or ; the shield verdured with bunches of bulrushes and slips of potato haulms, leaved and flowered proper. Here the potato flowers are borne to commemorate the fact that Parmentier first introduced the tuber into France, planting them in the plains of Sablonville on the outskirts of Neuilly.

Nettles are sometimes classed as potherbs, and possibly Nettle, co. Cork, who bore or, a chevron gules between three nettle leaves proper, may have been of this opinion. But the allusive intent of Malherbe, co. Devon, who bore the same coat, and Mallerby, of the same county, who improved upon it by emblazoning or, a bunch of nettles vert, was decidedly derogatory. An equally unpleasant association clings to the or, three birch twigs, sable of Birtles ; the sable, a fess between two birch leaves argent, of Birche, co. Devon ; and or, three birch twigs sable, of Birches.

Other rare charges are broom, heather, mistletoe and ivy. Broom is the *planta genesta*, the celebrated badge of our Plantagenet line of kings. It is borne by Broome, co. Somerset : argent, three broom branches, vert. Brugière, Baron de Barante, Auvergne, bears : argent, a branch of heather (French *bruyére*) vert. Walbert, Normandy : or, three bars gules, over all a branch of mistletoe, vert, fructed argent. The town of St. Ives, Cornwall, has this delightful composition : a branch of green ivy spreading all over a silver shield.

Thistles, when blazoned proper, have a blue or violet flower and green leaves. This is the badge of Scotland, and was given as a mark of honour by Scottish rulers in coats of augmentation. Leven bore : argent, a thistle slipped proper ; and this, the thistle Imperially crowned, was given as a coat of augmentation to Leslie-Melville, Earls of Melville and Leven. Teasdale bears : argent, a thistle between three pheons azure ; this, evidently, in allusion to the teazle thistle.

This brings us to flowers. Certainly among the earliest and most important of these were the quatrefoils and cinque-foils, but as these are intimately linked up with the rose forms, they will be considered in connection with the Queen of Flowers in a special chapter. A large proportion of blooms known to botanists have been used, but it will only be necessary to deal with some of the most characteristic.

Lilac is represented on a French coat in the form of violet or purple quatrefoils with star-shaped piercings. That is on the shield of the pleasant Paris suburb, Les Lilas: per bend gules and azure, a bend argent charged six lilac flowers,

two by two, purpure; the shield surrounded by a branch of lilac, flowered and leaved proper. Motto: "J'etais Fleur, Je suis Cité."

One group consists of the daisy or marguerite, the marigold, sunflower and chrysanthemum, which have a fundamentally religious significance or origin, for they are one and all representatives of the sun in glory and its fertilising powers. In the oldest symbolical renderings most of these

LES LILAS, PARIS.

are interchangeable and, indeed, frequently approximate to the pictorial renderings of wavy stars. As we have seen in a preceding chapter the daisy-like flowers on eleventh-century seals often merge into stars. In later heraldic representations the daisy is a pretty little flower of many white, red, or white and red petals, with a golden seed centre, and together with the marigold was adopted as a badge by many persons named Mary. It was this association that made it a favourite symbolical flower for religious bodies and persons, for they were both blooms of the Blessed Mary, and as in older systems, messengers of hope. The marigold and sunflower being flowers of Sol were also associated with gold, and were used by goldsmiths. The sunflower, shown as a huge flat seed-vessel surrounded by radiating petals, placed on a tall leaved stem, is generally borne in combination with the sun in splendour, towards which the bloom is turned, for it is the *girasole* or "heliotrope." On a seal of Margaret, daughter of Philip the Hardy, King of France, and consort of Edward I, an effigy of the queen stands, habited in a tunic "of England," with her paternal and maternal arms on either side, on a corbel, the base formed of ears of wheat and the cornice decorated with a row of marguerites. It was also the badge of Margaret of Anjou, queen of Henry VI, and of Margaret, Countess of Richmond, mother of Henry VII. This device was also used by many foreign princesses of this name. Daisie of Scotland bore : argent, three daisies gules, stalked and leaved vert. The Marquis Marguerie (Provence) : azure, three marguerites, stalked and leaved, argent. Pasquier (France) : or, trois marguerites (paquerettes) d'argent, boutonné d'or. Sunflowers being also known as heliotropes, we find Florio bearing : azure, a heliotrope or leaved vert, in chief a sun in splendour ; while the Marquises d'Espaynet (Provence) bore : azure, three marigolds on one stalk leaved or ; on a chief gules a sun in splendour. Within this group primroses may be included. We find Primrose, Earls of Rosebery, bearing a truly vernal coat : vert, three primroses within a double tressure flory counter flory or. Another Primrose altered the tinctures to gold and red, quite ruining the character of the delightful composition. Goldman bears : gules, a chevron or between three marigolds of the last, stalked and leaved vert.

Chrysanthemums are chiefly of interest as the sun emblems of the East. This flower is a constant recurring motif in Japanese design, for it is the Imperial and national badge. It has been conventionalised along two divergent lines : we see it as a figure constructed on purely geometrical principles, and also as a realistic simplification of the natural flower. It was obviously venerated as a symbol of the sun, for the Emperor traces his descent from the sun, Amaterasu, the glorious daughter of Izanazi and Izanami, and this we can see by the very treatment of the figure. The Imperial device, the kilku-mon, is a blossom with sixteen club-shaped petals radiating from a circular centre, the thick portions on the outer circumference, and a dot placed between each pair of petals. Its proper colours are red, with golden dots. It is known as the " Binding Flower," because as the bloom ties itself together in the centre, so the Mikado binds about him the hearts and souls of his people. It is, in fact, the sun

JAPANESE FAMILY MONS.

1. EMPEROR'S BLAZON AND MIKADO FAMILY BLAZON.
2. BLAZON OF THE TOKUGAWA SHOGUNS BETWEEN **MALLOW FLOWERS**.
3. SATSUMA AND BIZEN FAMILY BLAZONS.
4. HIRATO FAMILY BLAZONS.

131

ruling its satellites and sending forth its life-giving rays. On the other hand the device on the national flag is a form of sun in splendour suggested by the realistic representation of the chrysanthemum. A large red disc is placed to the left, and from it radiate sixteen wedge-shaped rays, the thick ends outwards. These rays are spaced irregularly; the three to the right, and longest, are placed more apart, and the thirteen (to left, top and bottom) closer together. The realistic conventionalised flower in older art is designed on the same lines, the ragged, single bloom being taken as a pattern, and a certain amount of irregularity introduced. In later art there is a greater approach to realism, and the use of the multiple petalled corolla blooms. In Europe the latter type has generally prevailed.

Japan heraldic art is almost entirely modelled on botany and geometry. The family or personal mons (badges) are usually placed in circular forms, and we rarely find any design which is not composed of flowers, leaves, or lines, though a limited use is made of animals. As we have seen, they have their own dragons, lions, unicorns and tortoises. But for the most part we meet with flowers. The Imperial family badge, the kiri-mon, is the blossom of the *paulownia*, three being used in a row, with three broad leaves below. Other mons include those of the Tokugawa Shoguns, three club-shaped leaves, points inwards, their stalks forming the circular outer frame ; the blossom and four leaves of Hirato is suggestive of the palm of Assyria and the thistle of Scotland ; Kaga have a well-defined cinquefoil; and Maeda, Higo and Soma have extremely conventionalised blooms evidently modelled on the Imperial chrysanthemum.

Blue-bottles is the heraldic term for cornflowers, which are not uncommon. Bothell bears : argent, a chevron gules between three blue-bottles slipped and leaved vert. Another favourite flower is the columbine, which in old examples is drawn so as to resemble a row of pea cods on a stem, but are now given their proper bell-shape. Coventry, Lord Mayor of London (1425) bore : argent, a chevron sable between three columbines azure, slipped vert. This was possibly derived

1. KAGA, NAGATO, AND KATO KYOMASA BLAZONS.
2. SEN-DAI (TWO) AND MAEDA.
3. HIGO (TWO) AND SOMA PRANCING HORSE.
4. HABESHIMA OF HIZEN (TWO) AND THE SOMA BLAZONS.

from the arms of the Cooks' Company, or Guild : argent, a chevron engrailed gules, between three columbines azure, stalked and leaved vert. Bessell bears : argent, two columbine slips crossed (in saltire) and drooping flowers purpure.

Pinks are known by the pretty old names of gilliflowers and also cloves, though the latter is misleading. They are of the single corolla type generally depicted in profile slightly conventionalised. Jollie bears : argent, three gilliflowers proper. Livingstone, Viscount Kilsyth : argent, three gilliflowers gules, pierced of the field. Cloves, the spice, are also borne. For instance, the Grocers' Guild of London has : argent, a chevron gules between nine cloves sable ; Duffield ; sable, a chevron between three cloves or ; and Clive : or, a camel passant between three cloves sable. Violets also appear and are the floral badge of the Napoleonic dynasty. Dickens bears : argent, a chevron sable fretté or between three violets purpure, stalked and leaved vert. Pol : argent, three violets purpure, stalked sable ; on a chief azure a spurrowel of eight points or.

Flowers and leaves are frequently borne in the form of wreaths, either as charges or as decorations for other charges, including human beings and beasts. Wreaths of flowers, such as of roses, are usually called chaplets. Rose chaplets are occasionally borne twined round caps, no doubt in allusion to the ancient custom of employing rose garlands on festive occasions, and with further reference to the flower symbolising among other things the duty of silence, for what was said *sub rosa* was sacred. Laurel, oak and palm wreaths are sometimes termed crowns. A figure or other charge bearing wreaths is said to be wreathed. Figures may be wreathed about the loins as well as about the head. A beast wreathed bears the chaplet about its head, but it may be gorged, or collared, with a chaplet of flowers or wreaths.

Cornucopias, or horns of plenty, are to be found as charges, as crests and as accessories to supporters. They have been employed as symbols of natural wealth and also of commerce from very remote times. They are shown brimming over with flowers and fruit. The cornucopia as a charge appears

on the arms of that popular seaside resort, Worthing, equally
known for its fisheries and its horticulture: argent, three

REPUBLIC OF PERU.

bars azure, each charged with a herring naiant; on a chief
or a horn of plenty gules.

The term proper usually applies to tincture, but a "rose
proper gules" or "a rose proper argent" refers to the
botanical variety as distinct from the heraldic convention.
But with regard to lilies, the natural flower is most frequently
referred to as "a garden lily," or "lilies of the Virgin," to
distinguish them from the fleur-de-lis.

CHAPTER XII

MARSHALLING

MARSHALLING is the art of blending two or more coats-of-arms to form one composition, so as to convey a definite meaning.

According to modern practice the various degrees of marshalling are: the assumption of arms of dominion placed either in a shield of pretence over all, or quartered, which may be the result of conquest, inheritance or election; the adoption of feudal arms connected with fiefs, acquired either by grant, inheritance, purchase or exchange; the recording of matrimonial alliances, either by impaling, placing new arms in the shield of pretence or quartering; the assumption of arms or part of arms as the result of gifts or acceptance of directions under a will, usually associated with change of name; the use of arms attached to any particular office; the assumption of an augmentation granted by a sovereign prince.

Now let us see how this branch of the art has been evolved from very primitive forms of grouping.

Apparently the first idea connected with any change of arms resulting from conquest or the acquisition of fiefs was the substitution of the arms appertaining to the new property for the paternal arms. This was done even by knights who married heiresses. And there are records where the holder of a fief agreed to sell it, together with all rights in his feudal arms. But the more usual way was to group a set of shields on seals, surcoats and horse caparisons, an arrangement specially rife in the thirteenth century. On seals we see three shields grouped in triangle, four or five in cross; at other times one shield or more may hang from a tree; or we have the effigy of the owner in armorial surcoat or robe, holding one shield or more. Sometimes we may have the paternal shield surrounded by crests, badges or charges from other arms. For, as Wyrley says in his " True Use of Arms," "divers did add unto the mark of their own house some part of the device of the family from which their mothers descended," even " some part of the device of him who advanced them." On surcoats we may find the chief coat on chest and back, with different bearings on the ailerons or short sleeves. Much the same practice was adopted with horse caparisons, the covering of the body having the chief bearings, that of the neck other arms.

Reverting to seals, we find the arms of the husband on the seal, and that of the wife on the counter seal. Ela, Countess of Warwick (*circa* 1240), daughter of William Longespée, Earl of Salisbury, on her widowhood married Philip Basset. All this is recorded quite plainly on her seal, for we find her effigy bearing in her dexter hand a shield of the arms of Longespée, in her left a shield of the arms of Newburgh, Earl of Warwick, while on the counter seal are the arms of Basset. Sometimes the effigy stands between shields charged respectively with the husband's and the paternal bearings. Another daughter of Longespée married a knight of the name of Audele, and their son, Sir James Audele, bore over his paternal arms a label azure, with a lion rampant or on each point, to denote his maternal descent. Instances of this method are numerous. The seal of Margaret Logie, second wife of David II of Scotland, is placed between three shields : Scotland, Logie (her first husband) and Drummond (paternal). Another interesting seal is that of Elizabeth de Clare, daughter and heiress of Gilbert de Clare, Earl of Gloucester, a niece of Edward II. She was a much married *grande dame*. The central shield is that of Roger d'Amori, the third husband, which is surrounded by three lions passant-guardant of England to show her royal descent. A cross of tracery embraces four armorial shields, the upper one being that of John de Burgh, Earl of Ulster, her first husband ; in base we see the fret of Theobald de Verdon, her second hus-

band ; and on either side are the arms of Clare. In the four
angles are trefoil compartments, two containing castles, and
two having lions rampant, these being borne in allusion to her
grandmother, Eleanor of Castile and Leon, wife of Edward I.
We see this system also on the royal seals. On the Great
Seal of Edward II, the King's effigy is flanked by two hexagonal castles representing his descent from Eleanor of Castile ;
and on the second Great Seal of Edward III, we find fleurs-
de-lis placed close to his throne, which refer to his mother.
Robert de Clifford bore : chequy or and azure, a fess gules,
and on his seal attached to the Barons' letter to the Pope
(1301), the shield is surrounded by annulets, which he
derived from his mother, Isabel, daughter and co-heiress of
Robert de Vipont, who bore : or, six annulets gules. John
de Dreux, Earl of Richmond, son of John, Duke of Brittany,
and Beatrice Plantagenet, second daughter of Henry III
(born 1266), bore : chequy or and azure (for Dreux), a canton
ermine (for Brittany, an heiress of that House having been
married), surrounded by a border of England, *i.e.*, gules,
charged with lions passant-guardant or, to record his descent
from Beatrice and Henry III. Both the canton and the
border were constantly used for this purpose. John of
Eltham, second son of Edward II and his queen Isabel of
France, differenced his royal arms of England with a border
of France.

Mention of the label for the same purpose has already been
made in connection with the de Longespée descent. Other
famous examples may be adduced. Edmond Crouchback,
Earl of Lancaster, second son of Henry III, after his marriage
with Blanche, daughter of Robert, Comte d'Artois, bore :
England differenced with a label of France, *i.e.*, azure a fleur-
de-lis or, on each point. His grandson, Henry Plantagenet,
first Duke of Lancaster, bore the same label. Edmond in
this matter followed the example of his father-in-law, for
Robert d'Artois, brother of St. Louis, bore France ancient
differenced by a label of Castile (gules, a castle or on each
point). Lionel, Duke of Clarence, Earl of Ulster, third son
of Edward III, after his marriage with Elizabeth de Burgh,

who as heiress of her father brought him the Earldom, bore a label with the red crosses of Ulster. Sir John Bourchier, Baron Berners (*circa* 1475), bore a label of England, each of the points being charged with three gold lions, in allusion to his mother, Anne, daughter of Thomas, Duke of Gloucester, sixth son of Edward III. His brother, William Bourchier, Lord Fitzwarren, bore a label of France.

A curious use of the label to denote descent, where the paternal arms had been abandoned in favour of a feudal coat, occurs in connection with Charlton of Powys, who bears Powys: or, a lion rampant gules, with a label vert, on each point an eagle or; the old arms of Charlton being: vert, three eagles or. This was a change resulting from succession to what amounted to a fief. A similar abandonment of paternal arms and the assumption of specially marshalled arms of dominion is seen in the case of Richard, Emperor of Germany ("King of the Romans"), Earl of Poitou and Cornwall, son of King John. The arms of Poitou are: argent, a lion rampant gules, crowned or; those of Cornwall: sable, bezantée. So he bore the arms of Poitou within a border of Cornwall. His son Edmond placed his shield over an Imperial eagle, the shield being suspended from the guige held in the supporter's beak. Richard's natural son, Richard of Cornwall, bore the same arms, but had the border engrailed. His successor, Sir Geoffrey de Cornwall, having taken the Duke of Brittany prisoner, changed his field to ermine; the Brittany arms being ermine plain. We find the same thing happening in France. Hugo, third son of Henry I of France, Earl of Vermandois by marriage with an heiress whose county he thus acquired, abandoned the lilies for: chequy or and azure. Robert, fourth son of Louis le Gros, Earl of Dreux, also changed his lilies for the chequy or and azure of Dreux. Pierre, fifth son of Louis, having married the heiress of the House of Courtney substituted their three torteaux for his fleurs-de-lis. According to the metrical historian of the Siege of Carlaverock Sir Nicholas de Segrave bore a lion sable, his father having discarded his ancient sheaves of corn. Now, it is found, by the seal of John de Segrave attached to the

Barons' letter to the Pope (1301), that he bore a lion rampant crowned, the shield being placed between two garbs. These are instances of changes in connection with feudal domains. A famous example resulting from maternal descent is afforded by Edward Tudor, Earl of Richmond, eldest son of Owen Tudor and Queen Catherine of Valois, widow of Henry V. He discontinued using the Tudor arms, bearing France and England quarterly within a border of France. His brother Jasper, less appropriately, bore the same arms within a border and Edward the Confessor (azure, five martlets or).

FRANCE AND BRITTANY IMPALED. ENCIRCLED BY THE CORDILIÈRE.

Ultimately, however, impaling was introduced, the two coats of husband and wife, or of son and mother, being borne side by side on one shield. In simple impalement the two entire coats are marshalled side by side ; but the practice of dimidiation was also long followed. In dimidiation only half of each coat is shown, the dexter half of the paternal arms and the sinister of the maternal. Some extraordinary combinations have resulted from this practice, which was the fashion in England from about 1270 to 1300, but persisted even much later. Margaret of France on her seal dimidiated her arms with the three lions of her husband, Edward II. It has been shown how by dimidiating the royal lion of England with the hulks of the Cinque Ports, the herrings of Yarmouth, lion-boats and lion herrings have been produced. In Germany we have seen a kind of Siamese twin eagle-bear. A dimidiation of Harcourt-Deke (1330), gules, two bars or (Harcourt) and gules, a cross moline argent, results in a weird piece of ironwork, suggestive of a Middle Age door hinge. Perhaps these awkward combinations suggested partial dimi-

diation, when the husband's arms were borne entire joined
to the sinister side of the wife's. This was reversed by Diane
de Poitiers, mistress of Henry II of France, who bore her
full coat with the dimidiated arms of her husband, the Duc
de Brézé. Dimidiation per bend was for a time practised
in Germany. And per fess is also seen. A Scottish example
is Lawrence-Archer. A partial retention of dimidiation is
still the rule with bordered coats, the inner part of such
borders always being omitted.

Originally impaled coats were merely used to show alliances,
or the holding of an office. A husband places his wife's arms
on the sinister side of the impaled coat, and usually also
bears a full shield of his own. A wife places her arms on the
sinister side of her husband's. A Bishop, a Herald or other
office holder having the right to official arms, bears an
impaled shield—the official coat on the dexter side, and the
personal on the sinister.

Allied to this form of marshalling is the bearing of two
armorial shields accolée,
that is, side by side. The
same rules as to position
prevail as in impalement.

Another way of mar-
shalling feudal or terri-
torial coats is by placing
these in subsidiary shields
beneath or round the
chief one, as we have seen
done on seals. They may
also be placed on suppor-
ters, as we see in the
cases of the German,
Austrian and Russian
eagles. Then again, sup-
porters and crests may

TWO QUARTERED SHIELDS ACCOLÉE.

bear armorial banners of the different fiefs. This is commonly seen in Germany and the Netherlands.

When marshalling by grouping and by combination was

seen to have disadvantages, quartering was introduced. This occurred early in the twelfth century, though the first instance occurring in England was late in the thirteenth century, with the quartered coat of Castille and Leon of Eleanor, wife of Edward I. Then on the obverse of the seal of Margaret of France, second wife of Edward II, we find a quartered shield ; England, France, Navarre and Champagne. A simple quartered shield is divided into four equal sections, the chief arms being placed in the first and fourth quarters, and the next in the second and third. If three coats have to be mar-

shalled then the principal arms again occupy the first and fourth quarters, and the two others the second and third respectively. If four coats are in question, then each has a division. But a shield may be almost indefinitely divided, though it is always said to be quartered. We may have an irregular number, say five (three in chief and two in base). If the divisions are of regular number and there are not enough different coats to fill up all the spaces, the principal arms appearing in the first quarter are repeated in the last. Sometimes a quartered shield has to be

DOMINION OF CANADA, WITH
SEVEN QUARTERINGS.

dealt with. This is always treated as an entity, occupying one division, and is called a "grand quarter." Impaled shields are treated in the same way. On the Continent divisions of irregular forms are admitted. Thus a bearing may be "enté en point," that is, a reversed pile with curved sides is placed in base, as in the case of Granada on the shield of Spain.

A "champagne" is the base of the shield cut off by a horizontal line, and it may be occupied by one, two or more bearings. Other irregular divisions are quartering per saltire (in Italy and Spain), tiercy or division by thirds. This may be done per pale ; per fess ; or per chevron and per pale, or per chevron reversed and per pale. The latter form is also called " en pairle." The grant of arms made to Christopher Columbus illustrates one or two of the points discussed above. These arms are : quarterly, (1st) gules, a castle, triple towered or (for Castile) ; (2nd) argent, a lion rampant gules (for Leon) ; (3rd) azure semé of islands and half surrounded by terra firma argent, all bearing palm trees vert, semé of golden grains ; (4th) azure, five anchors in saltire or ; (5th) enté en point, barry wavy argent and azure.

An escutcheon of pretence, also called a " surtout," is used to marshal arms of dominion, of an electoral domain, or of an heiress. This occurred on our national and royal arms with Oliver and Richard Cromwell under the Commonwealth, who, however, reversed the order, placing their paternal arms in pretence over the quarterings of the United Kingdom and Ireland ; William III, who placed the shield of Nassau " en surtout," and between 1801 and 1837, when the arms of the Hanoverian dominions were so borne. On a somewhat different principle the children and grandchildren of Queen Victoria and the Prince Consort place the arms of Saxony " en surtout." It is curious to observe that in early days sons occasionally bore their mothers' arms in this way. For instance, Richard, Duke of York (1460) on his seal bore a surtout on his arms with the bearings of his maternal grandmother, Joan, the Fair Maid of Kent. As a rule, however, the shield of pretence is reserved for the arms of an heiress, so borne by the husbands. Their children inherit these arms and quarter them.

Quartering, then, is utilised both for recording territorial or titular possession, and also descent. The " Ecu Complet " of Austria has nine grand quarters, containing sixty-two quarterings, including six crowned surtouts.

A curious Continental custom in connection with marshalling must be mentioned. As a rule all charges in heraldry are turned towards the dexter, any exceptions to this requiring special mention. But many foreign heralds when marshalling either by impaling or by quartering, place their charges (and more particularly animated charges) " contourné," so as to face each other. It is a peculiarity that has to be carefully borne in mind, as it may be misleading.

Marshalling of augmentations offers some peculiarity and opens up a wide field full of interest. Augmentations are additions made to existing arms by sovereign princes by way of reward or compliment. They may take the form of a charge or a complete composition. In the latter case they may be borne in an escutcheon of pretence, on a chief, a canton or even a bend. As regards charges, our own kings have granted lions of England, roses (of York, of Lancaster and Tudor) and fleurs-de-lis ; the Scottish kings were lavish with the double bordure flory counter flory, especially to record family alliances, and have also granted thistles ; the French kings bestowed the fleurs-de-lis ; the Emperors the Imperial and also the Apostolic eagles. In later time Napoleon I bestowed his Imperial bees and eagles, and the Cross of the Legion of Honour, the last course also being adopted by his nephew ; while the Emperor of Germany has bestowed the Iron Cross of Valour. Among famous single charges are the red heart of Bruce, long borne crowned by the Douglas family ; the blue sword borne palewise supporting a royal crown, seen on the shield of Setons, and granted to Sir Alexander Seton for his defence of Berwick about 1320 ; the arms of Scotland, but with a demi lion vulned in the mouth by an arrow, granted to Thomas Howard, Duke of Norfolk, by Henry VIII, to commemorate his victory at Flodden Field and the slaying of James IV. To Sir John Clerk for his capture of the Duc de Longueville at the Battle of the Spurs, Henry VIII granted : on a canton azure a demi ram saliant argent, armed or, in chief two fleurs-de-lis gold, over all a baton of the second. The Duke was a grandson of Jean, Duc d'Orleans, and he bore France differenced with a label, and a ram for crest. Of a different nature were the grants made by Richard II. Not only did he himself assume the mythical arms of Edward the Confessor, bearing them impaled with his own, but he bestowed them on his kinsmen the Hollands, Dukes of Surrey and Kent, and also on Thomas Mowbray, Duke of Norfolk, who quartered them with their paternal arms. Richard also gave to Robert de Vere, whom he created Duke of Ireland, the mythical arms of St. Edmund, which about that time became regarded as the insignia of the sister isle. In the same order of affairs Henry VIII granted to Thomas Manners, Earl of Rutland, in token of his descent from Anne Plantagenet, a chief quarterly of France and England, which the Dukes still bear. He also made grants of elaborate augmentations to most of his wives, as described in Chapter XXIV, which, however, contain very confused and misleading ideas of alliance.

With us the eighteenth and nineteenth centuries were prolific in military and naval augmentations. Nelson was granted a chief wavy azure, waves of the sea, from which a palm tree issues between a disabled ship on the dexter and a ruined battery on the sinister. Admiral Duncan, for his victory of Camperdown, had to remove his family chevron to make room for a representative of a medal of honour presented to him by the King, together with the word "Camperdown." Lord Hawke, for his victory over the French fleet, 1759, was awarded : argent, a chevron ermine between three boatswains' whistles, erect, proper. Supporters, dexter, Neptune with a trident, standing on a dolphin ; sinister, a seahorse holding a flag staff with Union Jack in its paws. The Duke of Marlborough received a chief : argent, a cross of St. George, thereon an escutcheon of the arms of France. That granted to General Gerald Lake, created Baron Lake by George III, for his victory over the Maharatas, is curious as taking us back to ancient symbolism. He bears on a silver chief the fish of the Mogul Emperors, per pale or and vert, banded vert and gules, surmounting the Goog and Ullum in saltire. This is the Mahi Maratib, a golden carp, partly enveloped in a mantle of green brocade, the badge of the kings of Oudhe, placed over their wands of office. The Duke of Wellington was granted the Union badge (Union Jack) to be borne on a shield in the honour point.

More peaceful in character was the grant made to the father of Captain John Speke, in recognition of his dead son's exploration of the Nile. On a chief is a river with the word " Nile." The crest is a crocodile, and the supporters a crocodile and a hippopotamus.

CHAPTER XIII

DIFFERENCING AND MARKS OF CADENCY

DIFFERENCING practically forms a branch of Marshalling. It is the art of introducing certain variations in armorial bearings with a view to give individuality to the shields of each member, or group of members, of a family, without losing the main characteristics which unite them all. This, of course, includes the modern system of recording cadency by the introduction of small charges on the shields of each son. These are called Marks of Cadency, which are assigned as follows : a label to the eldest son, a crescent to the second son, mullet to the third son, martlet fourth, annulet fifth, fleur-de-lis sixth, rose seventh, cross moline eighth, double quatrefoil ninth. These are generally placed on the honour point of the shield, and should also be borne on the crest and badge, if any. These marks of cadency may themselves be charged. Thus the eldest son of a second son would charge his father's crescent with a label, and so on. If we adhered strictly to this system, such differencing should go on indefinitely, either until older branches die out or some permanent difference, such as the introduction of additional charges, or quartering, produce new bearings. It must be confessed, however, that the use of marks of cadency is not observed with any degree of precision with us, and our system is not recognised in its entirety by authorities abroad.

Before the fifteenth century great diversity was shown in methods of differencing. Of our present-day marks of cadency practically only the label received general recognition for this purpose. The methods adopted were substitution of minor charges, addition of minor charges, introduction of some ordinary, variation of tinctures. Apart from all this, there was the important branch of differencing to indicate illegitimacy, for which purpose considerable ingenuity was displayed.

Labels are, undoubtedly, the earliest of the marks of cadency. A label is a horizontal bar, with pendent squares attached to it, called points. The number of these points varies. As many as ten are seen in old French examples. With us they rarely exceed five, and it is curious to find individual members of the House of Plantagenet bearing labels both of five and three points, sometimes even on the same seals. These labels may be of any tincture, and further distinguished by charges, generally placed on the points. As a rule, prior to the sixteenth century the label is carried right across the shield near the top. In later practice it was couped, being carried only partly across, and the points were converted into wedge-shaped pendents, the broad ends downwards. The three Edwards of the Plantagenet line bore labels during the lifetime of their fathers, and this gradually became the predominant mark of cadency for royalty, though this did not become general for a long time, and is subject to exceptions. On the Continent the label has never been confined to the eldest son, and it was not with us up to the fifteenth century. On the Roll of Carlaverock Sir Patrick Dunbar, son and heir of the Earl of Lennox, has his father's arms with a blue label. Sir John de Segrave bore his arms undifferenced, but all his younger brothers bore a red label. On the Roll of Arms of the reign of Richard II we find Sir Richard le Scrope bearing the arms full; Henry le Scrope has a label argent, William a label gules, John a label argent with three bars gules, and Thomas in place of the label has an annulet sable. On the same roll we find Lawrence St. Maur using a label vert, Nicol a label of France (that is, blue semée of fleurs-de-lis), and another Nicolas of the same family places a single fleur-de-lis on each point, whilst Ralph not only bears a green label, but changes the tincture of his arms. A list of royal labels is appended at the end of this chapter.

In a like manner the mullet was largely used by cadets in Scotland during the fourteenth and fifteenth centuries, but by no means always by the third sons, or descendants of third sons. Evidence of this is afforded by mullets on the seal of Robert Stewart, Earl of Fife, and later Duke of Albany, who was the second son of Robert I.

Sir Thomas Basset (early fourteenth century) bore : ermine, on a chief indented gules three mullets or. His brother, Sir John, merely replaced the mullets with escallop shells.

A change with a political complexion is afforded by the O'Kellys, who in Ireland bear : azure, a tower triple towered between two lions argent, two chains or pendent from the battlements. A branch of the family who settled in France under Louis XV removed the lions and substituted fleurs-de-lis.

Adding some charges was not uncommon, and often these bore some allusion to descent. The large and powerful family of Nevil give many examples. In the reign of Edward II the Nevils of Enderby, Leicestershire, showed an extraordinary variety. Sir Robert bore gules, a fess indented argent, a border indented or ; Sir Philip, gules, a fess indented argent, in chief three moles or; Sir Richard, gules, a fess indented argent differenced with a label azure. It is probable that this fess itself was a modification of the original charge, for Robert de Nevil in the preceding reign bore on his seal four fusils in fess and a border charged with roundels. Fusils borne in fess easily assume the aspect of a fess indented if carelessly drawn. Another branch of this house bore in the reign of Edward III gules, a saltire argent, which was used without difference by Sir Ralph. Alexander Nevil bore : gules a saltire argent, a martlet sable. Nevil of Hornby changed the tinctures thus : argent, a saltire gules. Thomas Nevil, Lord Furnival, placed the Furnival martlet on his saltire, and his brother used a mullet. Ralph Nevil, first Earl of Westmorland, had twenty-one children by two wives. Six of the sons became peers. The eldest, John, bore a label; Sir Ralph of Oversy, a silver label charged with

three hurts; Sir Richard, Earl of Salisbury, eldest son by
the second marriage, a label gobony argent and azure, this
being derived from his mother, a Beaufort, who bore the
royal arms within a border gobony of those tinctures. George,
Lord Latimer, placed an ogress, or possibly an annulet, on
his saltire; Robert, Bishop of Durham, used two annulets
interlaced; William, Lord Fauconberg, Earl of Kent, a
mullet; Edward, Lord Abergavenny, a rose, possibly in
allusion to his mother's royal Lancastrian descent. Others
of the family used fleurs-de-lis and cinquefoils. A remarkable heraldic arrangement is that of the Zouches in the
fourteenth century. Alan le Zouche, head of the family,
bore: gules, bezanté. On his seal his shield hangs from the
neck of a demi lion and is surrounded by six lions, to show
his descent from Ela, daughter and co-heiress of Stephen de
Longespée, who bore six lions rampant. His nearest cousin,
William le Zouche of Haryngworth, charged the shield with
a quarter ermine; William, of Leicestershire, a label azure;
Oliver, a chevron ermine; Amory; a bend argent; Thomas,
on a quarter argent, a mullet sable.

Another fine series is connected with the Cobham's gules,
a chevron or—younger members placing on the chevron three
mullets, three lions, three cross-crosslets, three fleurs-de-lis,
three crescents, and three martlets, in every case of sable hue.

A very good example of modern difference, conceived in the
best heraldic tradition, is seen in the arms of Colonel
du Pré Penton Powney: sable, a fess cotised and couped
argent, between five mascles, four in chief and one in
base, also silver. He derives through the distaff side from
the Powneys of Old Windsor, who bore: sable, a fess argent
in chief three mascles of the last. For crest, a demi eagle
displayed charged on the breast with a mascle argent.

As regards the introduction of ordinaries or sub-ordinaries,
the border was long the favourite with younger members of
our royal family. Edmund, Earl of Kent, younger son of
Edward I, bore England within a border argent. Thomas of
Woodstock, Duke of Gloucester, youngest son of Edward III,
bore France and England quarterly within a border argent.

Humphrey, Duke of Gloucester, youngest son of Henry IV,
bore the same quarterings, first within a border of gobony
argent and sable, and then within a plain border of argent.
John Plantagenet, Earl of Kent, second son of Edmond of
Woodstock, sixth son of Edward I, bore England within a
border argent. Richard, Earl of Cambridge, grandson of
Edward III, England within a border argent charged with
ten lions rampant gules. Then we have the famous Beaufort
difference. John and Henry Beaufort, sons of John of
Gaunt and Catherine, widow of Sir Otes Swinford, after their
legitimation, placed the royal arms within a border gobony
argent and azure. Thomas Beaufort, Duke of Exeter, the
third son, had his border at first of azure and ermine, but,
after his creation as Duke, altered it to gobony argent and
azure semée of fleurs-de-lis. Thomas Holland, Earl of Kent,
son of Thomas Holland and Joan Plantagenet, Fair Maid of
Kent, was granted by his half-brother Richard II, the arms
of England within a border argent. His brother John Holland
had a border of France, as did the third son of Henry. The
border, plain or charged, was largely used in noble families
of the west of England and Scotland for the same purpose.
While de Vere, Earl of Oxford (1266), bore : quarterly, gules
and or, a mullet in the first quarter, his brother differenced
with a border indented sable. The Lyon Register of Scotland
introduced a regular system whereby the first cadets had a
plain border of the tincture of the principal charge ; other
cadets had the border engrailed, invected, etc. ; while the
third generation had theirs charged ; and with the fourth the
border was divided per pale, per fess, or quarterly. The
border wavy and engrailed was unfortunately adopted as a
mark of illegitimacy. So that while we find Walter Stewart,
son by the second marriage of Robert II, bearing (1389)
Scotland within a border chequy argent and azure, we also
see the illegitimate Douglas of Drumlanrig, and the Stewarts,
Earls of Lennox, differencing with engrailed borders.

Just before the marriage of Princess Victoria of Battenberg
to the King of Spain, a warrant was issued assigning her the
arms of her father : quarterly, first and fourth azure, a lion

rampant double queué, barry of ten gules and argent, crowned, and holding in the right paw a sword proper (for Hesse), within a border gobony of sixteen pieces of the third and second; second and third, argent, two mullets sable (for Battenberg), the whole within a border of England, the supporters carrying banners of the royal arms of England.

Abroad the border was also largely used to difference the bearings of younger members of royal houses, in Spain and Portugal, these being charged so as to show maternal descent. Philip of France, Duke of Burgundy, bore France within a border gobony and gules.

Chevrons were introduced into their arms by younger members of French families, the same thing taking place in Scotland and occasionally in England. The canton was essentially the mark of cadency in the Low Countries and was sometimes used by us for the same purpose, having the advantage of being treated like a subsidiary shield whereon descent or alliance can be shown. In France the Bourbons, in addition to the border, showed a predilection for bends of different kinds. The Dukes of Bourbon used for brisure a bend cotised gules; the Dukes of Montpensier, a bend gules, the upper part charged with the cross of the Dauphiné; the Prince of Condé, a baton couped in bend; the Princess of Conti followed suit, but added a border gules; the Counts d'Estampes, France ancient differenced by a bend gobony gules and ermine; the Counts of Evreux, a bend gobony argent and gules; the Bourbons of la Roche sur Yon, France modern, a cotice in bend gules, charged with a silver crescent in chief.

Several instances of changes of tincture have already been given. This was the method adopted by the Balliols (*temp.* Henry III). The Berkeleys originally bore gules, a chevron or; but the chevron is also found changed to silver, and for further distinction other members added crosses patée and roses both argent, and the branch in Leicestershire, cinquefoils. In France we find Bourbers-Abbeville-Tunc bearing: argent, three inescutcheons gules; while Abbeville-Bourbers-Tunc bore: or, three inescutcheons gules.

As to powdering the field, we find this done by Sir Edmond

Dacre of Westmorland (*temp.* Edward II), who, to difference his shield from that borne by the head of the family gules, three escallop shells or, added a powder of golden trefoils.

Coming to the problem of differencing for illegitimacy it must be remembered that, however hard the law treated bastardy, in the social life of the Middle Ages and even long after, little distinction was made as regards birth, of course apart from questions of inheritance. Bastards filled important offices, intermarried with the legitimate issue of great houses, and so, provided both parents were of gentle blood, no difficulty was made about their bearing armorial shields. Only these had to be clearly differenced, and from earliest days the bend sinister, or preferably its diminutive the bendlet sinister, was that mark. This seemed quite appropriate, for it came from the " coté femme " of the shield, drawing a debruising mark right across the field. This mark of bastardy is mentioned in various Ordinances of different countries. But the regulations were never strictly observed. Soon, indeed, the bendlet was couped at both ends, and so we have what the French call the " baton perri en barre," whence have come the popular but erroneous phrases of " bastard bar " and "bar sinister." Another modification was soon introduced. In order to make the debruising less conspicuous the bendlet sinister was frequently carried under and not over any ordinary used as a charge.

The use of the bend sinister for debruising suggested another system of marshalling, that of placing the paternal arms on an ordinary, such as a bend, a fess, a chevron or a canton. The Beauforts, sons of John of Gaunt and Catherine Swinford, before the legitimation by Parliament, bore the arms of their father (gules, three lions passant-guardant, or, differenced with a label of three points ermine) on a bend, placed on a shield per pale argent and azure. Sir Roger de Clarendon, the reputed illegitimate son of the Black Prince, marshalled his father's " shield of peace " arranged on a bend, bearing : argent, on a bend sable three ostrich feathers bendwise, enfiled with a scroll argent. The same practice was adopted abroad. It was done by Mathieu, Baron de la Roche, le

Grand Batard de Bourbon, who bore a bend of France, debruised by a cotice gules, on a silver shield. Antoine, Comte de la Roche, le Grand Batard de Bourgogne, did the same with his quartered coat, the field being gold. The fess was used for displaying his arms by Charles Somerset, eldest son of Charles Somerset, Earl of Worcester, bastard son of Henry Beaufort, third Duke of Somerset, but the practice was soon abandoned, and his present-day descendants use the coat of the legitimate Beauforts. The fess arrangement was adopted by Jean, Batard de Bourgogne, Bishop of Cambray (*obit* 1479); while Philippe, Batard de Bourgogne, seigneur de Fontaines, illegitimate son of a legitimate son of Antoine, " le grand Batard," marshalled his quartered coat in a chevron placed on a gold shield.

Most of the illegitimate offspring of the English and British kings debruised their arms with bends or bendlets sinister, but there were other exceptions besides the Beauforts. Sir John de Clarence, natural son of Thomas, Duke of Clarence, son of Henry IV, bore : per chevron gules and azure, in chief two lions counter-rampant regardant, in base a fleur-de-lis or. While we have here the royal charges, the composition produces something quite new. Henry Fitzroy, Duke of Richmond and Somerset, natural son of Henry VIII, was granted : the royal arms within a border quarterly ermine and counter gobony or and azure, debruised by a baton sinister argent ; over all an escutcheon of pretence : quarterly, gules and vaire or and vert, a lion rampant, argent, on a chief azure a castle between two bucks' heads silver, attired gold. It is impossible to say what this escutcheon may have been intended to convey, but it is on a level with the muddled heraldry of the king's many wives. Another unusual marshalling was that of James Fitzroy, Duke of Monmouth, natural son of Charles II : quarterly, first and fourth, ermine on a pile gules three lions of England ; second and third, or, a shield of France within the royal tressure of Scotland. This, however, was soon abandoned for the royal arms debruised with a bendlet sinister, and with a shield of pretence of Scott of Buccleuch.

Apart from the natural children of royalty, the bendlet

sinister, or its diminutive the baton sinister, was practically disused in England after the sixteenth century, when borders, often wavy, were substituted. Even these mild reminders have frequently been dropped after a few generations.

LIST OF ROYAL LABELS

Geoffrey Plantagenet, Earl of Brittany and Richmond, fourth son of Henry II (1158–1186), a label of five points.

Edward I, as heir apparent, a label of five points azure; also one of three points. This label was also borne by Edward II and Edward III when heirs apparent. But Edward the Black Prince used a silver label of three points, and ever since his time this has been the label of the Princes of Wales.

Edmond, Earl of Lancaster, second son of King Henry III, a label of three points charged with nine fleurs-de-lis; also a label of three points azure with three fleurs-de-lis on each point or. His son, Thomas, bore the same label. All his descendants seem to have differenced alike.

Lionel, Duke of Clarence, Earl of Ulster, third son of Edward III, a label of three points argent, each charged with a canton gules.

John of Gaunt, Duke of Lancaster, King of Castile and Leon, third son of Edward III, a label of three points ermine. His son Henry, before his accession to the throne, a label of five points, the three to the dexter ermine, and the two to the sinister azure, with three fleurs-de-lis on each point.

Edmond, Duke of York, fifth son of Edward III, a label of three points argent, on each point three torteaux.

Thomas of Lancaster, Duke of Clarence, son of Henry IV, a label of three points ermine, each charged with a canton gules.

John, Duke of Bedford, third son of Henry IV, a label of five points, the two to the dexter ermine, the other three azure with three fleurs-de-lis.

Edward, Duke of York, eldest son of Edmond of Langley, a label of three points gules, on each as many castles or.

Richard II, during the lifetime of his father, a label of three points argent, the centre charged with a cross of St. George.

Richard, Earl of Cambridge, second son of Edmond of Langley (and grandson of Edward III), a label of three points each charged with as many torteaux.

Richard, Duke of York, son of the above, the same label.

Edmond, of York, Earl of March, third son of Richard, Duke of York, a label of five points argent, the two dexter points charged with as many lions rampant purpure, and the three sinister with nine torteaux.

Richard, Duke of York, second son of Edward IV, a label of three points argent, charged with a canton gules, which was also borne by the sixth son, George, Duke of Clarence; while the Duke of Clarence's son, Edward, Earl of Warwick, bore a label of three points gobony argent and azure.

Arthur Tudor, Prince of Wales, eldest son of Henry VII, a label of three points argent.

James, Duke of York, third son of Charles I, a label of three points ermine.

Henry, Duke of Gloucester, fourth son of Charles I, a label of three points argent, each charged with a rose gules.

George III. The sons bore their labels differenced as follows :

Duke of York, Bishop of Osnaburgh, cross of St. George in the centre point.

William Henry, Duke of Clarence (subsequently King William IV), a cross of St. George between two anchors gules.

Edward, Duke of Kent, a cross of St. George between fleurs-de-lis gules.

Ernest Augustus, Duke of Cumberland, a fleur-de-lis gules between two crosses of St. George. His son the second Duke, a label of three points gules, the centre point charged with the white horse of Hanover.

Augustus Frederick, Duke of Sussex, two hearts on centre point gules and a cross of St. George on the outer points.

Adolphus Frederick, Duke of Cambridge, a cross of St. George on the middle and two red hearts on each of the outer points. This label was borne by his son George, the second Duke, who placed immediately beneath it a label of five points gules.

Duke of Gloucester, a label of five points, on centre point a fleur-de-lis between a cross of St. George on the outer points. His son, the second Duke, had a label of five points, the centre one having a fleur-de-lis, and the four outer points crosses of St. George.

Charlotte Augustus, Princess Royal, Queen of Wurtemberg, a rose between two crosses of St. George. Her husband, the Prince of Saxe-Coburg, a label of five points, a red rose on the centre point.

Princess Augusta Sophia, a rose between two ermine spots.

Princess Elizabeth, Princess of Hesse, a cross of St. George between two roses gules.

Princess Mary, a rose between two cantons.

Princess Sophia, a heart between two roses.

Princess Amelie, a rose between two hearts.

Queen Victoria's children were all assigned silver labels of three points with the following charges: Alfred, Duke of Edinburgh, a cross of St. George on the central point and a red anchor on each of the outer points. His son, Duke of Saxe-Coburg-Gotha, a cross of St. George between two hearts. Arthur, Duke of Connaught, a cross of St. George and two red fleurs-de-lis. Prince Arthur of Connaught, a label of five points argent, the centre and outer points charged with a cross of St. George and the others with a fleur-de-lis azure. Leopold, Duke of Albany, a cross of St. George and two red hearts. Victoria, Princess Royal of England, Empress of Germany, a red rose and two crosses of St. George. Princess Alice of Hesse, a red rose and two ermine spots. Helena, Princess Christian, a cross of St. George and two red roses. Louise, Duchess of Argyll, a red rose and two red cantons. Beatrice, Princess Henry of Battenberg, a red heart and two red roses.

King Edward's daughters, granted while their father was Prince of Wales:

Princess Louise, Princess Royal, Duchess of Fife, a label of five points, the middle and outer points charged with a cross of St. George, the others with a thistle, slipped and leaved.

Princess Victoria, five points, the centre and outer points charged with a rose gules, the others with a cross of St. George.

Princess Maud, Queen of Norway, five points, the centre and outer points being a red heart, the others a cross of St. George.

CHAPTER XIV

CANTING ARMS

A REMARKABLE feature of heraldry, not only English, but of all countries, consists of what the French call "*armes parlantes.*" These "speaking arms" we describe technically as "allusive" or as "canting arms," the latter a term derived from chanting, to sing out, and are so called because they enable even the uninitiated to connect the coat-of-arms, crest and badge with its owner. They are, in other words, pictorial puns. This form of blazoning is very old. Some of the earliest examples of the twelfth and thirteenth centuries belong to this class. It served a useful purpose in its day, for it made the "cognisance" specially recognisable to both gentle and simple folk in the traffickings of peace and in time of war. But even in this direction we find warrant for the practice in quite remote days. Probably the heroes of antiquity began it on their metal or leather shields. Certainly Plutarch gives an instance of early emblematic punning. He tells us that when Cicero went as quæstor to Sicily, "he consecrated in one of the temples a vase, or some other offering in silver, upon which he inscribed his two first names, Marcus Tullius, and, punning upon the third, ordered the artificer to engrave a 'vetch.'" As we all know, Cicero was an inveterate punster, a weakness which caused him to commit many crimes against good taste and kindly fellowship. But his example was largely followed, emblematically as well as verbally.

In an old Herald's "Visitation Book," covering only a small part of England, of 1240–1245, we find no less than nine examples of these "speaking arms." It is somewhat curious to note, on the study of other Herald's "Visitation Books" and armorial dictionaries, that this peculiar form of human weakness was rather more widely prevalent in the North than in the South of England. Whether this was due to the slower spread of clerkly learning, or to the more steadfast clinging to feudal customs, it is hard to say; but later it became a mannerism, fostered, no doubt, by the lamentable proneness of man to give way to evil habits. One is the more induced to think this because of the shockingly bad work of some of the pictorial punsters. It is true that this is the reflection of a twentieth-century critic on the work of those of other ages and modes of thought and speech. Indeed, we find that some of those "speaking arms" are practically dumb to us, because we have re-christened many things and altered our phonetics. Thus, the family of Skenes bear three dirks (anciently skenes); the Lucies of olden fame, three fishes which turn out to be pikes, better known to our ancestors by the more poetic name of lucies. Our "fishy" friends are numerous. On the very old shield of the Comtes de Bar, who were so intimately connected with our Plantagenet kings, were two barbels (French, *barres*) embowed. Almost of equal age, the Troutbecks have a charming arrangement of mountain trout. The Turbuts have three turbots, the Whalleys can boast of three whales, and the Salmons three salmons. That once formidable man, Peter des Roches, Bishop of Winchester, had three roaches. This is curious, because the Norman name appears to be derived from *roche*, a rock, upon which their seigneurial castle was built. In fact, that grand bishop was named Stone Rock, his godparents being as guilty of tautology as the civic wags of Margate, who talk of Cliftonville. Argent, three eels naiant, azure, are the arms of Eeles. Then we have the following: Spratt: argent, a chevron sable between three sprats azure. Sturgeon: azure, three sturgeons naiant, argent. Mackerel: gules, three mackerel hauriant, argent. De Soles: gules, three soles argent. Robert, Lord Scales (*circa* 1300), descendant of Eschales of Lynn, Norfolk, bore: gules, six escallop shells argent. Sable, a fess engrailed between three whelk shells, stood for Shelley. Atsea bore: or, two bars wavy, gules, between three shrimps of the second ; and Sea : argent, a fish hauriant, azure, between two of the second, each charged with as many bars nebulé of the first ; for crest : two lobster claws erect gule, each clutching a fish argent.

Among the obsolete puns perhaps the arms of the Trusbuts, Barons of Wartre, should be included. They bore "trois boutz d'eau," or three water bowgets, those skins of animals used by the Crusaders for storing water—and sometimes for stronger liquids. In this instance the punster endeavoured to kill two birds at one " go," having a shy at the family name and baronial title with the three water bags.

Fruits, flowers, and plants are largely drawn upon, as we have already seen. Other examples are afforded. Pawne bore: argent, three peacocks in their pride proper, evidently in allusion to the French word *paon*. The far-spread Fraser family bear : azure, three frases, that is, strawberry flowers, from the French *fraisier*. Primrose bears: or, three primroses within a double tressure flory, counter flory gules. Azure, three lilies argent, stood for Lillie, and also for Beauty, whose appreciation of what is really beautiful and sense of humour are to be commended. Periton bears : or, a peartree vert, fructed proper ; and Warden : argent, three warden pears leaved vert. Argent, a fess sable, between three apples, gules, stalked vert, are the arms of the Appletons, of Surrey. By the way, it may perhaps be as well to state that every "mother's son" of us is fully entitled to the apple as an heraldic personal cognisance : that is, if we may believe the celebrated French herald Freron. This worthy sage declares that Adam after the fall adopted a fig leaf as his armorial insignia and that Abel and the rest of his progeny quartered the paternal arms with those of Mother Eve, who was an heiress, and bore: argent, an apple vert. Clearly then these arms are ours. But to return to our proper subject.

In the chapter dealing with animals in heraldry a varied array of punning coats has been given, but a few more instances may be mentioned here. Thomas Ramridge,

Abbot of St. Albans, bore: gules, on a bend or, between a lion rampant and a ram rampant argent, three eagles vert, armed gules. Argent, three eagles displayed gules, armed or, the arms of Queen's College, Oxford, are those of its founder, Robert de Eglesfield, Confessor to Philippa of Hainault, consort of Edward III. From pleasant wooded Surrey the Doves come with their shield bearing silver doves. Sir Roger de Merley (*temp.* Henry III) bore: barry of argent and gules, a border azure charged with golden merlots. Cocks crow lustily on the shields of the Cockaignes, Cockburns, and Cockerells. Lord Castlemaine, whose family name is Handcock, bears among other things a right hand between two cocks. Wolves prowl on shield or helm, for Lovell, Lovels, Lupus, Lovett, Lowe, Lows, Wolfe, Wolfton and Wolverton. An elephant represents the Oliphants. Norman-French puns are saddled on the Arundells, with their three swallows (hirondelles), the Tremaynes with their three hands, and the Malmaines with their three sinister hands. Baines from Scotland have bones of one kind or another as charges or crest. A family of that name hailing from Middlesex bear a human shin bone in fess, and another shin bone in pale, thus forming a cross. These white bones on a black field are suggestively presided over by a vulture; perhaps this last lugubrious addition has some occult meaning, for it does not help the pun.

Inanimate objects are frequently dragged in for this purpose. On the tomb of Sir Humphrey Stanley (*obit* 1805) in Westminster Abbey is a shield quartering Stanley, Clifton and Pipe. The third quarter is for Pipe of Pipe and stands thus: azure, crusily moline, two pipes in pale, or. Yates, of Lyford, Berkshire, bore: argent a fess between three gates sable; but Yate of Buckland in the same county preferred his coat thus: per pale crenelly, argent and sable, three field gates countercharged; while Yeates of Bristol bore: per fess crenelly sable and argent, three five-barred gates counterchanged. John Tyler, Bishop of Llandaff (1706-24), bore: argent, a bend gules between six tiler's nails sable. Probably this was a coat with a double meaning, to the vulgar a mere allusion to the bishop's name, to the bearer a perpetual reminder of the mystery of the Passion. Sir Ranaud de Coupenne (*temp*. Edward II) bore : gules six quill pens argent. The modern Cowpen have reduced them to three.

Occasionally the punning has, at it were, been curiously reversed—the badge has given its name to its bearer.

The Scotch family of Bannerman, who derive their name from the ancient office of Hereditary Royal Standard Bearer to the King of Scotland, have the following coat-of-arms: gule, a banner displayed argent, thereon a canton azure, charged with a St. Andrew's cross. Here we have a very good instance of a double event, a punning symbol on the name and an honourable badge of office. The celebrated French architect, Jacques Androuet, took for a badge a hoop or circle as a modest intimation of the infinitude of his art and its service to the Supreme Architect ; he became known to his own generation and subsequent lovers of art as Du Cerceau.

A very curious legend of the Black Forest tells us how one Kuno von Stein, a bold if not a bad Crusader, became irrepressibly homesick while away in Palestine, and there entered into the usual very one-sided compact with the Devil. His Satanic Majesty bound himself to send Kuno Stein back to his fatherland on the back of a flying dragon, only bargaining that if he, Stein, went to sleep during the long flight, then his body and soul would be ever forfeited. Stein, nothing fearing (or perhaps despairingly thinking that the end would be the same whatever he might do), got astride of the uncanny reptile, which immediately rose up and commenced a most prodigiously rapid flight. It was certainly in the right direction, but nevertheless Stein felt that he was lost, for the rapid motion lulled him towards a deadly sleep, which was only put off by the constant attention of a white falcon, whose strong beak reminded the nodding knight that he dozed at his peril. Thanks to these repeated and pointed attentions, Kuno arrived at his native home without once having actually closed his eyes. In token of gratitude to the white-feathered stranger, Stein adopted the falcon as his crest, emblazoned it thrice over on his shield and then, in the course of time, the Von Steins became Falconsteins. Sceptics may, of course, doubt the legend from beginning to end, but the fact that Steins preceded the Falconsteins in the Black Forest is beyond dispute, and also that the former bore a plain shield with a cross, and the latter bear falcons.

Even greater freedom was given to fancy when designing the personal badge and the rebus. Sir John Peché (early sixteenth century) used for his badge a peach slipped argent, charged with the letter E. A fructed peach branch was his crest, and he surrounded his arms with a beautiful wreath of peach leaves and fruit, each fruit bearing the letter E. Markham had a lion of St. Mark, its wings displayed, supporting a horse collar (hames). Sir Godfrey Foljambe, of Walton, Derby, had as one of his badges a human leg couped at the thigh, vestured per pale or and sable, spurred or. Catesby's golden leopard passant was probably intended for a cat o' mountain passing by. Ashton had an ash growing out of a tun, and Burton a bird standing on one. Bishop Thomas Beckington's rebus was a fire-beacon, a tun and the letter T. Oldham, that busy Lancashire town, used owls as supporters for its civic arms; and it is curious to find Oldham, Bishop of Exeter, adopting an owl bearing in its beak a scroll with the word Dom. Abbot Ramridge, whose arms have already been noticed, also sported a badge, consisting of a ram with a collar bearing the word " Ryge." Abbot Islip's chapel at Westminster Abbey shows two different versions of his rebus. The first represents a man falling from a tree, and exclaiming " I slip." In the second instance we have a human eye and a branch or slip from a tree. The Oxenbridge Chapel in St. George's, Windsor Castle, has sculptured over the doorway the founder's badge—an ox, a capital N, and a bridge. In St. Albans Abbey Church John Wheathamstede has a cluster of wheat ears between an eagle and a Paschal lamb, the symbols of St. John the Evangelist and St. John the Baptist. In Canterbury Cathedral the eagle, standing over an ox branded with the letters, N E, stands for John Oxney.

CHAPTER XV

THE FLEUR-DE-LIS AND ITS VARIATIONS

CERTAIN decorative forms seem to spring naturally from the human mind. This does not solely apply to the strictly geometrical figures. It is equally true as regards such conventionalised emblems as the cross with expanded limbs (the so-called cross patée, or more correctly formée, of the heralds), the tau and the ansata crosses, which we find in Egyptian, Eastern, and in Central American memorial carvings, some of which belong to periods long anterior to the dawn of our own era, in certain instances occurring spontaneously in each region. An example of this also appears to exist in the Fleur-de-lis.

In Europe from mediæval times downwards force of circumstance has conspired to endow the beautiful figure with a peculiarly French character. The French themselves say that they owe their lilies to Clovis, and it is worth noting that according to a very old legend they were a gift direct from heaven to the first Christian king of the Franks, they having been brought by an angel to a pious hermit for transmission to the monarch. This in itself is evidence of the extreme antiquity of these emblems, an antiquity which shrouded their beginning in obscurity. It is true that opponents of the miraculous have assigned amusingly divergent theories as to this origin. Botanists look upon it as the arbitrary form of the iris, supposed to have been used as a primitive sceptre for early chieftains ; others think it is the riverside flag, the yellow flowers of which were plucked by the victorious soldiers of Clovis after the battle of Tolbiac to adorn their flowing locks, and so adopted as a royal badge. We are also told that it may be a painter's rendering of the bee, very doubt-fully asserted to have been the badge of Childeric ; or even the three frogs which foreigners attributed to the Gauls. But the two great opposing schools are those who believe the emblem represents the garden lily, the white lily of the Virgin Mary ; and those who, with some show of reason, regard it

FRANCE ANCIENT.

as a war symbol, a beauti-ful partisan or pike head. If we consult old documents and monuments, evidence may be found to support each of these theories, and several more. Deeper study, however, can lead to but one conclusion, and that is, the fleur-de-lis is a conven-tionalised marsh or water flower. Its prototype may have been yellow blossom of the river flags, or the charm-ing iris (which, by a natural transition, would be over-laid with gold, for " painting the rose and gilding refined gold " has ever been a favourite pastime), or, again, it may have been the Eastern lotus. Egyptians and Asiatics held the lotus sacred, not only as a food-giving plant, but as a symbol of fertility, the product of earth and water vivified by solar heat, exhibiting the striking phenomena of opening and shutting with the rise and setting of the sun. Hence it was sacred to Phthah, to Osiris and Isis, all relating to the Nile and its wondrous floods. In the East, Vishnu issues from the floating lotus, symbolising the creation of the world from chaos. Possibly this lotus may have travelled westward through Greece and Rome. On the other hand, it belongs to the common fund of symbolism, and while the nenupha spoke of the life-giving overflowing Nile to the dwellers in Egypt, the lotus pictured fertility to the Hindus, the iris and kindred growths budding luxuriantly on the river bank foreshadowed spring to others. It is certain that we find the Greeks and Etruscans using a fleur-de-lis, and generally in much the same sense as the Egyptians did the lotus—as a sign of plenty and happiness. In this sense, too, was it employed by the Romans on some of their coins and medals—the French say chiefly in connection with Gaul. It is notable enough that many of the numismatic horns of plenty have a trifolated object in the mouth of the cornucopia, and this occurs on coins struck in Rome as well as in the distant provinces.

The fleur-de-lis belongs to the mystic triparted symbols so early venerated. In later times, like the shamrock, it told the devout of the Blessed Trinity ; while still later heralds saw in it a painted sermon, silently appealing to knights and squires, the three lobes standing for " Sapience, foy et prouesse." Finally the politically minded declared that the three lobes, and the three flowers on the royal shield, referred to the three early races of French kings.

One difficulty in treating this subject is that in spite of the great diversity of shapes given to the fleur-de-lis—though throughout its primal character is maintained—it is practically impossible to assign dates to these different varieties, as they are used simultaneously, especially so in the early days. For instance, we find a perfect conventionalised fleur-de-lis in the ancient hieroglyphics of Upper Egypt. In the Zodiac room of the temple of Denderah were to be seen three floral sceptres—one is topped by a bell-shaped flower, a mere outline of the symbolical lotus ; a second has a calyx formed of two sepals, with an inner lanceolate bud ; the third has at the top two steps, from the smaller of which springs an exact fleur-de-lis of the strictest Bourbon period. Perrot and Chipiez give a picture of a fleur-de-lis from a gem of the Mycenæan period. It is of the iris type, having a central oval petal, two curving outward petals, with ball anthers, a fillet, but no stalk.

A complete fleur-de-lis consists of three petals, a transverse fillet, and beneath this the stalk. Sometimes filaments are placed between the central petal and outer curved ones.

In one type we find the two curved outer petals joined together and forming a cup or calyx, from the midst of which springs an upright petal. Usually the fillet is absent, and the stalk is not triparted, but merely a straight stem.

TYPES OF FLEURS-DE-LIS.

Examples of this are seen in the flowers among Egyptian hieroglyphics in the Louvre, and Assyrian sculptures in the British Museum. The type is comparatively rare in heraldry. Dr. Bonavia regards this as the only true representative of *Lilium candidum*, or Madonna lily.

The outer leaves in the best examples are not too large, and are well curved over. If of nearly the same size as the central petal, and made to stand upright with only their tips curved, an awkward combination is the result. Frequently the under curved edge is serrated, unlike any true lily leaf.

The central petal may be long with a slight globular swelling near the top, or it may be of a more nearly oval form. Other favourite shapes are the squat club-like leaf seen on the Denderah sceptre, and the long diamond, of which rather handsome specimens are seen on French illuminations and on carved work taken to Scotland by Queen Mary Stuart. As a rule the petal is unmarked, but occasionally it has a ridge down the centre, giving it a convex appearance. This is particularly noticeable in the pike or lance-head designs, in which the central lobe is made to assume the appearance of a double-edged weapon with more or less curved cutting edges. However, it also characterises the three herbaceous-leaved lis, such as that seen as early as 1199 on the civic seal of Lille.

Perhaps the most puzzling part of the emblem is the fillet. It has no counterpart in the lily or iris, unless we take it to be a somewhat clumsy rendering of the calyx base, which has a rather marked series of protuberances in some of these flowers. This base may also account for the stalk of our typical lis. The fillet may be a thin, small band, constricting the emblem, or holding the separate parts together. At other times it is thick and long, very prominent. It is sometimes treated like a coronet fillet and studded with jewels. It may be double or even triple. Dr. Bonavia regards this as the essential part of the fleur-de-lis, which betrays its symbolical value. To him the fillet is a ligature, attaching two curved horns to an upright tree symbol. He argues that the central lobe is the Assyrian date palm, and the curved outer petals and their stalks are the luck bringing, evil spirit banishing sacred horns, actually attached to the trees. This theory is, of course, equally applicable to those lis which are shown with the outer curved parts springing from the fillet itself, and having only a central stalk. In the first case he sees two pairs of horns, in the second only one pair. This would be giving a definite birthplace to the symbol, which may have been brought to Europe either by the Crusading knights, or much earlier by means of the far-reaching Phœnician commerce.

As regards the heraldic stalk, we may have three short stems ; a short central and two long outwardly curved stalks ; a central long spike and two short curves ; or we may have practically a replica of the top part, and this repetition may be given such prominence as to detract from the elegance of the design. So far is this carried, indeed, that a double fleur-de-lis may be produced, as in the example drawn by Rey from a shield on a church at Altramura in the province of Naples. It appears to be the result of design, and not a mere whimsical exaggeration. It is constructed much on the principle of Jupiter's thunderbolt. Curiously enough we find a very similar object on the reverse of a British coin, ascribed to a king of the Iceni about A.D. 50. In many cases—and this is a characteristic of most of the badge lis on our Great Seals —the three petals and fillet form a single part, while the stalk is a small three-branched attachment.

It must be confessed that many European artists, even in early times, treated the symbol as though composed of three distinct parts, bound together by the fillet. Thus we have a central globular or lanceolate blossom with two leaves, each with distinct stalk, and not touching each other. In two quaint examples found on seals affixed to abbey charters in France this independence of parts is made quite plain.

GUILLAUME
BARON, 1260.

That on the seal of Theobald de Blangy, recorded at Bayeux, consisted of an upright ear of wheat between two ragged leaves. That of Robert Mahias, Knight Templar (Abbaye d'Aunay), has a central twig with alternate lanceolate leaves (perhaps this, too, may be an ear of wheat), between leaves having an upright shoot and an outward curved part. In this latter example there is no ligament. Yet in both instances, which belong to the thirteenth century, the general outline of the lis is preserved. Other examples closely allied to these are recorded at Aunay, Caen, and so on. This idea of the fruitfulness of the symbol is shown in another way. Often (both in heraldic painting and sculpture) the central lobe (and sometimes the three) is treated as though it were a pod partly burst and showing seed within. Or again we may have birds connected with the emblem. On the seal of Guillaume Baron, Knight Templar (Abbaye d'Aunay, 1260), we have a lis treated rather architecturally, the central lobe being a long oval cartouche with a fillet, apparently to represent a bud, between two curved leaves with serrated

NORMAN FLEUR-
DE-LIS, 13TH
CENTURY.

under parts, and a fillet. Standing on each leaf is a small bird pecking at the central bud. On the seal of Raoul de Carpiquet (Abbaye de la Sainte Trinité, Caen) is a fleur-de-lis composed of a curving calyx, fillet and triparted plain stalk, and a central oval seed pod, whence springs a sprig with seven filaments, having trefoil buds at the ends. Clinging to the pod on each side is a bird pecking at the lowest blossom. On the ancient seal of the town of Liskeard, Cornwall, we find a large fleur-de-lis, with filaments between the centre and outer petals, and on the anthers of these filaments are perched two small birds. I at first thought that these small birds were originally intended for the eagles of Richard, second son of King John, King of the Romans and Earl of Cornwall, for both he and his son Edmond used a sable eagle of Rome and the bezants of Cornwall; while another Earl of Cornwall, Piers de Gaveston, bore: vert, six eagles displayed or. But it was pointed out to me that the parish church of Liskeard was dedicated to St. Martin of Tours. Therefore they are probably allusive symbols, two martins. No doubt this explains the presence of the birds on the Liskeard seal, but those on the seals of the Crusading French knights suggest a curious connection with birds, winged figures, and men shown in Eastern symbolism as always guarding sacred trees, which Sir George Birdwood regarded as the

" witnesses " in connection with phallic worship. Did the supporting angels of the French king's golden lilies come from the same region ?

May we explain that extraordinary anomaly, the leopard's head, *jessant de lis*, in which we see a lis thrust through the mouth of a leopard, the stalk between its teeth and the three petals coming out at the back of its head, by a metamorphosis of the Egyptian and Hindu god-bearing lotus ?   On a beautiful sardonyx intaglio in the Demidoff Collection (shown in C. W. King's " Antique Gems and Rings ") we see Cupid rising from a pomegranate flower. On a sceptre shown in a painting at the Bibliothèque Nationale, Paris, attributed to a Roman consul A.D. 525, we see a winged child issuing from a lis. A gold sceptre found in the tomb of Philippe le Bel, at St. Denis, had a serrated leaf on each side of a rod topped by an eagle with half-spread wings. All these look very much like steps in the degeneration of the seed-bearing flower symbol.

The filament almost invariably springs upwards between the three petals, although a few rare instances are found of

FLORENTINE
FLEUR-DE-LIS.

fleurs-de-lis with filaments springing from the ligature outside the curved petals. Generally the filament bears at its end some kind of anther. This may be a mere ball, a concretion of small balls, or, as in the case of the so-called St. Louis example, it may take the form of a well-marked trefoil. On some early Florentine coins the anther partakes of the character of a trident, or an open fleur-de-lis. A daisy ornament tip is also met with as well as starred blossoms. When there is the filament with anther, and the petals are more or less decorated with serrations, curved over leaves, perhaps enclosing seeds, English heralds call it a " fleur-de-lis flowery." The French speak of it as *épanoui*, and the Italians as *giglio Fiorentino*.

A quaint form of decoration adopted by a few early herald painters was to diaper the three petals ; that is, to cover them with running floral or simple geometric patterns drawn in very faint lines. Occasionally examples of diapered fleurs-de-lis are met with in carvings and on seals.

I have said that the lis belongs to the triparted class of symbols. This is true as a rule, for the pictorial idea appears to guide even the sculptor. But there are exceptions. The Bourbon crest, worn on the helmet and apparently on some of their crowns and coronets, had four curved petals and a central upright bud, either ovular or carved so as to present four club or pike faces. This method has also been adopted with some sceptres, and more commonly when forming architectural finials.

It is generally assumed that the earlier French monarchs bore a lis " without number," " powdered," or " semeé," and that the use of only three, two below and one above, came in with Charles V, some say, as already observed, in honour of the Trinity, others to denote the three races of kings. As a matter of fact, from the earliest times heralds treated the lis as a symbol of such importance that it could be shown singly. The royal shields appear semée, with ten (placed 4, 3, 2 and 1), and with only three, long before Charles's day. It even occurs that the three flowers may be borne not as a pyramid, but placed two above and one below, technically, " mal ordonée." While most herald painters did not hesitate to slice off the lis in any way when decorating a " powdered " field, others strove to get in regular lines and only show complete flowers. But in course of time there was evolved a variety named a " fleur-de-lis au pied nourri," when only the top petals and filaments are shown. It was evidently derived from the royal sceptre or crown, and was probably an augmentation granted by kings as a mark of honour.

In England the fleur-de-lis was used at least as early as the first half of the eleventh century. A good specimen is seen on the coins of Harthacnut (1039–41). It is also seen on the coins of Edward the Confessor and of Harold. On the Great Seal of Edward we find the king holding a sceptre with a trefoil, three well-marked lobes forming a cross. On his crown we see trefoils round the band, but in the centre there appears to be a distinct fleur-de-lis. On the Conquerer's coins we find a lis sceptre and a flory cross. Henry II has a crown decorated with lis on his Great Seal, and so had the Empress Matilda, but her sceptre is tipped with a trefoil, not cruciform like the Confessor's, but approaching the form of the lis. After this the symbol appears on the whole series of our Great Seals. The sword of Edward I has a pommel shaped like a lis. On Edward III's first Great Seal we see a large castle on both sides of his throne, and above these a small top-heavy lis, the three petals being of almost equal size, and the stalk very small. On his second seal the castles disappear and we have two large lis, with a big lanceolate upright petal and two well-curved leaves, below the fillet small but well-defined stalks. On his third Great Seal we find the monarch on horseback,

TYPES OF FLEURS-DE-LIS.

with a shield quarterly, France ancient and England. These arms are on the horse's neck and hind quarters, while the background is diapered with lozenges containing a lis. The reduction of the fleur-de-lis to three on the royal coat-of-arms first appears on the second Great Seal of Henry IV. Henry VI had a special seal for French affairs. Thereon we see him with a fleur-de-lis sceptre : on his right is a crowned shield bearing the three lilies, on his left a shield quarterly France and England. On the coins of Henry VII we find both the fleur-de-lis and also a fleur-de-lis dimidiated with a rose. Elizabeth has on her second seal two big épanoui examples, with very small filaments, and each petal shaped as a separate bud enclosing seeds. With the House of Hanover the lis often becomes deplorably squat, sometimes looking much like ill-drawn three ostrich feathers.

St. Louis of France used many forms of the fleur-de-lis. On one of his seals it appears as a compact flower, with lanceolate central petal and two filaments with trefoil tips. It is sometimes named after him, but this variety was used both before and after his time. Indeed, many of St. Louis's lis are very suggestive of metal work—lance heads, pierced and otherwise.

Artists have often adorned the petals, sometimes placing a small crown on the centre lobe, or topping it with a Latin or a Lorraine cross. We have already seen that the side leaves may bear birds. But in heraldry the lis is never charged with another object ; on the other hand it is sometimes placed on a rose, castle, etc., and it may be dimidiated : for instance, half a rose and half a lis being stuck together, or half a lis and half an eagle. Its decorative value is very great.

Apart from its splendid possibilities for shield adornment, the fleur-de-lis became extraordinarily prolific in heraldry as a result of the liberality with which it was granted by both the French and the English kings as a mark of favour to armigerous persons. The change of the Chateaubriand golden pine cones for fleurs-de-lis, as already described, is an example of this. Charles VII bestowed on the brothers of Jeanne d'Arc the name of Lys, together with the following coat-of-arms : azure, a sword in pale argent, pommelled gold, supporting a royal crown on its point, between two fleurs-de-lis, also gold. Louis XII gave to Piero de Medici a roundel azure, thereon three fleurs-de-lis, to add to his collection of five bezants on his shield, for his military and political assistance. Other instances of the bestowal of lis have already been cited. Among these was the adornment of the Scottish tressure border with fleurs-de-lis. Crosses and other ordinaries and charges so decorated probably had a similar origin. Two of the oddest of these additions are seen on the shields of Woodmartin and Goldington, who bear respectively: (1) per fess dancetté argent and sable, each point ending in a fleur-de-lis; (2) or, a bend fleury counter-fleury, azure.

FLEURS-DE-LIS ÉPANOUI.

This last was much like the "bende d'aszure fleureté d'or" borne by Sir Motas de Latimer in the days of Edward II. Among the early English coats worthy of note are the following three. Robert Agulon (*temp.* Henry III) bore: gules, a fleur-de-lis argent. Sir John Deyville (*temp.* Edward II) bore: or, on a fess gules three fleurs-de-lis gold, between three fleurs-de-lis gules. But his descendant, Robert Deyville (*temp.* Edward III), bore: or, on a fess gules four fleurs-de-lis; whether gold or silver is not stated.

This emblem was also widely distributed among towns admitted to royal patronage. A notable example of this is, of course, the city of Paris. As now borne the arms are: gules, an antique ship with sail set, swimming on the river in base; on a chief azure, semée of fleurs-de-lis. But on the seal of the city of 1358 only two fleurs-de-lis appear, one on each side of the sail. In the seal of 1366, these have disappeared, but the ship flies a flag bearing three full and part of a fourth fleur-de-lis. Then the lis appear in the sky at the back of the ship, and it is only from 1426 onwards that the blue chief charged with fleurs-de-lis appears.

As already stated, true lilies have been otherwise distinctly conventionalised for ages past. On the Jewish shekels the lilies are the lilies of the field, shown on a rod with blossoms bell-shaped with trilobe petals. The Madonna lilies, as introduced in Christian art, and thence finding their way into heraldry, are quite clearly of the garden type, as may be seen on monastic and other seals. An excellent example is afforded by the arms of Eton College, for on their coat we have both the religious lilies and the royal fleur-de-lis. The arms granted by Henry VI to the College of St. Mary at Eton are : sable, three lilies slipped argent, on a chief per pale azure and gule a fleur-de-lis or, and a lion passant guardant or (of England). These same lilies appear on the coat of Magdalen College, Oxford : fusilly ermine and sable, on a chief of the last three lilies slipped in fess argent. These are the arms of the founder, William Waynflete, Bishop of Winchester, whose real name was Patyn. He added the chief to his paternal coat in acknowledgment of his debt to Eton College. Waynflete appears to have given the chief to Winchester College as well. Then we have the three silver lilies, in association with the golden roses of the Abbey of Barking, these flowers symbolising the Saviour and the Virgin.

As having much direct influence on the growth of the emblems, something must be said here concerning the lotus. This is a water-lily whose blossoms, buds and leaves enter largely into the whole range of decorative and symbolic art of Egypt and the East. The motifs were adopted by the Greeks and spread over Southern and Western Europe through Roman influence. It is a symbol of life and fertility. In Egypt the flower is white with a pink base ; in Persia it is blue ; in India red. The flower is represented in cup form, with large, broad petals, terminating in points, and has a golden seeded centre. The leaves are large and heart-shaped.

Both leaves and blossoms are borne on long, sinuous stems, and in Egyptian art are often found in combination with the papyrus plant, which has a bell-shaped flower and rush-like leaves. The Egyptians drew the blossoms as open in plan, as cup-like flowers in profile and as squat cone-shaped buds. The buds are often conventionalised, and we see a central club-like bud between two petals turned over to right and left, a primitive form of the fleur-de-lis ; it is frequently seen ornamenting the tips of sceptres. The buds, leaves and sinuous stalks are also employed to decorate friezes. A favourite combination of the lotus and papyrus is seen in the Egyptian column, which is either fluted or painted to represent a bundle of leaves, while the capital is in the form of a papyrus bell flower growing out of a lotus. The Persian blue and the Indian red lotus are generally represented as open blossoms, with two rows of pointed petals and a golden seed centre, and are allied in character and symbolism with the chrysanthemum of Japan. Vishnu is often represented as springing from a lotus, as is the youthful Horus, under the form of Harpocrates, the Egyptian god of love.

CHAPTER XVI

THE ROSE

QUEEN of Flora's glowing treasures the rose has long held a proud place in symbolism and in pure decorative art. It is the flower of innocence and of knowledge, of peace and of suffering, of passion and of secrecy. It was the flower sacred to worshippers of Adonis as a token of love and sacrifice, of life springing afresh from dead things. Legend says that Aphrodite hastening to the aid of Adonis, wounded unto death by the Boar of Mount Lebanon, trod on a white rose, thus staining the immaculate flower with immortal ichtor. According to Indian tradition in the Garden Paradise of the Brahmans is a great white rose, wherein are seen two lovely women, the Lady of the Mouth and the Lady of the Tongue, who, however, are one, and in the centre of the Silver Rose the Supreme Being has His permanent abode. Buddha was crucified for despoiling the sacred garden of a white rose, which thereupon became red. Again, it was amidst the frolics of Dionysius, or Bacchus, Cupid and Ganymede that the ruby nectar was spilled, causing the pallid blossoms to blush. These two seemingly divergent ideas (but really coming from the same root notion of the alliance between pleasure and sorrow, joy and sacrifice) rule the whole complicated symbolism of roses in the domain of decoration. So we find the flowers associated by the ancients with festivity, the roses with which they made chaplets to crown their heads as they quaffed libations to Bacchus and the mother of Cupid, which thus suggested the sacredness of words spoken at ceremonial mysteries or in friendly confidence. Adopted as a Christian emblem of He Who represents the Supreme Sacrifice, by a natural transmission, it was attributed to the Virgin Mary, whence we have rosaries, the beads corresponding to petals.

It is this flower that we find so lavishly displayed, occultly or otherwise, down the ages from a far-off past. In its earliest form both archæologically and in primitive heraldry, it is a conventionalised form of the wild or briar rose that we see. The rosettes seen on Phœnician sepulchral stelæ in the British Museum, and carved on soap-stone cylinders in those puzzling South African ruins at Zimbabwe, are practically identical with the quatrefoils and cinquefoils of heraldry, which are really the roses of feudal blazonry. These " daisy-like flowers " found on private and regal seals are the blossoms of the briar, emblematically and glyptically so apt to verge into the radiant star. Strictly speaking the quatrefoils and cinquefoils are formed respectively of four or five oval or squat club-like petals joined together. The quatrefoils are usually pierced of the field, having a circular hole in the centre. With the quatrefoil there is often a cruciform slit, with a pierced or raised centre. Sometimes the petals are slightly concave or convex, but quite as frequently perfectly flat. They may be of any tincture. Vincent bore: azure, three quatrefoils argent. The town of Leicester, for instance, bears : gules, a cinquefoil, pierced of the field, ermine. These are the arms of the powerful family of Beaumont, Earls of Leicester, whose bearings were borne by many other houses in blood or feudal alliance with the great earls. In the reign of Edward I the Lords Astley bore : azure, a cinquefoil ermine ; and under that monarch, at the siege of Carlaverock Hugh Bardoulf emblazoned his banner and shield azure, three cinquefoils or. Gilbert de Umfreville, Earl of Angus (1290), bore : gules, crusily, a cinquefoil or.

Apart from these somewhat nondescript charges, the rose has been treated in heraldry both conventionally and realistically, with equally charming effect. Certainly the early heraldic rose is modelled on the wild type. It is of this variety that Vulson de la Colombière says: " It forms a perfect symbol of beauty and gracefulness, although it possesses thorns and is doomed to fade." " The rose and the lily," declares the worthy squire, " are united in close amity, for the blending of these two flowers compose and truly represent the colour peculiar to the most perfect of human loveliness," so evidently he was thinking of the red rose, which is by far the most frequently seen in old blazonings. De Brue, a Crusader from Brittany (*circa* 1191), bore : argent, a rose of six petals gules, seeded or. In a Roll of Arms of the reign of Henry III we find Philip Darcy bearing : argent, three roses gules. In another Roll, of Edward II, Sir Robert Darcy is shown bearing : argent, three roses gules, within a border indented sable. His kinsman, Sir John Darcy, had : sable, a border argent charged with red roses. But at the siege of Carlaverock Simon de Fresel (or Fraser) bore : sable, six roses argent ; and a later Darcy of Platten bore : azure, three roses between seven crosses bottony argent. With regard to Fraser, it is to be noted that later his roses were converted into " fraisiers," and heraldically there is practically no difference between a strawberry flower and a cinquefoil.

This heraldic rose consists of petals, usually five in the early type ; small green leaves (the " barbs ") between each pair of petals, representing the sepals of the calyx ; and stamens, or cluster of " seeds." It is rarely " leaved and slipped " or " stalked." The petals are generally heart-shaped, slightly cup-like, with upward curving edges. Sometimes the barbs show between the petals, but more often only the tips appear at the edges. The " seeds " may be treated as a collection of tiny round balls, or the circular space is criss-crossed like a tartlet. In later examples two or more rows of petals are used, when we have a conventionalised rendering of the garden flower, as in the Tudor rose. Of course, this is merely a development and embellishment of the ancient rosette.

Side by side with this, however, a more realistic flower was being used. We hear of Edward I having for badge a gold rose with green stalk and leaves. In the oft-quoted Roll of Arms of Henry III, we are told that Le Comte de Rampanile bore : " dor a treis rosers ; sur chekune roser une rose ; chekune roser verte." These probably were rose branches, or slips, though they may have been rose bushes. Apparently, the field being gold, it was thought unnecessary to specify that the roses were red.

As for Edward's golden rose, it may have been derived from his mother, or perhaps borne in memory of her. For she was Eleanor, daughter of Raymond of Provence, where a cultivated variety of this flower had been introduced by Thibault IV and his knights on their return home from Cru-

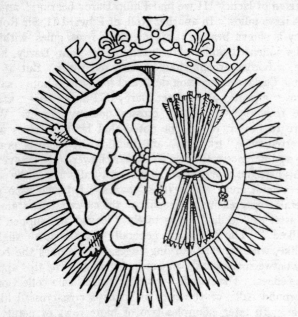

TUDOR ROSE EN SOLEIL WITH THE ARROW BADGE OF ARAGON.

sading. Roses of Provence were celebrated, and quickly found their way into local heraldry. A good example is afforded by the coat of d'Espinassy, of that province : or, a rose between three buds proper, slipped and leaved sable. These dusky blooms were of the botanical type. Edward III decorated his Great Seal with small roses, and his grandson, Richard II, placed them on Garters which he bestowed on a few honoured courtiers. But it was most likely from the exotic rose, rather than from the " daisy-like flower " and the briar blooms on the Great Seals, that the famous Yorkist and Lancastrian badges were derived. It is surmised that John of Gaunt, Duke of Lancaster, fourth son of Edward III, adopted the red rose, for cadets often used their fathers' cognisances somewhat differenced. In spite of the generally received idea, there is no direct evidence that the white rose belonged to Edmond of Langley, Duke of York, fifth son of Edward III. It seems far more likely that it was assumed by Edmond's second son, Richard of Coningsburgh, Duke of Cambridge, for he took as his second wife Maud, daughter of Thomas, Lord Clifford. From a manuscript in the Harleian Collection we see that a white rose was the badge of the Castle of Clifford, possibly in allusion to " Fair Rosamond " of Clifford. However this may be, these two badges were worn on a lavish scale during the long-drawn-out dynastic turmoil known in history as the Wars of the Roses. Edward IV, who had a diaper of small cinquefoil-roses and stars on his Great Seal (a design copied by Richard III on his Great Seal), placed his white rose on the Sun in Splendour badge of Richard II. Thus was produced the first of a long line of " roses en soleil," for both the red rose and the united blooms were later treated in the same manner.

To what extent the " wearing of the rose " entered into the national life may be gathered even by considering the byways of land tenure. A few out of many instances are worthy of mention. Sir Marmaduke Darel held the Manor of Fulmer, Bucks, direct from the King by the service of one red rose yearly (*temp*. Henry VI), while the Buckinghamshire Darrells bore : azure, a lion rampant or ; a branch of that family had : argent, three bars sable, on the first bar three silver roses. Sandes held land at Northampton from the King at a rental of one rose. In 1348 Sir John Poulteney " gave and confirmed to Humfrey de Bohun, Earl of Hereford and Essex, his whole tenement called Cold Harborough [Coal Harbour] with all the tenements and key adjoining, and appurtenances, on the way called Hay Wharf-lane for one rose at midsummer." Some overlords, however, actually stipulated for a rose at Christmas and a snowball at Midsummer, which was tantamount to a tenancy terminable at will of the grantor. We find that Edward Leigh in the thirty-second year of the reign of Queen Elizabeth died possessed of the Rose Hospital in West Smithfield, but this was almost certainly in allusion to the religious emblem. That was evidently the case as regards the Rose Manor in Southwark, which was referred to as a messuage called the Rose when Edward VI made over the Manor of Southwark to the City of London. We know that Henslowe and Alleyne's Rose Theatre must have been close by. Edward Alleyne received a grant of arms, which were: argent, a chevron between three cinquefoils gules. Now, he left his fortune for educational purposes and to benefit his native parish of St. Botolph, Bishopsgate, and the parishes of St. Olave's and St. Saviour's, where he had amassed much of his wealth. It is interesting to find the tradition still carried on, for St. Olave's and St. Saviour's Grammar School as late as 1668 gave a lease of a certain field (which has become very valuable property) for over five hundred years, at a rental of a red rose annually.

However, to return to the royal badge of the radiant rose.

ROSE EN SOLEIL BADGE.

Sometimes the rays, which are almost always of gold, project equally on all sides, producing a series of circles; but as a rule they are of varying lengths, arranged in such a way as to give the composition a diamond shape. This figure is seen placed within a mascle (or pierced diamond), and that again within a voided (or outlined) quatrefoil, the words " Dieu et mon droit " being written in the open spaces of the lobes. Henry VII, having united the opposing factions by his marriage with his cousin, blended the two badges, producing the Tudor rose. The first of these was borne quarterly red and white.

More generally the Tudor rose consisted of a row of red petals, then a row of white, and the golden circle in the middle, the bloom having three or more rows of petals round the golden "seeds." Occasionally the roses were dimidiated, being united per fess or per pale, one half red and the other half white. There are often more than two rows,

BADGE OF RICHARD, DUKE OF YORK AND EARL OF CAMBRIDGE.

when the colours alternate row by row, not petal by petal. These Tudor types are usually barbed, rarely stalked and leaved, though instances occur of this, and also their appearance on slips and bushes. Thus in a manuscript of the Heralds' College we find that Henry bore "a red rose surmounted of a white rose, with two buds slipped vert." They are treated as "roses en soleil," and Sandford gives a curious specimen in his genealogical work on our Royal Houses, for it bears in the centre a small crucifix. Martin Luther appears to have used as badge a red heart ensigned with a black cross, placed in the middle of a silver rose, surrounded by the golden circle of Eternity, the whole on a blue field. These may be compared to the Buddhist legend already given, and to the mystic symbol of the Rosicrucians, a white or silver rose on a red cross—the crucified rose. Henry VII placed on his Great Seal a Tudor rose on each side of the throne; the background of the obverse is fretty and powdered with roses and fleurs-de-lis, the latter being fixed at the intersections of the frets and the roses in the interspaces. On his standard he bore both the red and white roses, barbed and seeded proper, separately. Henry VIII, who had on the obverse side of his Great Seal a large Tudor rose in the sky, and two more on the caparisons of his charger, bore the stalked white rose within a red rose with two buds, like his father, as well as a separate red rose.

MARTIN LUTHER'S BADGE.

With his wives and children, even greater variety was introduced. Catherine of Aragon united her native pomegranate with the roses of her adopted country. In the early examples this was done in a strange way, the seed pod is shown bursting on both sides, the dexter exposing the purple pomegranate grains, the sinister showing a half-emerging Tudor rose. Later, thorough dimidiation per pale was adopted, and this badge Henry bore at a tournament in honour of his queen. Round her coat-of-arms she placed a wreath of livery colours, the white and green ribbons entwining red and white roses and golden pomegranates. Anne Boleyn's chief badge was a golden stump of a tree, with a crowned falcon standing thereon, bearing a sceptre in his sinister claw, while in front of it were rows of red and white roses on green stalks. Jane Seymour had a curious circular double silver castle; over

TUDOR ROSE, QUARTERLY RED
AND WHITE.

ROSE AND POMEGRANATE, BADGE
OF CATHERINE OF ARAGON.

the port was a hawthorn bush proper, flowered gules, and crowned; while on the green mound of the upper tower a golden crowned phœnix rose from flames of fire, a red and a white rose stalked vert being on either side of the pyre. Catherine Parr united the Tudor rose with her own family badge, derived from Ross of Kendal, of a demi-crowned queen. The arrangement is rather odd than pretty. Above small green barbs we see a row of four large red petals, then three of white, with a row of four smaller leaves of red, and out of the top of this pyramid issues a demi-queen proper, crowned,

BADGE OF CATHERINE PARR.

habited and crinned gold. Edward VI had much the same design for his Great Seal as that of his father, only the Tudor roses in his case are crowned, and on the obverse, in the foreground is a stump of a tree sending forth a network of fine twigs bearing roses and fleurs-de-lis, this forming a delicate and graceful diaper on the background, behind the equestrian figure of the youthful king. Queen Mary used the crowned Tudor rose and the impaled rose and pomegranate of her mother. She also impaled the Tudor rose with another badge of Catherine, the bundle of golden arrows, with silver barbs and feathers banded with a red ribbon. These arrows were placed on a half-circle divided per pale vert and azure, and the whole badge is surrounded by sunrays and ensigned by a royal crown. On their Great Seal Philip and Mary had a diaper of roses and fleurs-de-lis. On Queen Elizabeth's Great Seal the crowned roses, though small, have well-defined petals. Her badges comprised a crowned rose with the motto " Rosa sine spina," and the curious stump, falcon and rose device of her mother. Henry Fitzroy, Duke of Richmond and Somerset, the bastard son of Henry VIII, used a badge quite reminiscent of that borne by Catherine Parr. It was a rose divided per pale red and white, stalked and leaved vert, and rising from the centre a silver demi lion rampant, ducally crowned and chained or.

The Cæsars, a family founded in England by Cesare Adelmare, Italian Physician to Mary and Elizabeth, bore : gules, three roses argent, on a chief of the second three roses of the first ; these white and red roses obviously being adopted in honour of his royal mistresses. James I did not introduce much alteration in the design of his Great Seal, though he added a crowned harp on the obverse and replaced the badge-decorated caparisons of his charger by draperies of the full royal blazonry, this type being also adopted by the two Charleses and James II without the caparisons. James I had, on his succession to the English throne, adopted the Tudor rose, a red and white rose growing from one stalk ; and also dimidiated the Tudor rose with the Scottish thistle. Queen Anne, on the obverse of her Great Seal, had a large Tudor rose and a thistle growing from one stem, which was placed under a crown on her second seal, the exergus being decorated with small roses and thistles on one stem.

By an Order in Council of November 5, 1800, the badge of

the United Kingdom was determined thus : an heraldic Tudor rose (a rose gules, barbed vert, surmounted by a rose argent, seeded or) between a thistle and a shamrock, growing from the same stalk, leaved vert ; to be alternated by a rose between a shamrock and a thistle growing from the same stalk, both ensigned by a royal crown. That is the badge which subsists to-day.

On Queen Victoria's Great Seal there is a finely modelled wreath of oak leaves and acorns adorned with six large botanically conceived Tudor roses, placed at regular intervals. This is the old type of the chaplet of roses, such as Ralf Fitzwilliam bore at the Siege of Carlaverock, his banner, barry argent and azure, carrying three chaplets of roses proper (*i.e.*, red roses on a wreath

TUDOR ROSE AND SCOTCH THISTLE.

of green leaves). Nairnes of Scotland bear : per pale sable and argent, a chaplet with four quatrefoils all counterchanged. A branch of the family settled in England differenced this as follows : sable and argent, a chaplet of roses counterchanged ; and another : paly of three sable and argent, a chaplet of four roses leaved proper. These chaplets, besides being borne alone as charges, are sometimes seen enfiling swords or lances, circling cups, and used as collars or necklets and crowns. In the last case it has generally a religious significance, as in the arms of the Mercers' Company. While the early type of chaplet showed a wreath of leaves adorned with roses, the later examples show a string of blooms with just a few leaves, both being very beautiful. The wreath is occasionally seen treated as an orle, forming a border round the shield. Fields are also borne powdered with roses, as in the seals mentioned above. Bendlice's or, a rose leaf in bend sinister vert, refers to a leaf of the shrub ; but in Sir John Rose's gules, a chevron argent between three rose leaves silver, we have petals. A curious bearing is that of Tudman : argent, two bars azure, over all a lion rampant or, holding in the dexter paw a rose branch gules, probably referring to some family alliance. But we also see a wild boar with a rose and leaves in its mouth. Alten bears : argent, a bend of lozenges and roses alternately disposed gules.

CHAPTER XVII

THE IRISH HARP IN HERALDRY

HERALDICALLY the Irish harp is a thing of no great antiquity, owing its birth to the political instability of Henry VIII. As a racial token it becomes a link between the moon-worshippers' cup-markings and the three conjoined legs (naked in sunny Sicily, clothed in Mona), types of the Trinacria of the Latins, the Triskele of Scandinavians, themselves mere forms of the sun-worshippers' cramponed cross-wheel, that elaboration of the curved crossed snakes or swastika of the East. For the Welsh bardic harp and the Irish cruit were alike enlisted in the praise of Baal, the sun god, bestower of life, whose powerful rays gave rise to elemental harmonics. The bard and his instrument were held in high honour by Celt and Cymri, and the Saxon poets called the harp " the wood of joy." It might form an interesting subject of inquiry whether the Tudor prince in adopting a new badge for his kingdom of Ireland had not been guided by Welsh traditions, domestic or political.

Long prior to the rise of the House of Tudor the official arms of Ireland had been three golden crowns in pale on a blue field. These were the mythical arms of Edmund, King and Martyr, and probably owed their transplantation to the fact that the Anglo-Norman invaders, when setting about their conquest, invoked the protection of St. Edward and St. Edmund. These crowns were so far recognised that we find them on the Irish coinage, and when Richard II created Robert Vere Duke of Ireland, he assigned him as an augmentation to his arms, a blue field with three gold crowns, borne two in base and one in chief. Misliking these symbols for their supposedly Romish symbolism, Bluff King Hal established an undatably ancient Celtic emblem of concord as the national badge. Its first appearance seems to have been on his Irish silver sixpenny-piece, struck in the thirty-eighth year of his reign. It is found on the back, crowned, and between the small crowned letters H and R. Its form is decidedly peculiar, for we find its sounding-board broadening upwards, and its seven pairs of strings stretched between the neck and front pillar. Thus it is a complete reversal of the

IRISH HARP, *temp*. HENRY VIII.

musical instrument. Much the same shape was retained on the Irish coins of Mary, Philip and Mary, and Elizabeth, though the harp is longer and more upright, but the topsy-turvy idea still prevails.

A legend, fabricated long after the event, tells us that this harp of Henry VIII was the instrument which once awoke sweet echoes within the marble halls of Tara, seat of the suzerain kings of Erin. This antique relic of Brian Boru was supposed to have been sent by the Pope to King Henry VIII, though there is no evidence that it ever was in Rome, or in London. Some years after that robust swashbuckler and conqueror Brian was slain at the battle of Clontarf, A.D. 1014, his son Donogh murdered his brother Teague. As a reward for his villainy he was deposed ; but he astutely took possession of his father's crown, harp and regalia (so runs the legend), with which he fled to Rome to make his peace with the Pope. Adrian IV, it is said, claimed that holding these regalia he became manifestly King of Ireland, which warranted the transference of these rights to Henry II. Of this regalia, as further evidence of royalty, Henry VIII received the harp. So far tradition. It is certain that a very old, richly decorated harp, said to be the identical instrument, is preserved in the Museum of Trinity College, Dublin, but Dr. George Petrie, in a learned article contributed to Edward Bunting's "Ancient Music of Ireland" (1840), proves that the harp really belongs to the fourteenth century, or perhaps even the early part of the fifteenth century. It is a beautiful instrument, 32 inches high, with a sound-board of red sallow, a pillar of oak, and a neck of such charming contour that it has been named the "harmonic curve." The sound-board has four holes and there are thirty strings. The whole harp is richly adorned with carvings of modified Celtic ornamentation, silver, brass and crystal incrustations, and bears a rude representation of the O'Neil arms, as well as religious initials. From its form and decoration Dr. Petrie held that it probably belonged to one of those O'Neils who flourished as Bishops of Clogher and of Derry during the latter end of the fourteenth century. In this connection it is perhaps interesting to note that the Bishops of Derry now bear a harp on their coat-of-arms.

Although this instrument had nothing to do with Henry VIII, it is interesting because undoubtedly very old ; thus demonstrating the true form of the Irish harp. It is the form which should prevail on our royal and national escutcheon. The true guiding lines for the Irish heraldic harp are those of the scalene triangle : the long straight line (sound-board) leaning slightly back, the shorter line (pillar) bulging outwards, and the top line (neck), curving inwards. These lines —as we shall see—were abandoned, the isosceles triangle becoming the base of the draughtsman's sketch ; then by an easy transition (*facilis descensus averni*), the neck was stretched out and we had the almost perfect equilateral triangle, which practically prevailed up to within the last twenty years. The error is an unfortunate one, though it must be confessed not the worst treatment meted out to the symbol.

A crowned harp appears on the counter seal of Elizabeth's

second Great Seal. It is in the form of a badge. It is of excellent shape, for in conventionalising the emblem the artist retained the true main lines.

When James I ascended the throne, the Irish harp was, for the first time, introduced on the royal shield, the fourth quarter being emblazoned : azure, a harp or, stringed argent. The harps shown in the two Great Seals of James are fairly good, though there is a quaint neck added on the top of the sounding-board to connect it with the true neck, while the front pillar is too straight. The crowned badge harps on the counter seals are purely conventional ; they become spade shaped, the neck showing an inverted semicircle, little difference being made between the sound-board and pillar. We find the spade harps on James's gold sovereigns and double crowns, and his silver sixpences. It is on his coins that the erroneous equilateral triangle begins to prevail. The lines are also too florid ; the sound-board is made quite short, a slim curved arm, to connect it with the neck, being added. Moreover, the end of the neck is brought too far over, and, being unduly ornamented, foreshadows that other grievous sin, the feminine headed harp. At first, the end is merely a floral embellishment, but in his later gold coins and in the money struck in Ireland, it becomes distinctly the head of an animal. In the Irish form it is the head of some fabulous bird. I conjecture this was an Anglo-Saxon enormity, for in an illuminated coat-of-arms of James I by Sir William Segar, Garter King (Harleian MSS.), the pillar and forearm of the harp are joined by the mask of a satyr, a wild man of the woods, for the features are devoid of the culture and repose we should associate with the inspired bard.

With Charles I the equilateral triangle outline is pronounced. On the early coins and Great Seals the ornamentation is too florid, though the Celtic idea is not lost sight of. The flourish at the neck end, however, soon develops into a beak. In another illuminated MS. (Harleian Collection), we find the mask of a leopard. But the form of this harp is altogether rustically eccentric. It is to be noted that we find two tendencies at work here, the desire to join the neck and pillar

by a knob, or mask, and, on the other hand, the development
of the florid curved ends into heads, hair and wings. The
head is first finished off with floral continuations, then it
gradually develops a well-marked bust,
terminating in foliated drapery, as we
have it to the end of the Victorian
period, and the simple bowed pillar is
gone. From the head sprout floral adjuncts, which eventually become wings,
and so the gracefully curved neck of
the instrument is lost. The full-fledged
female harp is also an English invention.
It makes its first appearance on the
silver crown-piece struck at York, which
consequently cannot be earlier than 1629.
We also find it on the two St. Patrick's
halfpennies, so-called because they bear
on the reverse effigies of St. Patrick exhibiting a shamrock to assembled dis-

IRISH HARP, *temp*.
JAMES I.

ciples in one instance, and banishing reptiles in a second.
The obverse of both of these coins bears a crown, and the
kneeling figure of David crowned playing the harp. These
harps, though differing slightly, have the winged female
figure, with bust well developed.

It is to be presumed that the heralds, having evolved a
female form out of the chaos of their florid scrolls, dubbed her
Erin. There seems evident intention of symbolism in the
later forms of the figure.

Some time towards the latter end of the seventeenth century the French heralds tried their hands at the Celtic harp,
requiring it to emblazon on the regimental flags of the Irish
legions in the French king's pay. They produced a weird
arrangement, suggestive of an ill-treated gridiron, with a satyr
head stuck on one corner.

During the Commonwealth the ugly female harp was
frankly adopted. We find it on the first two " geographical "
seals, which show excellent maps of England, Wales, and
Ireland (Scotland being totally omitted). In the top part

of these seals, between England and Ireland, is a shield bearing the arms of St. George, while the harp is seen on a shield just outside the Irish Channel. But apart from the female figure the shape is elegant, scalene triangle lines being perfect, were it not for the woman's obtruding head. The same style of harp, though somewhat more approaching the equilateral triangle, is seen on the Protectorate seals of Oliver and Richard Cromwell. Generally speaking, on the Commonwealth coins the same type of harp is used as that found on the early seals, but there are some variations. The copper farthings have three remarkable patterns, all bad, because deviating from the true lines, while one is absurdly conventional. One of the sixpenny-pieces shows a harp with a very small sound-board, from which a female figure springs, turning her back to the pillar figure, the wings conjoined. On one of the shillings, and on half-crowns, we have a return to the goose and reptile heads.

On the Great Seal of Charles II the Irish harp occupies the second quarter of the shield, and is of a rather novel shape. The sound-board is narrow, upright and short ; the wings forming the neck curving upwards to the head, while the bust and foliated drapery (the pillar) form the segment of a circle. On his coins the harp is of inelegant, squat type, occasionally almost approaching a square, in such instances the head often sticking upright like a useless handle.

With James, Queen Anne, and the sovereigns of the Houses of Orange and of Hanover, little that is new is to be remarked. We can only note a tendency to confirm the equilateral triangle, to develop the female figure, and with the Victorian seals and coins unnecessarily to broaden the sounding-board. On the first Great Seal of George IV, however, on the counter seal, there is an allegorical figure representing Ireland, leaning on a tall harp on the true scalene triangle lines, but remarkable because the pillar is a complete winged female figure, nearly nude.

Meanwhile, a pretty and fairly accurate form of the Irish harp had been evolved from the royal emblems. We find Celtic form usually adhered to in the achievement of Ulster

King of Arms, and also in the modern bearings of the see of Derry.

When Edward VII ascended the throne and became Sovereign of the Ancient and Noble Order of the Garter, it was necessary to have the King's Royal Banner as Chief of the Order in St. George's Chapel, Windsor Castle. This banner was embroidered at the Royal School of Needlework, from the design of Mr. G. W. Eve. He adopted a thoroughly Celtic outline, though perhaps the pillar broadens too much towards the neck. But it was a vast improvement on the female harp. At the last moment objection was raised to this design and the beautiful harp was ruthlessly cut away and replaced by a Victorian instrument. As regards Mr. Eve's design, adverse criticisms were advanced by ultra-scientific heraldists, at the decoration of the harp with Celtic markings, the argument being that a charge should be plain. But in this instance the gold embroidered designs gave a characteristic touch to the Irish harp, and we may well ask why diapering— or the filling up of blank spaces with diminutive conventional designs—should be allowed on a field, and not on a charge, where they happen to emphasise symbolical value. Certainly old herald artists did not hesitate to diaper charges. We should endeavour to retain the Celtic feeling, and the harmonic curve of good Bishop O'Neil's hymnal harp.

IRISH HARP DESIGNED
FOR GARTER BANNER
OF EDWARD VII.

One or two instances of the harp on the shields of private persons may be given. It appears quite appropriate that Everest should bear : argent a harp gules ; Harpfield : argent, three harps sable, stringed or ; and Harpman : sable, a harp argent, stringed or. The charge is also found in the arms of Dobbin and Fogarty, and is occasionally met with in Continental practice.

CHAPTER XVIII

FEATHERS AND HORNS

FEATHERS are found under many different aspects. Mention has been made of the polychrome wings of angels, and a good deal will be said about wing and plume crests. Wings when borne in pairs, joined at the pinions, but without a bird's body intervening, are called a " vol " if the points are elevated, or a " vol abased," or " abaisé," if the points are lowered. A single wing is a " demi vol." These wings appeared to be very natural decorations for helmets, and are seen quite early, evidently as survivals of the bird-helmet. But in time they were treated with considerable eccentricity, as we see more particularly on studying German practice in the fourteenth and fifteenth centuries. We find crests of two wings with the lower parts covered with the " eyes " of peacock's feathers, the flight feathers being those of eagles.

In the case of John III, Duke of Brabant, the peacock wing borne has a gold scalloped border, ermine spotted flight feathers, and standing up between the vol is a plume of peacock's feathers. The crest of John, King of Bohemia, appears to have been indifferently a couple of eagle's wings, and a vol, the lower part sprinkled with linden leaves.

Another type consists of the pair of eagle flight feathers borne erect, one on either side of the helmet, as in the case of the Bishop of Cologne, whose plumes are used as flagstaffs. His crest is also interesting as showing another use of feathers, as a decorative border, which is also seen in the case of the Hanoverian crest.

The " panache " might take the form of a compact crown

of several "heights," as in the Mortimer crest, or a plume after the Dacian type. This leads us directly to the famous ostrich plumes of the Princes of Wales. As is well known this crest consists of three grouped silver feathers, the middle one curling forwards, and the others, slightly shorter, curling outwards. Three such feathers were borne by Edward, surnamed the Black Prince, it is said, as a crest or badge. Contemporary evidence, however, shows that he did not bear them as a triparted group, but placed three silver ostrich feathers, each enfiled with a scroll, on a black shield, and this he specifically describes in his will as his "badge of Peace." The best known example of this is from the illuminated charter granting him the Duchy of Aquitaine. It is interesting as showing the realistic treatment of the plumes, and also the purely decorative use of angel supporters. How did the Prince come by this badge? It is matter of doubt and controversy. William Camden gave currency to the legend that the Black Prince took it from the helm of John, King of Bohemia, Duke of Luxem-

CRESTED HELM, JOHN III.
DUKE OF BRABANT.

WINGED HELM, JOHN, KING OF
BOHEMIA.

burg, whom he is supposed to have slain at the battle of Crecy.

SEAL OF COMTE DE PORHOET,
BRITTANY, 1231.

John Aderne, a physician who appears to have been in the service of a knight belonging to the Prince's forces, certainly mentions the story, and in a medical treatise actually gives a picture of the single ostrich feather. But a difficulty arises inasmuch as John of Luxemburg is not known to have used such a crest, for all evidence goes to show that he bore eagle's wings. The only known connection with the family and the plumes is the ostrich badge of Anne of Bohemia, granddaughter of Duke John, and queen of Richard II. But this appears to have been a purely personal badge. Sir Harris Nicolas fancies the plumes really came from Philippa of Hainault, queen of Edward III, and mother of the Black Prince. She is known to have had plate adorned with a black shield with ostrich feathers. Possibly, he conjectured, it may have been a family badge allusive to their County of Ostrevant. There is, however, no evidence of this. But we do know that Edward III on one of his seals placed the

OSTRICH BADGE OF ANNE OF BOHEMIA.

shield of the royal arms between two ostrich feathers. He
also bore a silver ostrich feather with gold quill placed on a
banner. As shown in a previous chapter, John of Gaunt,
brother of the Black Prince, used the ostrich feathers, evidence
of which we have at Canterbury Cathedral, on his seals, and
in the allusion to the " deux plumes d'ostrich blankes "
found in his will. Over his tomb there was
a black shield bearing three ostrich feathers
of ermine with gold quills. Another brother,
Thomas of Woodstock, Duke of Gloucester,
had an ostrich feather borne in the beak of
the Bohun swan. Many other members of
the royal family bore the feathers in some
form or other. Richard II used them both
during and after his father's death, and bestowed them as a mark of honour on Thomas
Mowbray, Duke of Norfolk. It is to be
noted that these plumes were always treated
as single feathers. It was not until the days
of the Tudor princes that the three single
feathers of the Black Prince were grouped
together.

THOMAS, DUKE OF
GLOUCESTER.

Briefly, then, Edward the Black Prince bore a silver ostrich
feather enfiled with a gold scroll, or three such feathers
placed two and one on a black shield, as his " badge of
Peace." Edward III used a royally crowned silver ostrich
feather with gold quill. John of Gaunt bore three ostrich
feathers of ermine with quills and scrolls of gold. Thomas,
Duke of Gloucester, had his silver ostrich feather borne by
the silver swan of Bohun, a style followed by Henry V.
Richard II as Prince used the same badge as his father, and
as King he also bore gold ostrich feathers. John of Beaufort,
Duke of Somerset, bore silver ostrich feathers with quills
gobony silver and azure. Margaret of Beaufort, Countess
of Richmond, mother of Henry VI, also had ostrich feathers.
So had Edward Plantagenet, Duke of York, and his brother,
Richard of Coningsburgh, Earl of Cambridge. Henry IV,
while yet Duke of York, bore silver ostrich feathers entwined

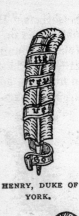

HENRY, DUKE OF
YORK.

HENRY IV.

JOHN, DUKE OF
BEDFORD.

EDWARD V.

ARTHUR TUDOR.

EDWARD, PRINCE OF WALES,
temp. HENRY VIII.

EDWARD PRINCE OF WALES,
temp. HENRY VIII.

with a scroll bearing the motto: "Sovereigne." When King, the ostrich feathers appear on his seal, supported by two couchant lions. John, Duke of Bedford, used the ostrich feathers; and his brother, Humphrey, Duke of Gloucester, used the black shield and three silver feathers. This same shield of peace appears on Henry V's seal of the Duchy of Lancaster. Henry VI as Prince and King used the feathers, occasionally borne in saltire. Edward V, as Prince of Wales, had a diaper of roses and feathers in the interstices of a fret on his seal; on the obverse his armorial shield is placed between two lions sejeant holding ostrich feathers. With Arthur Tudor the feathers were held erect by dragons. Henry VIII appears first to have grouped them together, much as we see them to-day.

MODERN BADGE, WITH WELSH DRAGON. (ROYAL WELSH FUSILIERS).

Practically the same reasons which gave the eagle, peacock and ostrich feathers such importance (the birds themselves possessing the highest symbolic values) brought horns into special honour. Apart from the "attires" of stags, and the official or territorial badge of the bugle-horn, horns are not often seen as charges, but they hold a striking place in the array of crests, especially in Germany. These are the great straight or curving horns so lavishly used on the war helmets of the Vandals and Norsemen, which were also modifications of the ox-head helmets such as were worn by the chieftains of the Marks. Of so high symbolical value were these horns that many great feudal estates in Germany, as well as with us in Saxon and early Norman days, were held in virtue of the mere possession of charter-horns bestowed by prince or Palantie noble. These horns, often borne in several pairs as supplementary to ordinary crests, represented fiefs. They were constantly adorned with feathers or other cognisances, either placed as a border or at the tip. This ultimately led to the tip being cut off to receive the bunch of feathers or flowers, and in due course we had that curious device which has often been described as " an elephant's trunk." Such a thing for German crests naturally puzzled many people ; but as a matter of fact there was no puzzle, but only an awkward rendering of the very ancient, much honoured war and territorial buffalo horn.

CHAPTER XIX

SHIELDS AND THEIR OUTER ORNAMENTS

HERALDIC shields present considerable diversity of form. These variations, for the most part, correspond closely to the diversity found in the designs of the actual war shields. At the dawn of the Middle Ages the influence of Roman practice was manifest, for the shields were very large, circular, oval, oblong and curved, as with the legionaries. It will be found on studying the subject that with the advance in the construction of defensive armour the importance of the shield diminished. When armour was little more than hardened leather, or quilted woollen cloth, strengthened by chain shirts, and plaques of beaten metal, the shields were designed to cover the body as much as possible. They were long, broad, considerably concave and decidedly unwieldy. With the introduction of more complete armour, the shield became smaller and lighter, something to be moved rapidly to ward off blows or thrusts. It was soon after this that fancy was brought into play in shaping the shield.

During the eleventh century two main types prevailed: (1) the kite, which was long and narrow, straight at the top, with gradually sloping sides meeting in a point, and slightly curved to cover the body ; (2) the pear-shaped, with rounded top. Both forms are to be seen on the Bayeux tapestry, on seals and illuminated MSS. On the seals of William I and William Rufus, Henry I and Stephen the shields are worn by the equestrian figures on their offside arms, so that shape cannot very well be distinguished, though they appear to be of a squat kite type ; but on those of Richard I and John they are clearly shown. That of Richard is large, has a straight top, a projecting boss or horn in the middle, and the pointed base curved outwards, the whole being well bent to cover the body. This is much the same style as that of Geoffrey Plantagenet (about 1150), father of our Henry II, long preserved at Le Mans. This, too, has a central boss, from which radiate cruciform strengthenings, and is further adorned with lions rampant. On the Great Seals from John to Edward II the shields are approaching the " heater " type, being less long, rather broad, with straight tops, gently sloping sides ending in an obtuse point. The true " heater " shield made its appearance with us during the reign of Henry III and prevailed till the end of the fourteenth century. It is somewhat squat, and there is slight curving, or convexity. It is one of the most elegant forms of the shield.

It must be remembered that at this period, and for some time longer, armorial insignia were painted, carved or embossed on the knightly shields, those for warfare, for the tourney, and also on the " shields parade." Interesting examples of the latter are to be seen at Canterbury Cathedral and at the British Museum. The first-named is a large shield constructed for the funeral of the Black Prince. It is of cuir bouilli. A light wood frame, slightly convex, is covered with gesso, and over this is the embossed leather, still bearing traces of the old vivid colouring. The specimen at the British Museum is of German origin and belongs to the reign of Edward IV. It is 2 feet 6 inches long, 1 foot 6 inches across the top, is convex, provided with notch at the top side for the lance, is of leather covered with moulded gesso, painted and gilded. The device is of the fancy tournament type, representing a lady seated on the dexter side, holding a girdle. Before her is a knight resting on his bended knee, and behind him is a skeleton touching him on the shoulder. This composition is completed by the motto " Vous ou la Mort."

The fine " heater " shape was gradually broadened out, and then we had that modification known as the spade shield, in which the sides descend almost straight to about the middle and then curve to a point. This tendency to squareness was probably the result of having to crowd numerous charges, and even quarterings, on one shield. It gave rise to many patterns of rectangular shields on the Continent, including that very common and decidedly ugly squat type, which has straight top with pointed horizontal ears, straight sides for three-fourths its length and terminating in a squat triangle. Both Italians and Spaniards were fond of circular or oval targets. The Italians also indulged in twisted kites, surrounded by curiously contorted scroll-work. This scroll work invaded German armorial art, and also influenced English practice, but with us the style was always kept within bounds, partaking of the character of our strapwork tracery. Georges de Recy (in his "Decoration du Cuir") says that this originated at the tourneys. He adds that these shields, originally in pasteboard, of a kin to that at the British Museum described above, emblazoned with the arms of the contending knights, were suspended close to the lists. Their curved forms and cockled-up edges, the result of their being exposed to sun and rain, became an almost classic style, and in Italy grew to be very fantastic in outline. Both these and war shields have a notch in the upper dexter angle. (shields "à bouche"), this notch being intended to receive the lance when a knight held his shield across his chest. This notch is only appropriate for large and early types of shields.

Knights banneret had square or "banner" shields, and such are still used by a few old French families. With us women (except sovereigns) place their arms on diamond-shaped shields. But in Flanders married women use ovals and only spinsters the diamond-shaped shields. Our sixteenth and eighteenth century heralds placed merchants' marks, rebuses and other "illegitimate" forms of bearings on circular targets; but this form of shield was also affected by ecclesiastics when they gave up the gentle art of spilling blood on the battlefield. It must be understood, however, that these distinctions were not strictly adhered to in early days, for well into the fifteenth century we find women using ordinary shields, especially for impaled coats, and on the other hand, instances of knights using diamond shields on their seals are not unknown. One example exists on the Barons' letter to the Pope (1300). On the Continent, as we have seen, the circular and oval forms were widely adopted. Indeed, the Spanish royal arms are almost without exception blazoned on ovals.

Heraldic shields are frequently placed on the slant (" penché " or " couché "), with the helmet and crest, or the crest alone, placed on the top angle. In early examples the helmet and crest are as large as, if not larger than, the shield itself. The shield may be slung at an angle from the " guige " or double sword belt, or we may see the shield hung horizontally from two guiges, as in the fine example of the arms of Provence in Westminster Abbey belonging to Eleanor, queen of Henry III. In this case the belts are attached to two bosses carved respectively with a male and female mask. The fashion of showing armorial shields hanging on the slant, or pendent from trees, is undoubtedly due to the custom of challenging knights suspending their emblazoned targets on posts or trees outside their tents, or near the tourney lists.

Shields are occasionally borne as charges. Grant, of co. Elgin, bears: gules, a round shield between three antique crowns or. Sobieski bore the arms of the clan Janina: or, an oval buckler of bronze (otherwise purpure). The Rothschild family has as a "surtout," what may be regarded almost in the light of a clan badge: gules, a target (circular or oval, with pointed centre) argent. The borough of Derby: argent, on a mount in base the trunk of an oak tree with two sprouting slips proper, with the shield of Pallas hanging therefrom or, fastened by belts gules.

When a complete achievement of arms is borne, the shield is generally surrounded by some form of drapery. This is the mantling, or "lambrequins," as the French call it. Broadly speaking the mantling divides itself into two distinct types—the scarf and the robe of state. In the older examples it is the scarf which prevails, and is always associated with the helmet. It is in the shape of a waving, rather tattered piece of silk, often having different colours on the upper and under sides, and is sometimes fringed. It appears to have originated from two distinct items of military equipment. Firstly, we have a cap worn over the helm, generally adorned at the top with an upstanding crest, and having tails floating behind. This is the " capeline." Secondly, the scarf, worn somewhat like a turban, but with floating ends to protect the back of the head and nape of the neck from the sun. The first type persisted on the Continent well into the seventeenth century, and is seen in the form of a cape or diminutive robe of estate, just covering the helm and upper part of the shield, and often shown as floating to one side. Or again, in Germany, we see it as a curious looking elongated sack with one side open, which starts from under the crest and floats behind like a tail. This is the " calote." Both the capeline and the calote are usually parti-coloured, and may bear a replica of the arms on the shield, or some other coat of alliance. The calote often actually forms part of the crest. As a rule, however, the scarf is a more or less ragged piece of textile, floating all round the helm and upper part of the shield. It was gradually given a foliated scroll appearance, something like an attenuated acanthus leaf, which is quite incongruous and misleading. The scarf may be of the two predominating tinctures of the arms, or the livery colours if these happen to be distinct, and I have seen tartans used for Scottish coats. In France when these were embroidered with gold and ornamented with precious stones, they were called " hachements." But the prevailing practice, at least in England, is to have them of gold and ermine for peers ; and of crimson and silver or white for others—tinctures also adopted for the larger mantle. In a fine contemporary example of the blazoning of Edward IV, the elaborately tattered scarf is crimson and white, and is fitted between helm and the cap of dignity. An allowable diversity is the replacing of the scarf by a number of long twisted ribbons. These represent the favours bestowed by fair ladies at tournaments, and they look quite effective. The precedent for this is of quite a respectable antiquity. In the old Monastery of the Preaching Brothers at Poictiers there was a coat-of-arms belonging to the Duke of Bourbon who fell at the battle of that name (1356). The shield is ensigned with a closed helmet and with a ducal coronet and panache of peacock's feathers. From the coronet are a number of streamers, silver on the dexter and azure on the sinister side, powdered with the letter E, the tincture counterchanged, this being the ribbon of the family Knightly Order of Esperance. In this monastic collection recording the fallen knights of that memorable fight. the ribbons appear in two other cases, associated respectively with a scarf and half a robe of estate, both on the dexter side. In the first case the ribbons are sable, pendent from a crest of a nun, hooded sable. This was the crest worn by knights for a year when mourning for their spouses or mistresses, or when about to take monastic vows. In the other case two of the ribbons are silver, two sable, which also seems to suggest mourning.

As for the robe of estate, it should be ample, so as to cover the whole of the shield and its surroundings, such as collars and supporters, but the helm and crown or coronet, if any, and the crest may be placed at the top, as though fixing the robe in its place. According to modern practice a sovereign's robe of estate is of gold brocade lined with ermine ; a peer's crimson velvet lined with ermine ; and that of a knight and gentleman either crimson silk lined with white, or of the livery colours. But in former times much greater fancy was allowed, adding beauty and practical interest to the piece of drapery. On the Garter plate of the first Duke of Clarence in St. George's Chapel, Windsor Castle, the lambrequin is powdered with white roses of York. Sir John Bourchier, Lord Berners, has the lining of his cloak powdered with water-bowgets from his arms and the Bourchier knot badge, while the crimson part is powdered with golden billets derived from one of the quarters on his shield. According to Sir William Fraser (in " The Douglas Book ") James, seventh Earl of Douglas, is represented in St. Bride's Church, Douglas, by a coat-of-arms surmounted by a peacock's head as crest, and the lambrequin is powdered with peacock's feathers. An even more instructive piece of heraldic work was the mantle of Olivier van

Noort, the Dutch Admiral who first took the Netherlands fleet through the Straits of Magellan. It is of blue, powdered with golden stars. The Kings of France had a tent of blue powdered with golden fleurs-de-lis, lined with ermine. Napoleon I and his nephew powdered their purple mantle with golden bees. As just stated the Kings of France replaced the robe of estate, or mantle, by a large tent, with the flies open, displaying the blazoned shield with its angel supporters, collar of the St. Esprit and so on. This tent is usually planted on a green mount, is of blue velvet lined with ermine, has a tasselled canopy charged with a radiant sun, and ensigned with the royal crown, behind which is a lance with the old banner of France, azure semée of fleurs-de-lis or. A tent is also occasionally used by the Royal House of Savoy, and by the King of Prussia, who charges the crimson cloth with golden crowns and black eagles. Knights use the robes of their orders as mantles. In many cases canons of Continental cathedrals employ their aumuses, or hoods and tippets of grey fur in place of lambrequins. An altogether excellent idea was carried out by Mr. C. M. Chadwick in his " Ontarian Families," where he gives scarves, capelines and full mantles of appropriate tartans to the arms of Scottish families.

In dealing with " Crowns, Coronets and Caps," mention is made of the knotted cords pendent on each side of ecclesiastical shields from the priestly hats. Other forms of cords are used by ladies. The cordon or cordelière was introduced by Anne of Brittany, widow of Charles VIII of France, who initiated an order for women, with a knotted cord as emblem, as a reminder of the cords and bonds of Christ. This cordelière she placed round her shield, and it soon became the sign of widowhood when thus used. It was of twisted black and white silk, or plain black. Abbesses also adopted the device. It never came into great favour in England.

Knights place the collars of their orders round their shields.

Office holders frequently place appropriate badges either behind, at the sides or beneath their escutcheons. Thus bishops place behind their shields two croziers in saltire, or one in pale. Patriarchs place the patriarchal cross in pale behind the shield. Priors affected the bourdon, or knobbed pilgrim's staff, in pale behind their shields. Generals and knights placed swords or batons in saltire, or in pale. Our own Court officials are entitled to such badges. Among these are: The Lord Chancellor, two maces in saltire; the Earl Marshal, two golden rods tipped with black; the Lord High Chamberlain, two keys; the Master of the Household in Scotland, two red staves powdered with thistles. In France Marshals of the Old Régime had crossed blue batons powdered with golden fleurs-de-lis, and those of Napoleon substituted golden bees. The list of official badges in France is a very long and elaborate one and may be read in Gourdon de Genouillac's "Grammaire Heraldique." Finally, it may be mentioned that the Marchessi Savelli, Marshals of the Papal Conclave, have a golden key on each side of their shield pendent by a knotted cord from the coronet.

Wreaths, or "cointices," on which crests repose, must be left for consideration when describing crests. But two other adjuncts must be mentioned. These are the scrolls borne under the arms, or over the crest, and inscribed with the motto. They are usually represented as broad ribbons of colour lined with metal, or metal lined with colour, and fringed or tasselled. It is preferable to place ordinary mottoes beneath the escutcheon, and to reserve the scroll above the crest for war cries, the *crisde guerre* of the French and the *slogans* of the Scottish clans. It is quite certain that at first mottoes were regarded as personal to the bearers, but the adoption of war cries and pass words and then punning references to the bearer's name or his heraldic charges, caused them to be regarded as part and parcel of the hereditary bearings.

CHAPTER XX

CRESTS, HELMS AND BADGES

CRESTS are among the oldest of heraldic compositions. Our own word crest, and the French *crête*, clearly show their original, the feathered crown of barbarian warriors, later translated into the cockscomb ridge of the Greek and Roman helmets, and the " panache " or vari-coloured plume. Greek vases and sculptures show that these plumes were occasionally replaced by figures of animals, as with the owl of Pallas ; and in this they were followed by the Romans, who, moreover, found the custom prevailing among many of the nations whom they conquered and partly absorbed—for instance, the Dacians, and apparently also the Gauls. The Vikings had wild boar, dragon and swan crowned helms. The custom was practically universal. When the Spaniards invaded Mexico they found the Aztecs wearing helmets shaped like the heads of beasts. They are a refined form of the fierce war masks of the savage and barbarian tribes, which are seen approaching the true era of heraldry by way of the ox-head helmets worn by the chiefs of the ancient German Marcomanni.

ROMAN CRESTED HELMET.

DACIAN CRESTED HELMET.

PERSEUS WITH EAGLE HELMET, ANCIENT GEM.

Wherever the idea of a feudal aristocracy has taken firm root the crest has assumed an importance practically overshadowing that of coat armour itself. It was so within the whole wide range of Germany, and also in France. Indeed, Gourdon de Genouillac goes so far as to say: " Toute armoirie timbré appartient à un noble. Tout blason non timbré est à un bourgeois." Two points have to be observed here. The term *timbré* includes helm, coronet (if any), wreath-crest and all appertaining thereto. It was even made to include the supporters, motto scroll and mantling. Secondly, "noble" here means the military territorial lords, for the *petite noblesse* was docked of many privileges. Thus, in

CRESTED HORSES, EARLY EGYPTIAN PERIOD AND HENRY VIII.

Germany a newly ennobled family had to submit to a probationary period, extending over three generations, during which they surmounted their armorial shields with a steel helmet in profile, the visor partly open. It was only the old nobility who bore the full-faced helmet with open visor. Thus the crested helm was an emblem of military leadership, which became an essential part of knightly equipment at those most strictly regulated and jealously guarded war-games, the tournaments. Therefore the wearing of a crested helm was regarded as a proof that the bearer was of tournament rank ; in other words, had satisfied the heralds of his nobility.

The feudal nature of the crested helm in Teutonic customs is well brought out by the German practice of surmounting their shields with quite a number of such helmets. The Margraves of Brandenburg-Anspach have thirteen of them. Each represents a fief. Family alliances are represented by the small armorial or badge-bearing banners placed at the back of the helmets, and often each crest has a panoply of many such banners.

An early form of the crest, which, however, was rather ornamental and of practical utility than a cognisance, was the two fan-shaped wings, borne towards the top of the helm. These are developments of the old cockscomb, and were of service in warding off blows. They long persisted, are constantly seen in association with regular crests, and no doubt in some instances having been peculiarly adorned were finally adopted as hereditary crests. This appears to be the origin of many of the double or single winged crests of Germany, often adorned with heraldic charges, even complete coats-of-arms. These wings are usually either those of eagles or of peacocks. They were often sprinkled with linden leaves, and sometimes curiously tinctured. Thus the Counts of Tanau bore : per pale argent and sable ; and their crest consisted of a pair of wings, the dexter argent and the sinister sable. Bertrand du Gueclin (*circa* 1365) had an eagle's head between a pair of wings, or " vol," each wing having a bend charged with his arms. These fan crests and " vols " seem to have developed into the " panache," or parti-coloured plumes, which were ap-parently mere indications of rank, rather than family emblems. For they by no means always de-scended from father to son. We find the Duc de Bourbon who fell at Poictiers bore a plume of twenty-four peacock's feathers in

BRUNSWICK CREST.

four rows, or " heights," the crest divided per pale, azure and argent, the eyes counterchanged. Yet the crest of the Bourbon of this line was a double fleur-de-lis. The pea-cock's feather was held in high esteem both in Germany and France, possibly because of the ceremonies and gallantries associated with the tournaments. Many German crests of quite another nature are adorned with peacock's feathers, as in the case of the Brunswick sickle, with its outer edge fringed with the bright coloured "eyes." This use of the feathers of Juno's bird, and the variability of crests is well shown in the case of John III, Duke of Brabant. In one case his crest is a peacock's tail between two wings of ermine, powdered with bees, bordered with gold and having an outer edging of the "eyes" of peacock's feathers. In the second instance, he bore a wing with peacock's feathers placed between two long gold plumes, the whole issuing from a black cushion bordered with gold.

JOHN III, DUKE OF BRABANT.

With us, crested helmets came in early, but were not general. Our royal seals are practically crestless until the reign of Edward III, whose equestrian effigy in armour wears a helmet with a statant crowned lion issuing out of an open crown. The same crest is shown on the seals of all his sons. But Richard I is represented as wearing a crest of a lion statant between two fan-shaped vols. Both the helm and crest of the Black Prince are preserved in Canterbury Cathedral. The crest is of *cuir bouilli*, is statant and has a very long tail trailing behind. It is placed on the chapeau or cap of maintenance, which is in turn placed on the large, pointed helm. On an illuminated MS. belonging to Edward IV, his arms are represented ensigned by a golden helm in profile, the visor closed, bearing a cap of dignity whereon is the crest of the statant lion, his extended tail supporting a fleur-de-lis.

This long tail of the lion is very characteristic of the twelfth to fourteenth century crests. Some of these, like that of the Black Prince, were of *cuir bouilli*, but very large, so as to cover the whole helm, which assumed the form of a beast or bird, or the head of a beast or bird. When bird crests on such a scale as this were produced, the tails, or the neck feathers, were prolonged, replacing the floating scarf. At other times it was the capeline, or hood, itself which was built up into the shape required, fitting on tight over the helm, the long flap streaming behind in a single piece or split into two or more strips. Many of these were so large that the mouths of the beasts became the visors, and the whole appearance is strongly suggestive of the grotesque war masks of China, Japan and even savage races. It is to be presumed that such constructions were only worn at tournaments or the festivities connected therewith.

CRESTED HELM, ROGER DE QUINCY, EARL OF WINCHESTER (1195–1265).

Curious as these were, the heraldic engravers and painters added many touches of exaggeration. But no matter how far the exaggeration was carried, crests, whether graven or painted, were always such as could actually be worn on helmets. Ships tossing on waves, floating islands, trees sheltering men and beasts and all such unsuitable compositions came in with the sixteenth century, when the real motive of the crest had been lost sight of, and a florid taste was given full play.

This fatal leaning towards the incongruous with British heralds was undoubtedly fostered by the fact that a very large number of grants of arms had been made without assigning crests. This was because in the beginning the crest was looked upon largely as a matter for personal choice and nobody thought of adopting one who was not a knight.

Then when formal grants were made and the crest became part of the hereditary bearings, this addition was purposely omitted when a grant was made to a non-warrior. But such grantees, though never thinking of surmounting their shields with crested helm, very generally adopted some form of badge. Many of these were personal and purely for temporary use. Others became definitely annexed by a family, though only used as cognisances. Later, when the heralds made their Visitations, claimants who had no right to crests thought that their bearings were incomplete, and so put forward their badges in place of them, and got many of these recognised and registered. As very often they were quite unsuitable to be fixed on helmets in the orthodox way, they were simply placed on the wreaths. Thus a vitiated public taste and too complacent officers of arms perpetuated the absurdity of accompanying all grants of arms with crests, and moreover of disassociating them from the helm. There is no justification for a crest resting on a wreath alone, a fact fully recognised among the Germanic nations, and for the most part also among the Latins.

STAG'S HEAD ERASED ON WREATH.

Wreaths, the French "torse" or "cointise," are merely twists of linen or silk, forming a kind of coronet, and originally really part of the mantling. Modern practice has introduced the fashion of having these wreaths of a colour and a metal, usually those predominating on the shield, and supposed to determine the livery. Formerly, however, three or more tinctures were used, and even chequy wreaths were not uncommon. This wreath should be placed on the top of the helmet, to represent the old cap or scarf. It should have six twists.

Helmets vary considerably in shape. The heraldic type at first was certainly influenced by those worn by Goths and

Norsemen, who are generally represented with ridged and winged helmets, the wings springing from the sides, just above the ears. These wings become the fan-like ornaments of our crests, and were modified under Teutonic influence during the Middle Ages into two tall spikes, often in the form of single feathers, starting from the sides and rising far above the crest. In heraldic art these spikes or plumes are sometimes adorned with armorial banners, becoming mere flagstaffs. As already stated, crests or plumes surmounted both the war and jousting helmets, and sovereigns placed crowns on theirs. Helmets of the

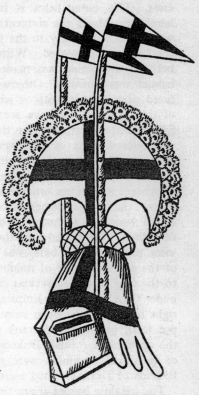

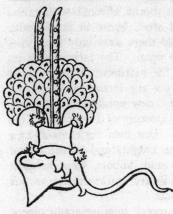

CRESTED HELM, JOHN III, DUKE OF BRABANT.

CRESTED HELM OF BISHOP OF COLOGNE.

eleventh and twelfth centuries are cylindrical with flat tops, box-like. Those of the thirteenth century onwards are rounded to the shape of the head. These have four distinct parts, of which the visor or beaver (in one piece or barred, and movable), the gorget, or neck piece, and the crest, or top and back, are the most important. The cylindrical type sometimes has the sides painted with badge or even a coat-of-arms. Towards the end of the Middle Ages knights when in actual combat bore a second helmet tall and square, resting on their shoulders and topped by the crest. This outer helm is frequently shown in Teutonic heraldry. About the sixteenth century peculiar importance was given in heraldry to the type, material and position of the helmet represented. With us until the reign of Elizabeth no distinction was made, except that the sovereign's helmet was crowned. Otherwise, they were borne either full faced or in profile, with or without visor, at the discretion of the artist, as we have seen in the case of Edward IV. Subsequent to that, however, the sovereign's helmet is of gold, with closed visor of six bars, lined with crimson, borne affronté; that of peers is of silver, garnished with gold, with closed visor and borne in profile; that of baronets and knights is of steel with silver ornaments, borne affronté with raised visor; that of gentlemen is of steel, borne in profile with closed visor. In Germany of old there were only two types of helmets, the closed and the open. The latter, with its visor provided with bars, was the attribute of every grade of the military caste of nobility; the former was assigned to the first three generations of " new nobility." However, under the Holy Roman Empire, Doctors of Law claimed the right to assume the open helm. Our own Serjeants-at-Law put forth pretensions to rank as knights and to the use of the open helm. Such Bishops and Abbots, who by right of territorial dominion were military commanders, as our Bishops of Durham, used helmets.

The heraldic helmet bears the crest, now generally placed on a wreath, but of old forming part of it. The helmet is placed above the shield and resting on it, or if a coronet is used, springing from that. In Mediæval design, and in the Teutonic work of a much later period, the helmet and crest are usually much larger than the armorial shield which they ensign. Helmets are frequently found as charges. Basset, Lord Mayor of London (1475), bore: gules, three helmets or.

David Dolben, Bishop of Bangor (1632), and John Dolben, Bishop of Rochester and then Archbishop of York (1638-9) bore: sable, a close helmet between three spear heads, points fessways. Daubeny: sable, three tilting helmets argent. Moriens, small steel skull caps, are also borne.

It has been shown above how badges, or cognisances, have often become confounded with crests. In their origin, how-ever, they served a different purpose. They are devices, sometimes of a strictly heraldic character, at other times more pictorial, adopted as personal or family symbols. They were placed on banners, on the liveries of retainers, carved, stamped or painted on buildings and movable property. In fact, they were marks of possession, and something by which the owner could be recog-nised. Some of these ap-pear to have been adopted in quite remote times. Such are the rampant bear and the ragged staff, which were later brought together and seem to have been associated with the Earls of Warwick " from time immemorial," the badge being adopted by the various families who enjoyed the title. While these cognisances became an important adjunct of social and political life and were registered by Officers of Arms, no laws existed for their regulation, and as a matter of fact, it was only exceptionally that they became hereditary. In the majority of cases a badge lasted the lifetime of its owner, perhaps was used only for a short period, though a son or daughter might also use it. We see this side of the practice in connection with the royal badges, for most of our sovereigns had two or more peculiar to themselves, while some were continued, possibly with a slight difference, by their successors. The bear and ragged staff of Warwick has been mentioned.

HELMET OF THE SOVEREIGN.

Other well-known examples are the buckle of the Pelhams
(which is part of the buckle and sword strap of the captured
King John of France, adopted by the captor, as already
explained), the Percy crescent, the Howard double manacle,
the Bohun white swan, the Hungerford sickle, the Peverel
garb, the Stourton golden drag or sledge, the Hastings sable
maunch, the de la Warr gold crampet (end piece of a
sword scabbard), the inside borne per pale azure and gules,
charged with the letter R. We may see how even hereditary
badges were subject to variation by considering that of the
Dacres. The first we hear of it is in connection with " The
Lord Dacre Fynnys of the South," when it appears as the
letters T and D united by an elaborate knot of "tassled
silken cord." Lord Dacre of Gisland replaced the letters by
an escallop shell and a ragged staff of silver, the cord being of
red. While some have regarded the staff as a symbol of the
hereditary forestership of Inglewood, others trace the shell and
staff to the marriage of Lord Dacre of Gisland to a daughter
of Lord Greystoke, while Planché is of opinion that the knot
is derived from descent from Bourchier, and the shell and
ragged staff from the Nevilles. However, it may be observed
that the Bourchier and Dacre knots are of an entirely different
design. The escallop shell is taken from the Dacres's own coat :
gules, three escallops or.

Knotted cords are found among the heraldic charges. Sir
James ap Owain (*temp*. Henry III) bore : gules, a chevron
between in chief two true-lovers' knots and in base a lion
rampant or ; which appears to be a modification of : gules,
a chevron between three tristrans or true-lovers' knots argent,
borne by Bowen, Abowen, and Owen. On the Continent we
find Guilbert, of Normandy, bearing : azure, a true-lovers'
knot between three mullets sable ; and Hughe, Netherlands :
azure, a lion rampant or in a true-lovers' knot argent, between
four fleurs-de-lis gold, their stalks turned to the fess point.
But it was as badges that these devices were chiefly used, and
though mainly decorative, often allusive in the punning sense,
they were also symbolical of some guiding thought or principle, as the Heneage motto shows, the whole system being

borrowed from the ancient symbolism of magic, white and black. Many of the mystic incantations and ceremonies were associated with the tying or untying of cords and thongs. The Gordian knot which Alexander severed with a stroke of his sword belonged to the region of magic. Another phase of the power of knots is seen in the legend concerning a long and languishing illness from which Mahomet suffered. It was found to be due to Jewish magic, they having fashioned a waxen image of the Prophet round a few of his hairs, then piercing it with eleven needles and finally binding it round with a bow string, fastened by eleven knots, upon each of which an incantation was breathed. It was only by the discovery of this, the untying of the knot by repeating certain verbal formulæ, and removing the cords, that Mahomet recovered. The system of magic knots was strangely elaborated in Egypt, where we see cords, snakes and the stems of plants (as in the union badge of Upper and Lower kingdoms, the lotus and the papyrus), and by the wandering Egyptians, or gipsies, the system was introduced into Europe.

Something of the fatalistic tendency is seen in the Heneage knot, which is formed of a flat thong or ribbon, with a lower and two upper loops, the loose ends hanging down, the whole fashioned into the shape of a human heart, and accompanied by the motto : " Fast though untied." It is an open knot, which, however, can be pulled tight. The Bowen knot is square, with a loop at each corner, thus we have a play on the word bow, and the presentation of the Greek letter B. The Bourchier knot is composed of two thongs or withies, bent into horseshoe shape and interlaced. The Wake knot (once a badge, now used as a crest), is constructed on the same principle, only cords are used and a more rounded style adopted. The famous Stafford knot, which has been annexed from the family by a whole county, for it is found on the arms of the town of Stafford, and is a badge of the Staffordshire regiments, is the true-lovers' knot, merely a piece of cord with the two ends turned in one upon the other, the most primitive method of making a knot. The Lacy knot is quite suggestive of the magic maze, consisting of a Bowen knot (but with small corner loops) interlaced with a similar figure placed diamond-wise. We have seen how the Dacre knot was utilised to unite other badges. The same thing occurred when Lord Hungerford married Catherine Peverel, and a knot was made to embrace the Hungerford sickle and the Peverel garb. Such badges as these were not only used to decorate personal property, but were worn by dependents and followers embroidered on the chest, on the arm, or as a jewel attached to a collar. It was thus that Queen Philippa of Hainault, consort of Edward III, bestowed her badge of an ostrich with a key in its beak on certain of her trusted

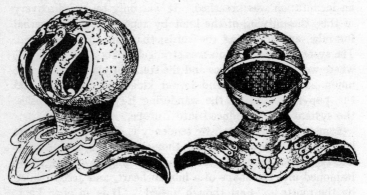

HELMET OF PEER.   HELMET OF KNIGHTS AND BARONETS.

courtiers, that Richard II distributed his badge of the white hart to those whom he wished to bind on his side, while the Lancastrian and Yorkshire factions were fostered in the same way, by the liberal distribution of the collar of S.S. and that of roses and suns.

Our royal badges bring out the essential difference between the true crest and many badges. The following list is fairly complete.

Stephen is supposed to have adopted a sagitarius.

Henry II, an escarbuncle, derived from Anjou; a genet cat passant between two slips of broom. This badge Edward IV bestowed on his natural son, Arthur, Viscount Lisle, as a crest.

Richard I. a star within a crescent; a star and crescent separately; a sprig of broom; and, according to Guillim, a sun on two crossed anchors.

John, a star within a crescent.

Henry III, a star within a crescent.

Edward I, a rose, slipped; on his seal for use beyond the Tweed a bear standing against a tree.

Edward II, a hexagonal castle with hexagonal tower, derived from his mother, who used the castles and lions of Castille and Leon as badges on her seals to denote her descent.

Edward III, rays from clouds; a stump of a tree with two sprigs (delightfully suggestive of a flourishing issue); an ostrich feather; falcon; and on private seal a griffin.

Richard II, sun in splendour; sunrays from behind clouds, called a sun or cloud burst; a branch of broom (on his robe on his tomb); a white hart couchant, gorged and chained or, probably derived from

HELMET OF GENTLEMAN.

his mother, who had as badge a white hind. This white hind was also borne by Thomas Holland, Earl of Kent, her son by her first husband. Another of Richard's badges was a white falcon, derived from Edward II.

Badges of the Lancastrian princes were the red rose, the red rose en soleil, and the collar of S.S.

Henry IV, a genet; an eagle displayed; the tail of a fox; the swan of Bohun; a white antelope; a crowned panther and a crowned eagle.

Henry V, a beacon in flames, which had a political meaning, reflecting on the necessity of guarding our coasts; hence the badge was subsequently adopted as an Admiralty badge.

Henry also had a white hart and an antelope gorged with a crown; a swan gorged with a crown (the Bohun badge), sometimes combined with a beacon; and as Prince he bore a swan carrying an ostrich feather in its beak. According to an old MS. in the Harleian Collection when Henry interviewed Charles of France at Melun, his headquarters were under a huge tent of blue and green, richly embroidered with the silver hart badge, and a displayed eagle placed over his tent. The French King's tent was of blue, powdered with fleurs-de-lis, but over it was a large winged white hart, probably borne in compliment to the English monarch. When Henry's body was brought back to England, the coursers in the funeral procession had trappings of blue and green velvet decorated with the white hart.

Henry VI, an antelope collared and chained; two feathers in saltire; spotted panther passant guardant.

Badges of the House of York were the white rose, the white rose en soleil and the collar of white roses and suns.

Edward IV, a falcon within a closed fetterlock. John of Gaunt bore a falcon with a fetterlock in its beak. The sable bull of Clare; the black dragon of Ulster; a sun in splendour; a white hart and a white wolf.

Edward V as Prince, by his father's order, bore his falcon within an open fetterlock.

Richard III, a rose and a sun separately (on Great Seal); a falcon with maiden's head; a white boar; and the black bull of Clare.

Badges of the House of Tudor were the united roses; the red and white roses separately and crowned; a portcullis denoting their descent from the Beauforts.

Henry VII, a red dragon inflamed, derived from Cadwallader, Prince of North Wales; hawthorn bush crowned, adopted to commemorate the finding of Richard's crown on the may bush after the battle of Bosworth Field; a dun cow; a white greyhound courant collared azure, to denote his maternal descent from John, Earl of Somerset. The dun cow was also probably allusive to the Beaufort descent, who themselves descended from the Beauchamps of Holt, who claimed to have sprung from the mythical Guy of Warwick, slayer of the devastating Dun Cow of Warwick.

Henry VIII, a white greyhound courant ; a white antelope ; a red dragon of Wales ; Tudor roses ; flames ; fleur-de-lis ; an archer in a green coat drawing a bow. According to Holinshead, when Henry met Francis on the Field of the Cloth of Gold, his horse was gloriously caparisoned in trappings of russet velvet, on which were wavy bands of gold to represent his dominion over the seas.

Edward VI, a sun in splendour ; a cannon on a mount, belching fire.

Mary, a double rose (Tudor) impaled with a sheaf of arrows ; a rose and pomegranate conjoined ; these being derived from the badges of her mother Catherine of Arragon.

Elizabeth, a harp crowned for Ireland ; the Tudor rose.

Badges of the Royal House of Stuart were the Tudor roses ; the fleurs-de-lis of France ; the thistle leaved for Scotland ; the crowned harp for Ireland. James I and VI dimidiated the Scottish thistle with the Tudor rose.

The rose badge will be found fully dealt with in Chapter XVI and the ostrich feathers in Chapter XVIII.

Our present-day National badges are : For England : a white rose, seeded gold, within a red rose, slipped vert. For Scotland : a thistle, blue, slipped vert. For Ireland : a shamrock leaf, vert ; a golden harp, stringed silver. For Wales : a red dragon passant ; wings elevated, on a green mount (official) ; a leek, green leaves and silver bulb (unofficial) ; For the United Kingdom : a Tudor rose (as for England), a thistle and a shamrock growing on one stem ; the Union Jack on a shield. All these (except the dragon and the leek) are, as Royal badges, ensigned with an Imperial crown. Canada's popular badge is the red maple leaf, gold veined. Australia's unofficial badges are yellow-bloomed wattle, a kind of mimosa ; a kangaroo. India's a red lotus flower.

LIST OF SCOTTISH CLAN BADGES

Buchanan, oak or bilberry.

Cameron, oak or cranberry.

Campbell of Argyll and Breadalbane, fir club moss and bog myrtle.

Chisholm, alder.

Colquhoun, dogberry hazel.

Cumming, common sallow or cumin plant.

Davidson, box-wood; red whortleberry.

Drummond, mother of thyme; holly.

Farquharson, little sunflower; foxglove.

Ferguson, little sunflower; foxglove.

Forbes, broom.

Fraser, yew.

Gordon, rock ivy.

Graham, laurel spurge.

Grant, Scotch fir.

Gunn, juniper.

Johnston, red hawthorn.

Lamont, crab apple tree.

Logan, gorse.

MacAllister, common heath.

MacAlpine, Scotch fir.

MacArthur, bog myrtle; club fir moss.

MacAulay, Scotch fir.

MacBean, box-wood; red whortleberry.

MacCall, common heath.

MacDonald, common heath.

MacDonnel, common heath.

MacDougal, bell heath.

MacDuff, box-wood; red whortleberry.

MacFarlane, cranberry; cloudberry.

MacFie, or Mac Phee, Scotch fir.

MacGillivray, box-wood; red whortleberry.

MacGregor, Scotch fir.

MacInnes, holly.

MacIntosh, box-wood.

MacIntyre, common heath.
MacIvor, bog myrtle.
MacKae, fir club moss.
MacKay, bulrush ; broom.
MacKenzie, holly.
MacKinnon, Scotch fir.
MacLachlan, mountain ash.
MacLaren and MacLaurin, laurel.
MacLean, holly ; blackberry ; heath.
MacLeman, gorse.
MacLeod, juniper ; red whortleberry.
MacMillan, holly.
MacNab, common heath ; Scotch fir.
MacNaughton, trailing azalea.
MacNeil, sea-ware.
MacPherson, variegated box.
MacQuarrie, Scotch fir.
MacQueen, box-wood ; red whortleberry.
Menzies, Menzies' heath.
Munro, club moss.
Murray, butcher's broom ; juniper.
Ogilvie, hawthorn.
Oliphant, maple.
Robertson, five-leaved heath ; bracken.
Rose, wild rosemary.
Ross, juniper.
Shaw, box-wood ; red whortleberry.
Sinclair, whin (or gorse).
Stewart, oak.
Sutherland, butcher's broom ; cotton sedge.
Urquhart, wallflower.

The badge regarded as the older one is given first where the clan possesses two. It is clear that the second badge was not adopted to show the different septs as has been suggested ; Mr. MacKenzie MacBride points out to me that all the great septs of the MacDonalds for instance bore the same badge, and all the MacKenzies bear the holly, and the Campbells, all or nearly if not quite all, bear the bog myrtle and the fir club moss. Again, all the clans that formed the great clan Chattan bore the same badge, even though there was originally no blood relationship between some of them. Similarly the MacArthur Campbells, though of different origin, bore the badge of their chief the Campbell. He suggests that it is more probable that the second badge was adopted because the original one was sometimes out of bloom, and practically unwearable. The bilberry, cranberry and whortleberry are for long without berries, and the bearers of them, it is noticeable, have all a second badge. The broom is sometimes a mere podstick; the bog myrtle of the Campbells again fades very soon after being plucked, and this may have led to the addition of a less perishable second badge.

Chiefs wear three long feathers from an eagle's pinion, chieftains two, and gentlemen one, pinned to the bonnet or cap.

CHAPTER XXI

CROWNS, CORONETS AND CAPS

CROWNS have long been used in design to symbolise power, spiritual or material. The earliest types were the feather crests of warriors; then the ceremonial chaplets or wreaths, used during the performance of religious rites, and also bestowed upon victors in warfare or public contests. Feathers are usually grouped fan fashion over the forehead, from temple to temple, the tallest pens being placed in the middle. We have this type in the well-known Mortimer crest, a pyramid of four heights of feathers out of a crest coronet. On the other hand the feathers may be carried in single or double row from forehead to the nape of the neck. The former method undoubtedly suggested the fillet, whence sprang the diadem, for the fillet was useful in binding the feathers, and naturally was adorned with precious materials. In this form the diadem was worn on occasions when the feather war-crest was laid aside.

Most plants and flowers have been utilised to form wreaths and chaplets. The rose, as one of the floral attributes of vernal divinities, represented joy and conviviality, suggesting the festivities after the acceptance of sacrificial offerings. Partly from this idea of joy and partly in allusion to the pagan legend of the white rose having been encrimsoned by sacrificial ichtor, the rose red chaplet became a Christian symbol. The laurel or bay leaf was the attribute of Apollo and therefore awarded to poets, but it was soon assumed by the Romans as a symbol of victory and Imperial power. The wreath is usually in the form of two sprays tied by a bow

of ribbon at the back, and meeting in a point over the brows.
The oak wreath, treated in the same way, was the reward for
naval successes, and we often see a wreath composed of one
branch of laurel and one of oak. The myrtle, with small,
glossy, dark green, oblong leaves, tiny white or rose star-like
blooms and round black berries, was sacred to Venus, and
decorated the brows of magistrates and victors at public
games. Parsley wreaths were bestowed on victors of foot
races. Ivy and vines as the attributes of Bacchus, originally
an arboreal god, are usually twined into a wreath together,
symbolising plenty and conviviality. Olive branches are
occasionally used as wreaths, and as the symbols of agricultural riches and domestic felicity, represent peace. Palms
are also used as wreaths, two being united as with the sprays
of bays, and symbolise victory, or more often martyrdom.
Bulrushes, alone or twined with lilies or irises, are peculiar
to river divinities, and are used to symbolise the wealth
brought by great fluvial highways of commerce. In heraldry
the chaplet of rue, technically a " crancelin," seen in the arms
of Saxony, is a bend slightly arched, composed of a jewelled
band topped by conventionalised foliage. It is supposed to
represent a wreath of rue " which is for memory," claimed to
have been fashioned by the Emperor Barbarossa on the field
of battle and bestowed on his successful lieutenant, Bernhard
of Ascania, founder of the House of Saxony.

It has been said that the fillet supporting a feathered crest

RADIATED OR EASTERN CROWN.   VALLARY CROWN.

suggested the diadem. This is confirmed by the fact that
our earliest representations of crowns show them as plain
bands, and even more often in the radiated form. A
radiated crown has a fillet, quite rudimentary or in the shape
of a jewelled band, topped or heightened by triangular or

wedge-shaped spikes. This is the heraldic antique or Eastern crown. In later types the spikes are topped by round balls. Variations of this are the palisade or vallary crown, consisting of a number of palisades springing from a fillet and spiked at the top. Among the Romans it was awarded to those who first broke into or captured an entrenched camp. The Celestial crown is of the radiated type, though often we see tall and low spikes alternating, each topped by a star. It is the crown of the Virgin Mary and of martyrs.

CELESTIAL CROWN.

The earliest royal diadem extant is the Iron Crown of Lombardy, which dates from the late sixth century. It is composed of broad curved plates of gold, held together by an inner thin band of iron, traditionally said to have been forged from a nail of the true Cross. The gold plates are ornamented with rosettes in goldsmith work, coloured enamels and precious stones. The Votive crown of Recescuito, King of the Visigoths, seventh century, still preserved in Spain, is of the same type: it has a broad band of chiselled gold, with blue and greeny yellow uncut stones set in circles, and jewelled drops attached to chains pendent from the circlet.

Charlemagne's crown, eighth century, is a variation of this. It is composed of eight broad gold plates, arched at the top and hinged together. Four of the plates are encrusted with precious stones, four are ornamented in enamel with the figures of Solomon, David, Hezekiah and Christ. At a later date a Latin cross was fixed above the front jewelled plate, and from its base a single arch, composed of a band of eight miniature jewelled plates, was carried to the back plate. This type served as a pattern for the crown of the German Empire. It is composed of eight gold plates, arched, and slightly broader at the top than at the base. Four of these are ornamented with diamond Latin crosses and four with the Imperial German eagle. Two arches formed of four semi-hoops, spring from the plates to meet in a high point, supporting an Imperial mound topped by a jewelled cross. The tall domed cap is a network of filigree. Two broad, richly embroidered bands depend from the back plates.

St. Stephen's crown of Hungary is composed of two parts. The broad circlet, or diadem, dates probably from the eleventh century. It is a broad band, with beaded edging top and bottom, ornamented with figures of saints in enamelled panels and large precious stones. From this circlet spring a series of plates, alternately domed and pyramidal, richly jewelled. The central arched plate is adorned with figures in coloured enamels. To this Pope Sylvester II added a single arch in two half-hoops, supporting a pearl and a cross patée, when he bestowed the title of Apostolic King on Stephen. From the sides and back small jewelled trefoils hang on little chains.

ST. STEPHEN'S CROWN.

CROWN OF BOHEMIA.

The Byzantine crowns, represented by the series belonging to the Tartar Kingdoms and principalities of Russia, also show this built-up appearance. They have generally a broad fillet, topped by a conical cap formed of decorated metal plates. The Austrian and Russian crowns are modifications of this design, consisting of a broad fillet and a globular dome in two sections, leaving an open space between them, partly filled by an arch supporting jewels. In the case of Austria the headband is topped by large trefoil ornaments; in that of Russia the wreath idea is represented by two diamond sprays of laurel leaves and two palms.

In England the Saxon kings wore crowns made of gold

plates, consisting of a broad ornamental band, topped by trefoils placed at the jointing angles. On coins the crowns appear square ; showing three trefoils. King Edgar appears with a crown composed of a fillet, with three upright projections split at the top and curving to right and left, like an heraldic millrind. William I is variously represented as wearing a plain headband, topped by straight florated spikes ; and a jewelled headband, with single arch in two sections, and side chainlets with pendants. It is said that Alfred's crown was adorned with small golden bells, pendent from chains. The Norman kings wore crowns composed of a jewelled fillet topped by florated ornaments. The fleur-de-lis appears to have been introduced by the Plantagenets. But Richard II is represented with a crown consisting of a jewelled headband and crest ornaments of tall oak leaves and short trefoils (strawberry leaves) placed alternately. In de Meziere's book of the Coronation, presented to Richard II, we find the above type assigned to the English King,

ROYAL CROWN OF ENGLAND.

while that of Charles of France is a fillet surmounted by four tall and four short fleurs-de-lis. The ornamented headband was further adorned by two arches at the coronation of Henry VI. The usual arching is produced by four half-hoops, slanting outwards, slightly hipped at the points of bending and dipping to the centre, where a mound and cross patée are supported. The fillet is ornamented with four crosses patée and four fleurs-de-lis placed alternately, In the Imperial crown made for Queen Victoria the crown is a mass of jewels, the two arches being composed of diamond oak leaves with pearl acorns, and have no dip in the centre. The heraldic British Imperial crown is shown with raised and rather angular arches, forming a dome.

Many foreign crowns are closed with eight arches, for instance, those of France, Prussia, Brazil. The elder branch of the Bourbons had a jewelled fillet supporting eight fleurs-

CROWN OF THE BOURBONS.　　　　CROWN OF NAPOLEON I.

de-lis, from which sprang eight half-hoops, supporting a large six-leaved fleur-de-lis, four curved outwards and two forming the central bud. The Orleans branch replaced the fleurs-de-lis with strawberry leaves, the top ornamented by a royal mound, and placed a wreath of oak leaves round the fillet.

CORONET OF THE PRINCE　　　　CORONET OF ROYAL
OF WALES.　　　　PRINCES OF ENGLAND.

The crown of Napoleon I had a rim above the broad head-band supporting eight eagles, with long wings elevated above their heads, and eight palms springing from rosettes, the palms forming arches over the eagles and meeting in the middle to support an Imperial mound and trefoiled cross.

In England the Prince of Wales wears a coronet similar to the royal crown, only having a single arch of two half-hoops. The other sons and daughters of the sovereign have a similar coronet, but without the arch. The grandchildren of the sovereign have the fillet ornamented with two crosses patée, two strawberry leaves and four fleurs-de-lis, the crosses being placed back and front, and the strawberry leaves on the sides ; other princes of the blood have four crosses patée and four strawberry leaves.

The coronet of a duke was of an undecided type until the end of the sixteenth century. It is composed of a circlet and eight strawberry leaves. About the same period the marquises were assigned a coronet formed by a headband topped by four strawberry leaves and four pearl-like silver balls, placed alternately. Earls wore pearl-like balls on their coronets as early as the first half of the fifteenth century, but the present form, a circlet with eight tall rays adorned with silver balls, and a small strawberry leaf in each depression, came in with the sixteenth century. Viscounts were granted coronets by James I; they consist of sixteen silver balls placed direct on the circlet. Barons wear a golden circlet with six large silver balls placed direct on the top of the band. Continental practice differs slightly. For instance, in France, while the coronet of a duke is like ours, that of a marquess is adorned with four large strawberry leaves and a row of three small pearls between each pair ; or the pearls may be arranged in a trefoil. A count has sixteen pearls placed in the circlet. A viscount has four large and four small pearls, and barons a jewelled circlet entwined with a string of pearls. The old Vidames' coronet had a jewelled circlet heightened by four crosses patée. The German baron has twelve pearls on spikes.

Our Kings of Arms bear crowns composed of jewelled circlets heightened with sixteen oak leaves.

Crowns and coronets may be represented quite plain, or lined with caps of crimson velvet, with a band of ermine on the lower edge, topped, in the non-arched types, by a tassel of bullion.

The crest coronet used in heraldry and commonly but wrongly called a ducal coronet, is composed of a jewelled circlet and four strawberry leaves. Crests are often shown springing from such a coronet, which is also used as a gorge, that is encircles the necks, of heraldic beasts.

A crown of considerable symbolic value is the civic or mural variety. It may consist merely of a crenelated wall ; of four turrets joined by screened walls ; or of a tall tower with minor turrets. All three types are seen on Greek and Roman coins of very early date, worn by figures representing important cities. The mural crown was also assigned to those who captured a walled city in battle. In heraldic practice the mural crown was reserved for fortified towns and the conquerors of such towns.

The naval crown, consisting of prows of galleys alternating with square sails, placed on a head-band, is also of a classic origin, and denotes maritime dominion and victory.

NAVAL CROWN.

The vallary crown has already been described.

Caps of dignity, sometimes called caps of maintenance, are of crimson velvet, turned up with ermine, and have two swallow tails. They are worn by princes and great nobles and are found both as charges and as supports for crests. The Electoral Cap of Hanover, which appeared ensigning the shield of pretence in our Royal Arms when George I came over, is much of this style. It is a tall crimson cap on a circlet, turned up with ermine. Such a cap was borne by all the Electoral Princesses of Germany. In the case of Hanover it was converted into a crown when the Electorate became a Kingdom.

Mitres have varied considerably in shape. At first they were much lower than is now the fashion, and were worn sideways, as it were, showing two points and a considerable

depression between. Then we find they assumed the shape
of a triangle above the headband. They are worn by archbishops, bishops, and formerly by bishop-abbots.

In Roman Catholic countries the general ecclesiastical
timbres for armorial shields are the black biretta or black
large flat-brimmed hat, with cords having two tassels, one
above the other. The Pope's tiara is a tall dome-shaped
hat adorned with three fleury crowns, one above the other,
and topped by a mound and cross. It was originally a high
round cap without any crown ; Constantine is commonly
supposed to have granted the right of adding a crown, or
coronet, to their tiaras. Rees says, " Boniface VIII encom-
passed the tiara with a crown ; Benedict XII added a second ;
and John XXIII a third." The globe and cross over the top
were added at a later period, to denote the spiritual power
of the popes over the earth. Cardinals have the right to
mitres, to a red skull cap, and to the red broad-brimmed hat,
with knotted cords (" houppes ") hanging on both sides of
the shield, having fifteen tassels, united by cords and disposed thus : 1, 2, 3, 4, 5 ; so that the houpes broaden out at
the base. Archbishops have the mitre, as well as the ecclesiastical hat, only of green, the latter with cords and fifteen
knots, but the number is usually reduced to ten. Bishops
have the mitre, the green broad-brimmed hats with cords of
ten, or now six, knots.

It is to be noted that formerly many of the prelates and
abbots were either princes, dukes, or counts by virtue of their
office, and they wore the coronets of their rank, as well as
their ecclesiastical cognisances.

A curious cap of dignity is that belonging to the Corporation of the City of London. It is the fur head-dress of
the Sword Bearer, and is in the shape of a reversed truncated
cone. This is often placed above the coat-of-arms.

Crowns and coronets are constantly used as charges. We
also see figures, beasts and even inanimate objects crowned,
while beasts and birds are frequently gorged or collared with
coronets. Two forms of old crowns are borne : (1) the open
crown with the circlet heightened by four strawberry leaves

(three being shown), and (2) the radiate or Eastern crown, usually five rays being shown. The see of Ely bears the apocryphal coat of St. Ethelreda : gules, three open crowns or. Azure, three open crowns or, are the arms of Sweden. Earle, Bishop of Salisbury, (1663–5), bore : ermine, on a chief engrailed sable three antique crowns or ; Grant, Earls of Seafield : gules, three Eastern crowns or. Royal crowns are borne by Konig, Germany : azure, a royal crown or ; and they are found on many coats as augmentations, of which more will be said later.

Worthington bears : argent, three pastoral staves each ensigned on top with a crown celestial or. The same crown is to be seen in the arms of the Royal Borough of Kensington, representing the Virgin, patron of the parish church of St. Mary Abbot's. Rogers, of Wales, bears : or, a crown vallary gules between three stags trippant proper. Jourdain : gules, three mural crowns argent, masoned sable. These are commonly borne by towns, though strictly they should only belong to walled towns. Lenden (who captured a fleet of Commonwealth craft for Charles) bears : azure, a naval crown with an orle of twelve anchors or. Pellen : gules, a lion passant guardant, and in chief two wreaths of oak leaves and acorns or ; on a chief wavy azure a ship-of-war before the town of Algiers, proper. The Counts of Wrede, Germany : or, a laurel wreath proper, set with five roses gules. The Viscounts de Meaux : argent, five crowns of thorns sable (this was of religious origin, for the first bearer was a Crusader). Dasilva (Portugal) : argent, a lion rampant gules encircled by a wreath of brambles proper. Goodall, Suffolk : gules, an eagle displayed argent, armed or ; on a canton silver a chaplet of graminy (plaited grass) vert. The Drapers' Company, London : azure, three clouds proper, rays issuing therefrom downwards or, surmounted by as many tiaras gules, crowned gold. Mitres appear in the arms of many sees. They were also added to their paternal arms by bishops, for instance Clifford, Bishop of Bath and Wells (1401) and London (1407–21), bore : chequy or and azure, on a fess gules, a mitre stringed argent, all within a bordure of the second. Thomas de Beckington, Bishop of Bath and Wells (1443) : argent, on a fess azure a mitre or ; in chief three bucks' heads caboshed gules ; in base as many pheons, sable.   On the other hand, Robert Marshall, Bishop of Hereford (1404–16), bore simply : sable, three mitres or.   We also find Myerton, Newcastle, bearing : azure, three mitres or.   Holworth : argent, three caps of maintenance sable.

CHAPTER XXII

SUPPORTERS

SUPPORTERS are human figures, angels and fabulous creatures, animals (both natural and imaginary) and inanimate objects placed on both sides of an armorial shield, or on one side only, as though holding it in position. There are exceptions, for a supporter may be placed behind the shield, above or beneath it, or two on one side.

According to modern practice in Great Britain the use of supporters is strictly limited to certain persons, and subject to definite regulations. Those entitled to supporters are: the sovereign and members of the Royal Family, peers and peeresses, eldest sons of peers, younger sons of dukes and marquesses, a few commoners assigned them by special grants, some families who have used supporters before the restrictive regulations came in, and therefore have established a prescriptive right to them. Baronets of Nova Scotia at one time claimed the right to supporters, and many of these succeeded in securing registration by Officers of Arms, hence their more frequent use in Scotland. All the above are hereditary. Knights of the Garter and Knights Grand Cross of the Bath use personal supporters granted to them by the Heralds on their creation or elevation. Towns and corporate bodies having arms are also usually granted supporters. Since such rules have been recognised, the position, and all details connected with any given supporter have become stereotyped. Before that, there was great latitude both as regards those who used them and in their representation. Even when supporters became hereditary considerable freedom was shown

242

BOOK PLATE OF VISCOUNT HOOD.
Designed by Mr. Friend.

in their treatment, only their main characteristics being maintained, which was an immense gain to artistic effect.

This freedom of treatment was really inherent to their origin, for though there has been much controversy on the subject, it is clear that they were merely a device of heraldic artists adopted to fill empty spaces on seals and so on, with a view to set off the armorial shield to better advantage. Owing to the frequent appearance of savages, wild men of the woods, and similar figures as supporters, it has been asserted that they represented pages and squires in attendance on knights at tournaments. It is quite true that at some of the most famous of these, knights assuming the character of a hero of romance appeared in the lists disguised, accompanied by pages and squires dressed, or more accurately undressed, as wild men of the woods, or even beasts of the forest or as dragons. This is said to have occurred first at a tournament organised in Germany. There were many instances of such disguises at the celebrated tourney organised by James IV of Scotland in 1503, when, on the occasion of his marriage with Margaret, eldest daughter of Henry VII, he challenged the whole of Europe " in defence of the Savage Knight." Noble knights flocked in from all parts, with their attendants, appearing more of less in character suitable to the occasion. That this practice may have had some influence on artists is possible, but the fact remains that the earliest known examples of supporters are on seals, and these are either angels or reptilian creatures more or less circled round the shields. This also does away with the theory that supporters represent the two witnesses in attendance on candidates for knighthood. Both seals and armorial bearings carved on churches and other buildings show the adventitious character of supporters, and their gradual development into accessories of very considerable symbolical value.

As above stated, the first examples that have come down to us represent angels or some nondescript " worm," in the latter case usually forming a kind of collar round the shield. A shield of the arms of Richard II carved in Westminster Hall has an angel attendant on each side of it, a third is

BOOK PLATE DESIGNED BY MR. FRIEND.

behind the escutcheon and leaning on its top, while the escutcheon itself is resting on the back of a collared and chained white hart lying below. Thus we have a kind of frame of quasi supporters. Oliver de Bohun had three of the swan badges on his seal ; they are quite small, one being placed on either side and one at the top of the shield. The same thing is seen on the seal of an early fifteenth century Duke of Berri ; there the arms are surrounded by a ring of seven bears, walking with their feet touching the shield. An eleventh-century sculpture of the arms of the Porccini has a similar ring of small pigs, but they have their backs to the shield, except the top one which stands on it. We also sometimes see in old Italian armoury two heads of beasts, the mouths biting the dexter chief and the sinister base of the shield. Other arrangements of this kind are common enough, and denote that while the artist was giving a free rein to his fancy, he was also anxious to turn his embellishments to symbolical account.

At Canterbury Cathedral the richly carved cloister ceiling,

JOHN OF GAUNT

with its many bosses adorned with armorial shields, affords numerous instances. They date from the reign of Henry IV. The boss with the shield of John of Gaunt, Duke of Lancaster, as King of Castile and Leon, is extremely curious as showing this dual development. A small shield charged with a lion rampant is placed over a strange castle, composed of five turrets, knitted together by flying buttresses, and a dexter and sinister arm springing from behind the base of the shield, the hands grasping the outer towers. Two curved ostrich feathers, tied with a ribbon, form a wreath frame. On another compartment the arms of the King in a small spade shield are placed over a lion couchant gorged with the crown fleury. Farther on is an elephant, with a double-towered castle on its back, a sarcingle keeping in place a shield with the arms of Jerusalem. This refers to John de Beaumont, son of John de Brienne, who was elected King of Jerusalem in 1209. Probably the most instructive of all is a boss of compartment twenty-nine, referring to Lathom and Stanley. Here we see an eagle rising, clutching in his talons a child in swaddling clothes. On the dexter wing is a shield of the arms of the Isle of Man; on the sinister wing a quartered shield: first and fourth or, on a chief indented azure three bezants (for Lathom); second and third, argent, on bend azure three stags' heads caboshed or (for Stanley). Now, the eagle is the Lathom crest, from whom it descended to the Stanleys, subsequently Earls of Derby and Kings of Man. Legend ran that Sir Thomas Lathom of Lathom, co. Lancaster, in the reign of Edward II, having no heir, adopted a male infant discovered in an eagle's nest, who took the name of Lathom, and left an only daughter who became the wife of William Stanley of Stanley. The instructive point is, that we have here a crest, as a crest, used in place of a supporter. For another example of this we must go to the Monastery of Preaching Fathers at Poictiers, where there was long preserved a collection of armorial bearings of those French knights who fell at the battle of the same name (1356). One of these trophies shows a closed helmet ensigned with a crest coronet over the scarf, issuant therefrom a crowned swan, wings displayed, holding in its beak two tasselled ribbons, pendent from which is a quartered armorial shield.

Both anterior to and contemporarily with these, we find armorial shields on seals pendent from trees, held by effigies of the owners, or the arms may be emblazoned on their robes. When a lady is in question she may hold the armorial shield of her husband in one hand and that of her father in another.

Quite a late, though probably independent, development of this idea was recorded by Willement from a carving in the old mansion of the Rodes family in Derbyshire. It shows an impaled coat, the husband's being quartered. The supporter on the dexter side is a bearded gentleman in the stately robes proper to a man of position in the days of Queen Elizabeth. A cartouche tells us that this worthy is Francis Rodes. His *vis-à-vis*, if that expression may be used when both figures are heraldically "affronté," is a lady in the hoops and ruffles of the same period, the cartouche telling us that she is Elizabeth Sandford, who was spouse to Francis Rodes. Had the notion persisted, very valuable records would have resulted.

An intentionally sarcastic use of a badge as a supporter is to be seen in the "Wapenbock" (1334–1572) of Hynen, Gelre Herald. It records the alliance of many princes of Christendom under the French King against the Duke of Brabant, whose cognisance was a wild boar, and who is addressed as "Sire Sanglier." Gelre blazons the Duke's arms (quarterly: sable, a lion rampant or, armed gules, and argent, a lion rampant gules, forked tail, armed azure) on a tabard, which he fastens round the neck of a wild boar.

Gradually, however, the angels and nondescript beasts gave place to charges either taken from the shields themselves or suggesting descent or alliances. Edmond, Earl of Cornwall, son of Richard, Earl of Cornwall, elected King of the German Empire and styled King of the Romans, son of King John, used his father's arms, which he placed over an eagle displayed, the guige held in its beak. This eagle referred to the German honours. Much the same practice has long been carried out by the Kings of Prussia and the Emperors of Austria and Russia, whose single-headed eagle in the first case, and doubled-headed eagles in the other two, are charged with a shield on the breast. The Austrian and Russian Emperors, moreover, place many armorial shields on the open wings and spread-out tails. The eagle as a single supporter appears to have been common in Scotland between

1250 and 1400; sometimes a shield is placed on the breast between one on each wing.

Often supporters are merely adapted badges; hence we occasionally see inanimate objects, such as the swords of office formerly borne by Marmion of Scrivelsby, Hereditary Champions to the King of England; halberts; the tent poles of Dazell of Bins; and the more celebrated Pillars of Hercules of the Spanish monarchs (representing the Straits of Gibraltar); and the armillary sphere on which the explorer and sailor kings of Portugal placed their shields.

Derivation from badges is well shown by many royal supporters. With us Edward III is said to have used a golden lion and a silver falcon, and Richard II a white hart, gorged with an open crown of gold, and a white falcon; or two white harts; or two angels. As we have seen, there is actual evidence of the couchant hart sustaining the shield on its back, while non-armorial angels stand by. Coming to contemporary evidence we find Henry IV using, as prince two swans holding an ostrich feather in their beaks, as King, a golden lion of England and the white antelope of Bohun. Henry V, the lion (crowned) and antelope. Henry VI, gold lion and silver antelope; two antelopes; lion and heraldic tiger; the last sometimes making way for a panther charged with roundels of various colours. Edward IV, the golden lion of England and the black bull of Clare; two white lions of March. Henry V, the March lion and a white hart. Richard III, two white boars; or one of these with the gold lion of England. Henry VII, the red dragon of Cadwallader in pairs or in association with the white greyhound of Neville; the golden lion and red dragon; two silver greyhounds. Henry VIII, the red dragon and greyhound; two greyhounds; gold lion and red dragon; antelope and hart. Edward VI, golden lion and red dragon; golden lion and silver greyhound. Mary, a gold lion and golden dragon; a lion and greyhound; also the Apostolic eagle of her mother and her husband. Elizabeth followed her sister's example, except as regards the eagle, and like her father had an antelope and stag on her Exchequer Seal. In a splendid specimen of this monarch's bearings from a carving at Carhoys, Cornwall, the dexter supporter is a lion of England, the sinister an uncrowned dragon. They support the shield with their inner paws, while with their outer ones they clutch at scarves held by flying angels above, who support the royal crown over the shield. From the accession of James I the regulation supporters have been: dexter, the golden crowned lion guardant of England, and, sinister, the silver crowned unicorn of Scotland (which first appeared in the reign of James III).

TUDOR ROSE, WITH RED DRAGON OF WALES AND WHITE HOUND OF NEVIL, TOMB OF HENRY VII, WESTMINSTER ABBEY.

But there were variations on certain seals. Thus James I had on the Seal of Common Pleas a griffin and greyhound, an example followed by Charles II and George I. Charles I on his Exchequer Seal retained the antelope and stag of Henry VIII, and on his Session Seal for South Wales had a dragon and an heraldic antelope. James II on his Privy Seal for the Duchy of Lancaster had an odd arrangement of two greyhounds sejant addorsed, each holding an ostrich feather. It is to be noted that the consorts of our kings have usually used their paternal supporters, or one of these and a lion of England. This was done from at least the time of Margaret of Anjou, queen of Henry VI, the paternal supporters generally being placed on the sinister side of their impaled arms. Margaret of Anjou's father had two golden eagles, which he represented as crowned, but those adopted by his daughter in England have a plume of peacock's feathers on their heads. Elizabeth Widville, queen of Edward IV, had a silver greyhound, collared and chained or. Catherine

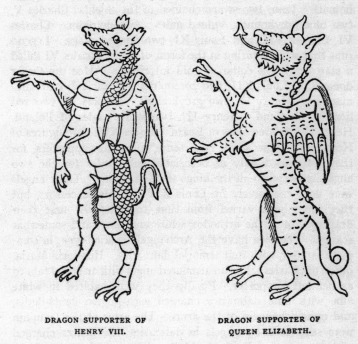

DRAGON SUPPORTER OF HENRY VIII.   DRAGON SUPPORTER OF QUEEN ELIZABETH.

of Arragon had an Apostolic eagle, sable, wings elevated, and crowned with a glory. Anne Boleyn, a silver griffin. Jane Seymour, a gold unicorn, collared and chained gules ; also a silver unicorn gorged with a wreath of white and red roses. Anne of Cleves, a black lion (of Juliers). Katherine Parr, an unclassified animal of the heraldic type, striped per bend of divers colours, gorged and chained. Anne of Denmark, a wild man. Henrietta Maria, an angel in armour, with the armorial tabard of France. Catherine of Braganza, a dragon.

Mary d'Este, a crowned eagle.   Queen Alexandra, a wild man.
Queen Mary, a stag.

French royal practice offers the same diversity.   Philippe
Auguste had two lions.   Louis VIII, the two wild boars of
Brittany.   Louis IX, two dragons.   Philippe III, two eagles.
Philippe V and Charles IV, two lions.   Philippe VI two greyhounds.   Jean, two swans chained to the shield.   Charles V,
two blue greyhounds, vulned gules ; two dolphins.   Charles
VI, Charles VII, and Louis XI, two winged stags.   Legend
runs that while hunting in the forest of Senlis Charles VI killed
a stag bearing a collar of gold inscribed : " Hoc me Cæsar
donavit."   Louis XII, two porcupines.   Francis I, two salamanders.   Henry II, two greyhounds.   Francis II, two red
lions of Scotland.   Henry III, two white eagles of Poland.
Henry IV, two red cows of Bearn.   Louis XIII, two figures of
Hercules.   These were, in a sense, personal supporters, for
they were used only as occasional substitutes for the two
angels common to all the kings since St. Louis.   These angels
were used exclusively by Louis XIV and his successors, but
they have been varied from time to time.   At first their
drapery was of the orthodox white and blue, and somewhat
scanty.   Then we have the Archangel Gabriel type, in complete armour, with rich armorial dalmatics.   Henrietta Maria,
queen of Charles I, had an armoured angel with armorial tabard
as her left supporter.   Finally they were habited in white
albs with blue dalmatics charged with golden fleurs-de-lis,
and upheld banners of the arms.   The arms of the Dauphin
were supported by angels in dalmatics, the dexter charged
with the arms of France, and the sinister with those of the
Dauphiné.   Princes of the Blood had angels in albs only.   A
fine example of a single angel supporter is given by Willement.
It shows a seated angel with outspread wings holding above
his aureoled head in his uplifted hands the shield of France.

Supporters in former days, and especially on the Continent,
were shown wearing capelines and volets (or small capes),
which were often armorial, or decorated with badges.   An
eccentric example is that of Aspremont, Lorraine ; the displayed eagle wears a long robe of state, charged with double-

headed eagles, and bears in front of it the armorial shield duly ensigned with crested helm. The eagle of Vivonne bears the shield on its breast and has its head within the crested helm. This enclosing of the heads of beast and bird supporters in crested helms was common in France and Germany, and was not unknown with us. Supporters both carry small shields and are themselves bearers of charges. Viscount Allendale's dexter supporter is a silver lion semé of red crescents (his arms are: gules, a lion rampant or between eight crescents gold). Baron Aberdare's two silver owls have collars with pendent shields charged with his arms. It is not quite clear what useful purpose this serves, as supporters are nowadays rarely used apart from the armorial shield, and therefore such external banners and escutcheons should be charged with other symbols. Baron Alington's two silver talbots are billety sable, and hold in their mouths red roses slipped vert.

Typical examples of supporters may now be given. As might be expected, military and naval exploits are well represented. We find warriors of all kinds, from the naked wild men armed with clubs, Roman soldiers, knights in armour, men-at-arms, to soldiers and sailors of our own days. The wild men are depicted as naked, wreathed about the temples and loins with verdure, and may carry uprooted trees as well as the more common clubs. Among the military type are the following: Lord Annesley has a Roman soldier in armour and a Moorish prince; while the Wards, Viscounts Bangor, have a Crusader and a chained Turkish prince. In keeping with their gibbeted naked man, the Earls of Carnwarth flank their shield with two Highland warriors in kirtles. These may be matched by Lord de Freyne's two ancient Irish warriors, dating back to the reign of Henry VII, when the family settled in Galway. Lord Napier of Magdala has a soldier of the Royal Engineers (early Victorian period) and a Sikh Sirdar. Barons Harris (granted to the hero of Seringapatam and of Mysore), a grenadier of the 73rd Regiment (of which he was Colonel) and a Malay, holding respectively a staff with a Union Jack flying over the banner of Tippoo Sahib, and the flag of the East India Company flying over Tippoo's banner, both staves wreathed with the French tricolour. The first Baron Keane, who distinguished himself in the first Afghan expedition, received an exceptional grant of supporters, these being a mounted Beloochee and a mounted Afghan. Baron Làwrence, an officer of the Guide Cavalry of the Pathan tribe and an officer of the irregular cavalry. The Pottingers, a China Mandarin and a Scinde soldier. Mackenzie of Seaforth, two Highland

SUPPORTER OF LORD
ARMSTRONG.

SUPPORTER OF LORD
WIMBORNE.

soldiers. Lord Roberts, a grenadier of the 92nd Regiment of Foot, and a Goorka soldier. Among the sailors, Lord Nelson has a tar in the dress of the eighteenth century. Lord Hotham also has two sailors of a later date, and Lord Fisher two able seamen of our own day. Lord Hood has a merman and a mermaid carrying respectively a trident and a hand mirror. The first Earl Camperdown was granted for supporters, dexter, an angel with celestial crown, resting on an anchor; sinister, a sailor holding up a blue banner, the staff wreathed with the Dutch flag. Viscount Bridport, Neptune armed with a trident and leaning on an anchor, and a sea lion with anchor. Lord Exmouth has for one of his supporters a man, the upper part naked, holding a broken chain and a cross, this commemorating the Admiral's successful attack on piratical Algiers, when he destroyed the fleet and arsenal and set free many Christian slaves. The Milnes have a

SUPPORTERS OF LORD ARMITSTEAD.

similar liberated slave for the dexter supporter; and for the other a sailor with cutlass and pistols. These were granted to Sir Alexander Milne as a reward for the valour of his father, Sir David Milne, second in command of the Exmouth expedition. Lord Aylmer, two sailors of George I. Lord Invercylde, as head of the famous shipbuilding firm of Burns, has two sailors of the Royal Navy, one resting his hand on an anchor, the other on a rudder. Among Colonial administrators we find Robert Palk, Baron Haldon, Governor

of Madras in 1763, with two Native Indians, naked, girt about
the loins and turbaned. Lord Seaton, at one time Governor-
General of Canada, a soldier of the 52nd (*temp*. battle of Water-
loo), and a Canadian Red Indian with tomahawk. Lord
Stanmore, a chief of the Fiji Islands and an Adiger of Ceylon.
Sir Hercules Robinson, Baron Rosmead, an ostrich and a
kangaroo. Lord Loch, a Chinese warrior and a Zulu with
assagais and shield ; he was with the Earl of Elgin's embassy
in China, and was taken prisoner ; subsequently he was High
Commissioner for South Africa. Exploring is commemorated
by the crocodiles and hippopotamus granted to the family of
Captain Speke, the African traveller. Literature is badly
enough represented, although we have Lord Burnham's
Clio, muse of History, and Hermes or Mercury the swift
messenger, appropriate enough for the proprietor of a great
daily newspaper ; and Lord Courtney of Penwyth's two
Doctors of Law of Cambridge. Law itself is by no means
so shy. Lord Aberdeen pairs his Earl in his robes with a
Doctor of Laws ; Scarlet, Barons Abinger, two angels of
Justice robed in blue and white carrying swords ; Gibson,
Barons Ashbourne, a figure of Mercury with sword reversed,
and blind Justice with sword erect and scales, both charged
with a shamrock on chest. Viscount Alverstone has two seals
collared, and with azure escutcheons pendent therefrom
charged with a silver swan. There are also many representatives of industry and commerce. Lord Wimborne has two
Tubal Cains with hammers resting on anvils. Lord Strathcona and Mount Royal had a railway navvy and a trooper
of Strathcona's horse. Lord Armitstead, a mechanic with a
cog-wheel and a carpenter with a hand-saw. Lord Armstrong,
two smiths, with sleeves rolled up, leather aprons, and sledge
hammers. Cubitt, Barons Ashcombe, a stonemason and a
carpenter. Sir David Graaf, a Boer farmer with rifle and a
miner with pick. Baron Cowdray, a diver and a Mexican
peon.

Landed interests and family alliances are responsible for
a large collection. Howison, of Scotland, held lands in co.
Ayr by service of holding the King's stirrup and presenting

him with a basin of water and a towel whenever he was in
the neighbourhood, and such service was duly rendered to
George IV. The grant is said to date back to James I of
Scotland, who when in the forests was attacked by robbers
and rescued by a farmer and his son, who brought their
sovereign a basin and towel and received in exchange the
grant of land. The family supporters are two peasants, one
with a flail and the other with a basin and towel. This
James was an unlucky body, to whom we owe another quaint
heraldic device. The Robertsons have a chained naked man
prostrate under the shield as sole supporter, who is said to
represent one of the king's murderers tracked down by the
trusty clansman. The only other similar position of a supporter in British practice I have noticed is the salamander
of Douglas. Sir George Mackenzie states that the first Earl
of Panmure adopted two greyhounds for his supporters
because he gained recognition from James IV when enter-
taining the king with sport over the moors of Monroben. In
1761 Sir Alexander Grant was licensed to bear as supporters
a Highlander and a naked negro, with cloth about the loins,
to commemorate his acquisition of a Highland estate and his
marriage with a Jamaican heiress. The two horses of the head
of the Antrobus family are those of the extinct barony of
Rutherford, whose estates were purchased by the newer peer.
Heathcote-Drummond-Willoughby have for their dexter supporter a grey friar habited proper, holding a crutch and
rosary (for the barony of Willoughby de Eresby), and, sinister, a wild man for Heathcote. Lord Ailesbury's two savages,
wreathed about the temples and loins vert, carry armorial
banners. Baron Charnwood has two roebucks supporting
banners of the arms of Thorpe, he having married an heiress.
This carrying of armorial banners by supporters is largely
indulged in by the Germans, among whom sometimes quite a
number of such banners are borne on each side of the shield.
Originally these all represented military fiefs in the possession
of the family, but later by extension alliances were also
recorded in the same way.

Heraldic practice in granting supporters during the

eighteenth and early part of the last century, was often deplorable. As an example of over particularising we may quote the official description of those of the Earls Amherst : supporters, dexter, a Canadian Indian of a copper colour, his exterior arm embowed holding an axe erect, proper, rings in his nose and ears, and bracelets on his arms and wrists argent, over his shoulders two buff belts in saltire, suspended from one his powder-horn on his right side and from the other his scalping knife on his left ; before him a short apron azure, tied round the waist with a belt gules, fimbriated or, on the legs blue gaiters, seamed gold, his ankles fettered together, and the chain, affixed to the bracelets on his exterior wrist proper ; sinister, a similar Indian, holding in his exterior hand a tomahawk, the lower end resting on his hip, and on the upper end a scalp proper.

The following were evidently adopted as " pièces parlantes," the first in execrable taste : Montagu-Douglas-Scott, Duke of Buccleuch and Queensberry, two female figures, habited from the waist downwards in blue kirtles gathered up at the knees, the arms and bosoms uncovered ; around the shoulders flowing mantles vert, suspended by the exterior hand ; girdles and sandals gules, and their heads adorned with a plume of three ostrich feathers argent. Seymour, Marquises of Hertford, two blackamoors, wreathed about the temples, or and sable, habited in short golden garments and in buskins, and girdled with feathers, holding shields charged respectively with a sun in splendour and a crescent. Hope, Marquises of Linlithgow, two female figures of Hope resting on anchors. Sir Alexander Hope, of Fifeshire, has the same supporters.

CHAPTER XXIII

COCKADES AND LIVERIES : THEIR USE AND ABUSE

ALTHOUGH immediately derived from the buttons and knots of ribbons which tied up the flaps of the old three-cornered and cocked hats, the cockade really has a more ancient and illustrious origin, as its name testifies. For it comes from the cock, that fighting bird whose comb suggested the headgear of barbarians, the helmet of the Roman legionaries coming down to us in the protective ridge at the back of helmets worn by our firemen and the City of London police. Both shape and colouring of cockade were also influenced by the coloured scarf or bunch of ribbons presented to a knight by his lady patroness before he entered the lists at a tournament, or went off to the wars. These colours were worn by a knight, his squires and pages.

On the Continent these little badges played a big part. They appear to have been introduced into the French army by Louis XIII. " Le Gentil " Bernard, Court poet to Louis XV, sings of

> " L'ornement galant et terrible
> Par qui, desormais invinsible,
> Je puis affronté les hasards."

Under Louis XVI they assumed immense political importance. On the dismissal of Neckar, his partisans assumed a black cockade, which was very widely worn as a direct contrast to the white one common to the royal servants and troops. Next Camille Desmoulins plucked leaves from a tree, and pinned them to his hat as a symbol of Hope, and it

259

was under this rallying badge that the Bastille was stormed and levelled to the ground, thus bringing into fashion a green cockade, to which presently the royal white was added. Then the National Guard, who had a cockade of blue and red as part of their uniform, and the populace adopted a tricolour cockade, red and blue being the heraldic colours of Paris, and white, that of the royal house. And in October 1789, the National Assembly decided that the tricolour cockade alone should be used. Lafayette told his brethren in the Assembly : " Messieurs, je vous apporte une cocarde qui fera le tour du monde " ; and Louis himself adopted it. Whether this Lafayette badge was the simple tricolour or one of the many fanciful designs introduced is not clear. Prudhomme, editor of the " Révolutions de Paris," however, tells us how he composed one which was accepted by the popular general, and this was to some extent armorial in character. The design shows France seated on a throne trampling underfoot title-deeds representing the privileges of nobility and clergy, holding in one hand the table of laws and in the other a bundle of lictors' rods, the axe being replaced by a club surmounted by a Phrygian cap. Pendent from the rods is a medallion of the King, and by his side is a shield bearing the Bourbon lilies. This design was printed in blue and red on a white background. But in secret royalists cherished the white, which gave rise to the introduction of the extremist red. This red at last ousted the tricolour, ruling during the Terror, and then making way for blue, white and red under the Consulate and the Empire, though a Napoleonic violet cockade became fashionable for a time. Under Louis XVIII and Charles X the white cockade again became the official badge, to be replaced once more by the tricolour under Louis Philippe, Napoleon III and the Third Republic. The red cockade made momentary reappearances during the revolutionary periods of 1848 and 1871.

In its modified form the cock's comb was represented by an aigrette pinned to the hat by a rosette and fan-like crest. In this form it was introduced among us by George I, who brought over with him the Hanoverian black cockade, and black it has remained ever since for the ordinary run of mortals. But of course the ordinary rosette and streamer cockade was known in England before that. On the expulsion of the Stuarts the dissatisfied Jacobites adopted a white cockade in contrast to the orange ones of Nassau, and the black of Hanover. It is a common fallacy that cockades should only be worn by servants of naval and military officers. As a matter of fact, its legitimate use extends much further, but as the law takes no cognisance of the subject, nor do the Heralds, there is considerable laxity displayed.

Etiquette recognises the cockade as a badge of service to the Sovereign, therefore it belongs to all holding direct office under the Crown, and should be worn by their servants. This is the view taken on the Continent, for all soldiers, sailors of every rank, and all uniformed civil servants, wear the small rosette cockade on the front of the cap or the side of the cocked hat, while domestics of Crown servants wear it in a modified form.

There are two forms of the cockade: the rosette and crested comb, usually assigned to the servants of those holding military rank, which include commissioned officers of the auxiliary services, Lord Lieutenants, and Deputy Lieutenants and others ; and the large plain rosette. This last has been particularly adopted by naval officers, and also by civil officials. Peers and Privy Councillors are members of the Court, and so are entitled to cockades, and it is very usual for widows of peers to adopt the rosette form.

The cockade is almost always black, and should be of crape when mourning is worn. For ordinary use very often the bow of tiny ribbon forming the centre of the rosette is made up of the livery colours. The coloured cockade is by the unwritten law of society a diplomatic badge, reserved for the servants of Ambassadors, members of embassies and by an allowable extension to Consuls. The colours used are the National colours. Thus the servants of the French Embassy wear cockades divided vertically into three, blue, white and red, with a blue fan and a red rosette with a white centre.

With us the cockade is always worn on the side of the

hat ; but on the Continent is usually placed in front on the undress livery cap. This method has been adopted with chauffeurs and footmen on motor-cars, if wearing caps. Official coloured cockades are worn on the Continent by members of the military, naval and uniformed civil services, as well as by the personal servitors of the royal houses and rulers, and, as we have seen, by servants of Ambassadors. In the following list of the most important, the first colour named appears on the dexter side in upright specimens :

Austria-Hungary : black and yellow.
Belgium : black, yellow and red.
Denmark : red, white and red.
France : blue, white and red.
Germany : (in rings from centre outwards) :
    red, white and black.
Baden : yellow, red, yellow.
Bavaria : white, blue, white.
Hesse : white, red, white.
Mecklenburg : red, yellow, blue.
Prussia : black, white, black.
Saxe-Weimar : yellow, green, blue.
Saxony : white, green, white.
Wurtemberg : black, red, black.
Greece : sky blue and white.
Holland : orange.
Italy : green, white and red.
Norway : red, white and blue.
Portugal : green and red.
Spain : red, yellow and red.
Sweden, blue and yellow.
Russia (oval, from centre outwards) :
    black, yellow and white.

Liveries give even more trouble than the cockade, because it is felt that a system should regulate these matters, yet there are so many exceptions to rules. While it may be laid down as a guiding principle that the livery colours are the chief tinctures of the armorial shield, and are those appearing on the crest wreath, now of six, three of metal and three of colour, there are numerous exceptions. This is natural, for the liveries, as the word implies, were something given, in fact, uniforms delivered by a sovereign or a feudal chief to his dependents, and these uniforms were of the donor's colours ; not necessarily those of his arms, but often those he displayed on his war or on his tourney banners. Therefore, in some of our old families we notice apparent anomalies due, either to the fact that they are using their tourney colours, or perhaps the colours of some long-forgotten overlord. For as Vulson de la Colombière observed even in his day, knights " bore helmet wreaths differing from the tinctures of their shields, composing them from the colours and liveries of their fair mistresses, or from those of the princes under whom they served, or even from the tinctures of arms belonging to their distinguished alliances."

Before entering upon a practical side of the question let us look a little more closely into its history. The word livery comes to us through the French *livrée* from the Low Latin *liberare*, to liberate or bestow, and is derived from the practice of Kings of the Carlovigian and Merovingian races to bestow on their officers and courtiers every eve of Noël and Assumption fine robes. Other courts and feudal chiefs followed the example thus given, because the advantage for a leader to have his followers in some sort of uniform which visibly associated them with his service was too evident to escape attention. Princes and feudal chiefs bestowed liveries as a token that they would maintain their followers either on the estates or by extending protection to them ; while the followers accepted liveries, wearing their patron's colours, to show that they were ready to support him and in return claimed his protection. Such liveries were not borne merely by menials, but by those in quite good stations, often living away from the actual domains of their lords. How this could be worked for good or evil is shown by that pious *ruse* adopted by Louis IX, who on the eve of Christmas made a most generous gift of liveries, not only to his immediate court, but to chosen men of mark. And they soon found that they were marked men, for the liveries bore the cross badge which dedicated them to the Crusade Louis was then meditating. Few dared attempt evasion. But what could be done by way of recruiting soldiers of the Cross for service against the Paynim, could be done by ambitious princes and nobles to further their own ends nearer home. With us the custom was early democratised, for when Edward II granted special privileges to Guilds, Confraternities and Mysteries, enacting that all citizens should become members of those regulating their trades, it naturally followed that sumptuary laws should be applied, every Guild and Mystery having its special colours and uniform. Hence arose the City Liveries, whose members alone could take part in civic governance. Thus all over the land there grew up a competition both in the bestowal and acceptance of liveries. Great rivalries arose, and owing to the ever-swelling retinue of clients who looked up to powerful noble houses, in opposition to the steadily advancing influence of artisan confraternities, faction fights constantly assumed dangerous proportions. Richard II in 1392 and 1396, Henry IV in 1411, and Edward IV in 1468 legislated against the abuses of livery and maintenance, the mischief of which had become particularly notable during the sanguinary fraternal strife of the Wars of the Roses. Ultimately the Statute of Livery and Maintenance of Henry VIII did away with the old practice of general bestowal of patron's colours, reserving the right to the Crown, and on a limited scale to the nobles, for only household servants could wear their lord's colours. It was then that some attempts were made to introduce regulations. As already stated, the task was a difficult one, for some livery colours had become hereditary. By a will dated 1550 it is evident that the black and white livery of the Lords Stourton had even then been long fixed, though the field of their arms is black and the principal charge is of gold.

It was probably so with a great many others. Yet early in the following century we find this curious state of affairs in connection with the influential house of Howard. According to Robert Treswell, Somerset Herald, Charles Howard, Earl of Nottingham (*obit* 1624), used for his livery colours an orange-tawny, with a braid of silver and blue ; while Doyle is our authority for the statement that Thomas Howard, Earl of Suffolk (*obit* 1626), used blue and dark green ; and Philip Howard, Earl of Arundel, who flourished about the same time, had for his livery colours red and yellow, with red, white and yellow plumes. Now, the field of the Howard arms is gules, and the principal charge argent, but those of the old extinct family of Arundel were gules and or. So while there is some explanation for the colours of Philip, Earl of Arundel, there is none for those of the Earls of Nottingham and Suffolk. Then Henry Algernon Percy, Earl of Northumberland (*obit* 1527), had for his livery colours russet, yellow and tawny, while the chief tinctures of his arms were azure and or. John Dudley, Duke of Northumberland (*obit* 1553), had a ceremonial standard of red damask, thereon a white lion ; but we are told that for his livery one half was black with gold embroidery, the other half black, white and red. While Edward de Hastings, Lord Hastings and Hungerford (*obit* 1506), had a ceremonial standard of " a lit blew and a sad," his descendant sported purple and blue ; and while George Hastings, Earl of Huntingdon (*obit* 1545), also chose purple and blue, the Earls Francis (*obit* 1560) and George (*obit* 1604) had blue for their livery colour. Then we find William Paulet, Marquis of Winchester, with a ceremonial standard of white charged with a golden falcon, while his livery colours were red and white, and his arms were : sable, three swords argent, garnished or, their points in pile. Other anomalies may be cited. The Wilsons of Crofton Hall have for the armorial colours sable and or, yet their liveries are dark blue with gold buttons, while the Hoziers (Barons of Newland) translate the colours of their chief, sable and or, into a black livery with silver buttons. Perhaps one more instance will suffice : the Berkeleys, whose servants wear an orange-tawny, have for their chief heraldic colours gules and argent.

Another cause for confusion arises from the unfortunate

fact that we cannot dress our servants for ordinary occasions in bright yellow, pure white, brilliant red or sky blue. So if a man's shield is gold and the chief charges red, he does not give his footman a yellow coat and a red waistcoat and breeches, but he translates yellow (or gold) into brown, and red into maroon, claret or chocolate. White (or silver) in the same way becomes a very light brown, or preferably some shade of grey, and azure is changed into a darker tint of blue. The proper colours, however—bright yellows, white, red and blue—are used for full-dress occasions.

In modern practice (though this is a matter of etiquette or convention, not of heraldic regulation) the rule is that the coat should be the colour of the field, and the waistcoat and trousers of the secondary colours. Frequently, however, for everyday use, the whole suit is made of the dominant colours, and the accessories, or what, speaking sartorially, we may call the trimmings (the cuffs and collar and the braiding or piping) of the secondary colour or colours. Very often when braid is employed, or piping of twisted cords, the two secondary colours are used. Or again, if it has been necessary to soften yellow into brown, or white into grey, the braid and cord may be plaited or twisted threads representing the true livery colours : say, gold and red, or silver and green. Then again when the braiding is wide it may be embroidered with some heraldic charge. This is frequently the case where the shield is adorned with an Ordinary, as when the chevron or bend forms a principal charge. An instance of this kind of thing is seen in the white braid ornamented with black spread eagles in the uniforms of the King of Prussia's servants. Chevrony, bendy, barry and paly woven braids are quite common. On the Continent an attempt has been made to give an idea of the character of the armorial bearings by the width, weaving and colour of the embroideries, extra wide representing ordinaries, medium sub-ordinaries, and narrow common charges. Striped waistcoats are often seen. The ground may be of the dominant livery colour with a thin stripe of the secondary tint ; or the stripes may be of equal width. The latter fashion is rarely adopted unless the field of the shield itself is parti-coloured, say, half of one colour and half of another, or striped in some form. Occasionally the waistcoat is treated on the same system as the braid : it is used to display the true livery colours where they have had to be modified in the coat and trousers.

Buttons should always correspond to the chief metal on the armorial shield ; a white metal representing silver, or white ; brass standing for gold, or yellow. Gold should always take precedence of silver, unless the field is of silver. It is allowable, however, to have the buttons covered with cloth, and this should invariably be the case when mourning is being worn.

A very common, but exceedingly bad mistake, is to adorn servants' buttons with the master's crest. This should never be done. The crest, as we have seen, is essentially something for the head of the family, denoting leadership, and should not be delegated to the servants. The proper adornment is the badge (if any), monogram, or coronet of any degree. But the crest may be converted into a badge by the simple process of removing it from its wreath, for then it loses its old knightly attributes, becoming merely an heraldic cognisance. It is also allowable, though not usual, to imprint the whole coat-of-arms, but without the crest, on the buttons.

Tartans are really the Scottish form of the old general livery. Diodorus Siculus speaks of the Gauls of Cæsar's days wearing vari-coloured garments. It is true that, as regards Scotland itself in early times, the ordinary run of folk appear to have worn costumes of one colour only, while chiefs had five colours and overlords six. But quite early we hear of the vari-coloured clothes. For instance, in a book entitled " Certayne Matters Concerning Scotland," issued in 1597, the author, speaking of the Highlanders, says that they " delight in marbled clothes especially that have long stripes of sundrie colours ; they love chiefly purple and blue." It seems quite clear that a settled policy of distinctive colouring of tartans had become adopted well before 1600, when these several compositions became not only peculiar to one clan, but common to all its members, from the eagle-plumed chief to the cottar's youngest bairn. Many of these tartans are pretty, and some quaint and others decidedly startling, for often there is a daring blend of brilliant coloured checks and stripes, giving a distinctive and outstanding character to each, as easy to recognise as an armorial shield, though in the mass quickly absorbed to the point of invisibility on the heather-clad hillside. Colour alone plays but a small part in the individuality of a tartan; it is the wonderfully complicated arrangement of checks small and large, stripes broad and thin which stamps the character of each. In the following notes on a few of the leading tartans it is only possible to indicate the dominant factors employed in their composition. Buchanan : a complicated arrangement of red, blue and green squares, with yellow and white stripes. Clan Cameron : a bright tartan of large red squares, with blue and black broad broken stripes and thin white stripes. Cameron of Erracht has a dark tartan of black, blue, green and red, with thin yellow stripes.* Campbell : dark pattern of blue squares with broad broken lines in green and black, and thin yellow stripes. The Campbells of Cawdor replace the yellow by thin blue and red stripes. Chisholm : a bright tartan of red squares, crossed by mixed green and blue broad bands and thin stripes of red and white. Cumming : another bright red squared pattern with green, mixed green and red broad bands, and thin white and green stripes. Farquharson : blue square crossed by dark blue lines, broad green stripes, within lines of red and yellow. Gordon : green and blue squares with broken black bands and thin yellow stripes. MacAlister : bright red ground crossed by groups of wide and narrow stripes of light blue, broken green and white. Mac-Donald : blue and green squares intersected by broad and narrow bands of broken black and red. MacLean of Ouart : bright red squares, smaller squares of light blue, crossed

* This is identical with the tartan of MacDonald of Glencoe, save that when it was chosen by Cameron of Erracht for the uniform of the Highland Regiment he was then (1793) raising, his wife (a Mac-Donald) gave her tartan, plus the yellow stripes still worn in the blend of the Cameron Highlanders, the 9th Regiment of the line.

by broad bands of broken black and blue, and thin yellow
lines. MacLeod: yellow ground, black squares, bands of
broken black and yellow, with narrow lines of yellow and red.
MacMillan: yellow ground with black bands of narrow red
lines. MacPherson, hunting tartan: grey and black bands
with a little blue and narrow red stripe; dress tartan: black
and white with narrow red stripe. Menzies: red ground with
white stripes. Rob Roy MacGregor: squares of red and
black, with squares of broken red and black. Stuart, Old:
green ground with a close pattern of blue, black and red
bands, both broken and plain colours; Hunting: green and
blue with black bands and narrow stripes of red and yellow;
Royal: bright red ground, with pattern of green, black and
blue, with white stripes; Dress: white ground with narrow
stripes of red and yellow. This last was an invention of
the Prince Consort.

ENGLISH ROYAL LIVERY COLOURS

Plantagenets to 1399, white and scarlet.
House of York, murrey and blue.
House of Lancaster, white and blue.
House of Tudor to 1603, white and green.

From the advent of the Stuarts the royal livery dress colours
have been gold and scarlet; undress, scarlet and blue. But
before coming to the British throne, William of Orange's
livery colours were blue and orange. It may be noted that
there is some evidence that in days prior to the coming south
of King James various members of the royal family had their
own individual livery colours. Mr. Fox-Davies conjectures
that the livery colour of Edward the Black Prince was black,
for his " shield of Peace," as it is named in the Prince's will,
is black with his badge of silver ostrich feathers. Then we
find the ostrich feather badge of Edward VI, when Prince
of Wales, shown on a rounded per pale sanguine and azure.
To this perhaps may be added the roundel per pale vert and
azure on which Catherine of Arragon placed her royal badge
of a bundle of arrows.

CHAPTER XXIV

ROYAL ARMS OF ENGLAND AND OF THE UNITED KINGDOM

ALTHOUGH much has been written about the armorial bearings of English kings before the Conquest, we have nothing solid to go upon until the reign of Richard I, except as regards one fact. In the long list of what we must hold to be the apocryphal arms of the Kings of England appear those of Edward the Confessor, which are described thus: azure, a cross patonce between five martlets or. Now, some such device was actually used by Edward, for we find on the reverse of different types of his coins a cross voided with a martlet, or possibly a dove, in each angle. Quite probably this was employed by the king as a kind of personal badge or emblem. Other semi-religious badges of a like nature were used by several of the earlier and later kings, but were not of a strictly heraldic character.

Tradition says that William I bore: gold, two lions passant guardant in pale on a red field. But there is no evidence of this on his banners or Great Seals. Nor have we anything to substantiate the assertion that Henry II added a third on his marriage with Eleanor of Aquitaine, whose paternal coat of Guyene was: gules, a lion passant guardant or. It is true that a seal of John Lackland, when Count of Montaigne, had on its obverse an effigy bearing a shield charged with two lions passant in pale. But this coat does not appear on the Great Seals. Richard I on his first Great Seal is seen on the obverse astride his charger, with a large shield on his arm, only half of which is visible. This shows a lion counter-rampant, which has caused the conjecture that at first he

270

used two lions combatant. On his second seal, however, we find the three lions passant guardant in pale, and ever since then the armorial bearings of the sovereigns of England have remained : gules, three lions passant guardant or, armed and langued azure. But while these lions " of England " have remained unchanged during all the past centuries, they have frequently been associated with other quarterings. The first change occurred under Edward III, who in 1340, in accordance with his policy of claiming the throne of France, added the golden lilies to his shield, which was borne quarterly thus : 1st and 4th, azure, semé of fleurs-de-lis or (for France Ancient); 2nd and 3rd, gules, with the three lions of England. Richard II adopted the practice of impaling the royal arms with the mythical coat of Edward the Confessor, placing these on the dexter side, with the quartered coat on the sinister. This was more or less of an unofficial act, for the impaled coat does not appear on the royal seals. Henry IV followed the lead of Charles VI of France, who adopted definitely the practice of reducing the number of fleurs-de-lis on the blue field to three. No further alteration occurred until the marriage of Queen Mary with Philip of Spain, when she occasionally impaled her husband's arms with her own, and sometimes bore them quartered with hers. These arms of Spain were very elaborate. They were : per pale, in chief quarterly ; 1st and 4th quarterly, Castile and Leon (1st and 2nd, gules, a castle or ; and 2nd and 3rd, argent, a lion rampant gules), 2nd and 3rd, Arragon impaling Sicily (or, four pallets, gules ; and argent, an eagle displayed sable). Enté en point Granada : argent, a pomegranate gules, slipped and seeded proper. In base : quarterly ; 1st, Austria Modern : gules, a fess argent ; 2nd, Burgundy Modern : azure, semé of fleurs-de-lis or, within a border gobony argent and gules ; 3rd, Burgundy Ancient ; bendy of six or and azure ; a border gules ; 4th, Brabant : sable, a lion rampant or. In a shield of pretence : Flanders impaling Tyrol : or, a lion rampant sable and argent, an eagle displayed gules, crowned and with the words " Klee Stengeln " on wings or. These arms appear on the dexter side on the Great Seal.

Queen Elizabeth bore the arms quarterly, France and England, but Willement gives an interesting example of an unusual marshalling. Three shields are placed under one crown and crest. They bear respectively England, France and Wales (quarterly, 1st and 4th, gules, a lion passant guardant : 2nd and 3rd, or, a lion passant guardant gules). These are the arms of North Wales. Those of South Wales were : gules, three lions passant regardant in pale cowé (with their tails between their legs) argent. These latter were used officially by Prince Edward, Earl of Chester, son of Edward IV, and by Edward V when Prince of Wales, and by Arthur Tudor, Prince of Wales.

With the coming of James there was a considerable change. The arms were borne : quarterly 1st, and 4th, France and England quarterly; 3rd, Scotland (or, a lion rampant gules, armed and langued azure, within a double tressure flory counter flory of the second); and 3rd, Ireland ; azure, a harp or, stringed argent. Charles I introduced no modification. As regards the arms of Ireland, it should be mentioned that a Commission appointed by Edward IV found them to be azure, three ancient crowns in pale or, within a border argent. These arms are the mythical arms of St. Edmund, but were undoubtedly associated with the sister island for some time ; they were assigned to Robert de Vere when created Duke of Ireland by Richard II, to be borne in his first quarter. But Henry VIII caused them to be abandoned, and substituted the present coat.

During the Commonwealth the royal arms were discarded and the following substituted : quarterly, 1st and 4th, argent, a cross gules (the banner of St. George, for England) : 2nd, azure, a saltire argent (the banner of St. Andrew, for Scotland) ; 3rd, azure, a harp or, stringed argent (for Ireland) ; in a shield of pretence, sable, a lion argent (for Cromwell).

Charles II and James II reverted to the practice of their father.

William and Mary impaled the arms of Nassau (azure, semé of billets, a lion rampant or) with those of France and

England quarterly. After Mary's death, the King bore France and England quarterly, and en surtout the arms of Nassau.

After the union with Scotland in 1707 Anne bore : quarterly, 1st and 4th, England impaled with Scotland ; 2nd, France ; 3rd, Ireland.

On the accession of George I the royal arms were borne thus : quarterly, England impaling Scotland ; France ; Ireland ; Hanover : tierced in pairle reversed ; 1st, gules, two lions passant guardant in pale or (for Brunswick) ; 2nd, or, semé of hearts gules, a lion rampant azure (for Luneburg) ; 3rd (in point), gules, a horse courant argent (for Westphalia) ; over all in an inescutcheon gules, the crown of Charlemagne, or (official badge as Hereditary Arch-Treasurer of the Holy Roman Empire).

After the Treaty of Amiens and the Union with Ireland in 1801, the arms of France were relinquished, and the coat marshalled thus : quarterly, 1st and 4th, England ; 2nd, Scotland ; 3rd, Ireland. Over all the Hanoverian escutcheon. This shield of pretence was at first ensigned with an Electoral bonnet, which was changed to a royal crown when Hanover was declared a Kingdom.

On the accession of Queen Victoria, the Hanoverian escutcheon was removed. Her consort, Prince Albert of Saxe-Coburg and Gotha, bore by special warrant : quarterly, 1st and 4th, the royal arms of Great Britain and Ireland differenced by a label argent, the centre point charged with a cross of St. George ; 2nd and 3rd, barry of ten or and sable, over all a crancelin, or coronet of rue in bend, vert. These arms of Saxony were borne in inescutcheons surtout by all the children and grandchildren of the Queen and Prince Consort, the bearings of the United Kingdom and Ireland being differenced by silver labels specially charged, as described in the chapter on " Differencing."

From an early date, certainly from the reign of Edward I, it has been the custom for the Queens to impale their paternal arms with those of England or Great Britain and Ireland, giving the latter bearings precedence.

The arms attributed to or really belonging to the earlier Queens are as follows : Matilda of Flanders, queen of William I, gyronny or and azure, an inescutcheon gules. Matilda of Scotland, first wife of Henry I, the arms of Scotland. Adelaide of Louvain, daughter of Godfrey, Duke of Brabant, his second wife, or, a lion rampant azure. The above are doubtful. Then Matilda, daughter of Eustace, Count of Bologne, wife of Stephen, or, three torteaux. Eleanor of Aquitaine, wife of Henry II, gules, a lion passant guardant or. Berengaria, daughter of Sancho IV of Navarre, wife of Richard I, Navarre Ancient : azure, a cross pommety argent (which is very doubtful). These arms are said to have been changed after the battle of Tolosa, when the King of Navarre broke through the chains surrounding the Moorish camp, and routed the Moslem hordes. Thereupon he, and a number of his knights, charged their shields with the Moorish chain defences. Isabel of Angoulême, wife of John, lozengy or and gules. Eleanor of Provence, wife of Henry III, or, four pallets and gules.

As stated, there are no actual records of any such marshalling. But we come to ascertained facts with Eleanor of Castile, wife of Edward I. On her seal her arms appear thus : quarterly, Castile and Leon, impaled with France and England quarterly, her paternal coat occupying the sinister side. Margaret of France, Edward's second wife, dimidiated England and France. Margaret of France, wife of Edward II : quarterly, 1st, England ; 2nd, France ; 3rd, Navarre Modern ; gules, a trellis work of chains in cross and saltire, connected by an annulet in the fess point, and a double orle of chains or ; 4th, Champagne : azure, a bend double cotised, each pair of cotices potent on the inner sides, or. It is a most irregular form of marshalling, conveying quite a wrong idea. Philippa, daughter of William of Hainault, Count of Holland, wife of Edward III, followed the above example, bearing : 1st and 4th, England, 3rd and 4th quarterly ; or a lion rampant sable (for Flanders) and barry paly or and gules (for Holland). Anne of Bohemia, wife of Richard II, impaled her coat with the impaled shield of her consort. Her arms were : quarterly,

1st and 4th, or, a double-headed eagle displayed sable (for the Empire) ; 2nd and 3rd, gules, a lion rampant queue fourché argent, crowned or (for Bohemia). Isabel of France, Richard's second wife, bore France Modern : azure, three fleurs-de-lis or. Henry IV's queen was Joan of Navarre, and she bore : quarterly, 1st and 4th, France Ancient, over all a bend compony argent and gules (for Evreux) ; 2nd and 3rd, Navarre Modern. Katherine of France, wife of Henry V, bore France Modern. Margaret of Anjou, daughter of Réné, Duke of Anjou and titular King of Jerusalem, wife of Henry VI, bore: quarterly of six ; 1st, barry gules and argent (for Hungary) ; 2nd, France Ancient, differenced with a label gules (for Naples) ; 3rd, argent, a cross potent between four plain crosses or (for Jerusalem) ; 4th, France Ancient, differenced with a border gules (for Anjou) ; 5th, azure, crusily fitchy, two barbels hauriant addorsed or (for Duchy of Bar) ; 6th, or, on a bend gules, three allerions or (for Lorraine). Elizabeth Widville, queen of Edward IV, bore : quarterly of six ; 1st, argent, a lion rampant double queue gules, crowned or (for Limburg) ; 2nd (quarterly), 1st and 4th, gules, an estoile of sixteen points argent (for Beaux) ; and 2nd and 3rd, France Ancient ; 3rd barry of ten argent and azure, over all a lion rampant gules (for Luxemburg) ; 4th, gules, three bendlets argent ; a chief per fess of the second and or, on the last a rose of the first (for Des Ursins) ; 5th, gules, three pellets vair, on a chief or, a label of three points azure (for Chatillon, Comte de St. Pol) ; 6th, argent, a fess and canton conjoined (for Widville). Anne Neville, wife of Richard III, bore : gules, a saltire argent, differenced by a label compony of the second and azure. Elizabeth of York, daughter of Edward IV, and wife of Henry VII, bore : quarterly, 1st, France and England quarterly, 2nd and 3rd, or, a cross gules (for De Burgh) ; 4th, barry of six or and azure, on a chief of the first two palets between two gyrons of the second, over all an inescutcheon argent (for Mortimer).

Now we come to that formidable group of marshallings connected with the wives of Henry VIII. Catherine of Arragon bore : quarterly, 1st and 4th, Castile and Leon

quarterly ; 2nd and 3rd, Arragon impaling Sicily ; enté en
point, Granada. Anne of Cleves, quarterly of five (placed
three and two) ; 1st, or, a lion rampant sable (for Julich) ;
2nd, gules, an escutcheon argent, over all an escarbuncle or
(for Cleves) ; 3rd, argent, a lion rampant gules, armed
azure (for Berg) ; 4th, or, a fess chequy argent and gules
(for Marck) ; 5th, argent, a chevron gules (for Rosenberg).
Anne Boleyn : quarterly of six : 1st, England, with a label
of three points (for Lancaster) ; 2nd, France Ancient, with
label of four points gules (for Angoulême) ; 3rd, gules, a lion
passant or (for Guyenne) ; 4th, quarterly, 1st and 4th, or, a
chief indented argent (for Butler), 2nd and 3rd, argent, a lion
rampant sable (for Rochfort) ; 5th, England, with a label
argent (for Brotherton) ; 6th, chequy or and azure (for
Warren). Jane Seymour : quarterly, 1st (of augmentation),
or, on a pile gules, between six fleurs-de-lis azure, three lions
of England ; 2nd, gules, a vol abaisé or (Seymour ancient) ;
3rd, vair (Beauchamp of Hacche) ; 4th, argent, three demi
lions rampant gules (Esturmi) ; 5th, per bend gules and
argent, three roses in.bend countercharged (Mac' William) ;
6th, argent, on a bend gules, three leopards' faces or (Cocker).
Catherine Howard : quarterly ; 1st (of augmentation),
azure, three fleurs-de-lis in pale or between two flaunches
ermine, on each a rose of England (Tudor rose) ; 2nd, Brotherton ; 3rd, gules, on a bend between six crosses crosslet fitchy
argent, the royal shield of Scotland, but differenced thus : a
demi lion pierced with an arrow through the mouth (for
Howard) ; 4th (of augmentation) : azure, two lions passant
guardant or, on edge of the escutcheon charged with four
demi fleurs-de-lis of France. Catherine Parr : quarterly, 1st
(of augmentation), on a pile of gules between six roses of
Lancaster, three roses of York, all barbed and seeded or ;
2nd, argent, two bars azure, a border engrailed sable (Parr) ;
3rd, or, three bowgets, sable (Ros of Kendal) ; 4th, vair,
argent and azure, a fess gules (Marmion) ; 5th, azure, three
chevronels interlaced in base, a chief or (Fitzhugh) ; 6th,
vert, three stags at gaze or (Green).
    Anne of Denmark, wife of James I, bore : quarterly, separ-

ated by the cross of the Dannebrog (a plain cross argent,
fimbriated gules), 1st, or, semée of hearts gules, three lions
passant guardant crowned azure (for Denmark) ; 2nd, gules,
a lion rampant crowned or, holding the Scandinavian broad
axe with curved handle, argent (for Norway) ; 3rd, azure,
three open crowns or (for Sweden) ; 4th, or, in chief a lion
passant azure, in base nine hearts in two rows gules (for
Gothland) ; on a champagne in base gules a wyvern, wings
expanded or (for Vandalia) ; on the centre of the cross a
quartered shield : 1st, or, two lions passant in pale azure
(for Schleswig) ; 2nd, gules, an escutcheon per fess argent
and of the field, between three nails en pairle, alternating with
as many demi nettle leaves, all of the second (for Holstein) ;
3rd, gules, a swan, wings expanded argent, gorged with an
open crown or (Stormarn) ; 4th, gules, a knight armed at
all points or, and mounted on a horse saliant argent (for
Ditmarschen); en surtout, per pale : two bars gules (Oldenburg) ; azure, a long cross or (for Delmenhorst).

Henrietta Maria, queen of Charles I, bore France Modern
and Navarre impaled.

Catherine of Braganza, wife of Charles II, bore : argent,
five shields azure, each charged with five bezants in cross,
within a border gules, charged with an orle of castles or.

Mary d'Este, daughter of the Duke of Modena, wife of
James II, bore : quarterly, 1st and 4th, azure, an eagle displayed argent, crowned or (for Este of Modena) ; 2nd and
3rd, azure, three fleurs-de-lis within a plain border of or and
gules indented in to each other (for Duchy of Ferrara).

Sophia Dorothia of Brunswick-Luneburg, wife of George I,
bore : gules, two lions passant or (for Brunswick), impaling,
or, semé of hearts gules, a lion rampant azure (for Luneburg).

Caroline of Brandenburg-Anspach, wife of George II, bore
an extremely complicated coat, of which the following
marshalling is considered to be the most correct. Quarterly
of fifteen : 1st, argent, an eagle displayed gules, " Klee
Stengeln " on wings or (for Brandenburg) ; 2nd, per fess gules
and argent (for Madgeburg) ; 3rd, argent, an eagle displayed
sable, armed gules, crowned or (for Prussia) ; 4th, azure, a

griffin segreant gules, crowned or (for Stettin) ; 5th, argent, a griffin segreant gules (for Pommern) ; 6th, or, a griffin segreant sable (for Cassuben) ; 7th argent, a griffin segreant bendy gules and vert (for Wenden) ; 8th, argent, an eagle displayed sable (for Crossen) ; 9th, argent, an eagle displayed sable, on its breast a crescent of the field (for Schwiebus) ; 10th, per pale argent and gules (for Halberstadt) ; 11th, gules, two keys in saltire, argent (for Minden) ; 12th, or, a lion rampant sable, crowned of the field, within a border compony argent and gules (for Nurnberg) ; 13th, gules, a cross ancre argent (for Camin) ; 14th, quarterly, argent and sable (for Hohenzollern) ; 15th, gules plain (for Regalien).

Charlotte Sophia of Mecklenburg-Strelitz, wife of George III, quarterly of six: 1st, or, an ox's head caboshed sable, ducally crowned gules, armed and buckled argent (for Mecklenburg) ; 2nd, azure, a griffin segreant or (for Rostock) ; 3rd, per fess azure and vert, in chief a griffin segreant or ; the base bordered argent (for Principality of Schwerin) ; 4th, gules, a cross couped patée argent (for Ratzeburg) ; 5th, gules, an arm embowed in armour issuant from clouds in the sinister flank, the hand holding a gem ring proper ; a scarf azure, tied at the elbow (for county of Stargard) ; 6th, or, an ox's head in profile sable, horned argent, ducally crowned gules (for Wenden). Over all an escutcheon of Schwerin County : per fess gules and or.

Caroline of Brunswick-Luneburg, wife of George IV, quarterly of twelve : 1st, Luneburg ; 2nd, Brunswick ; 3rd, azure, a lion rampant argent, crowned or (for Eberstein) ; 4th, gules within a border compony argent and azure, a lion rampant or (for Homburg) ; 5th, gules, a horse saliant gules (Lower Saxony) ; 6th, per fess (1st) gules, a lion passant or, (2nd) or, three bars gules (for Lauterburg) ; 7th, quarterly, 1st and 4th, or, two bears' paws addorsed sable (Hoja), 2nd and 3rd, per fess, in chief, barry of four gules and argent, in base, gyrony of eight argent and azure (Bruckhausen) ; 8th, or, a lion rampant gules, crowned gold (impaled with 11th) ; 9th, chequy argent and gules (for Hohenstein) ; 10th, argent, a stag trippant argent (for Klettenberg) ; 11th, azure, an eagle displayed argent (impaled with 8th for Diepholz); 12th, argent, a horn in bend gules, and another in bend sinister sable (for Regenstein and Blankenberg).

Adelaide of Saxe-Meiningen, wife of William IV: quarterly of nineteen: 1st, azure, a lion rampant, barry argent and gules, crowned or (for Thuringia); 2nd, Cleves; 3rd, Juliers; 4th, or, a lion rampant sable, crowned gules (for Meissen); 5th, Saxony; 6th, Berg; 7th, gules, an eagle displayed or (for Westphalia); 8th, or, two palets azure (for Landsberg); 9th, sable, an eagle displayed or (for Palatinate of Thuringia); 10th, or, semé of hearts gules, a lion rampant sable, crowned gules (for Weimar); 11th, argent, three bars azure (for Eisenberg); 12th, azure, a lion rampant or (for Pleissen); 13th, argent, a rose gules, barbed seeded or (for Altenburg); 14th, Regalien; 15th, argent, three nenuphar leaves gules (Brehna); 16th, Marck; 17th, gules, a column argent, the capital and base or (for Anhalt); 18th, or on a mount vert a hen sable, wattled gules (for Henneberg); 19th, argent, three chevrons gules (for Ravensberg).

Queen Alexandra, daughter of King Christian of Denmark, and wife of Edward VII. Quarterly, separated by the Cross of Dannenbrog: 1st, Denmark; 2nd, Schleswig; 3rd, per fess, in chief Sweden, in base gules, a stock fish argent, crowned or (for Iceland), impaling azure, a buck passant argent (for Faroë Islands), and azure, a polar bear rampant argent (for Greenland); 4th, per fess, in chief Gothland, in base Vandalia. On a shield of pretence: 1st, Holstein; 2nd, Stormerk; 3rd, Ditsmarchen: 4th, gules, a horse's head couped argent (for Lauenburgh). Over all: Oldenburgh impaling Delmenhorst.

Queen Mary, daughter of Princess Mary of Cambridge and the Duke of Teck, wife of King George V, quarterly: 1st and 4th, the royal arms as borne by George III, differenced by a label of three points argent, the centre point charged with a St. George's cross, and each of the other points within two hearts gules (for Cambridge); 2nd and 3rd, or, three stags' attires fessways in pale, the points of each attire to the sinister sable, impaling or, three lions passant in pale sable, langued gules, the dexter forepaws of the last; over all an inescutcheon paly bendy sinister sable and or (for Teck).

By a Royal Warrant the arms of the Prince of Wales were established thus : quarterly, 1st and 4th, England ; 3rd, Scotland ; and 4th, Ireland; differenced by a label of three points argent ; and en surtout on an escutcheon of pretence quarterly : or and gules four lions passant guardant counterchanged (for Wales). Crest : on a coronet of the Heir Apparent a lion statant guardant or, crowned with the like coronet, and differenced with a label three points argent. Badges : a plume of three ostrich feathers argent, enfiled by a coronet of fleurs-de-lis and crosses patée and motto " Ich Dien " (for the Heir Apparent) ; on a mount vert a dragon passant, wings elevated gules (for Wales), differenced with a label of three points argent.

The Royal crest is a golden crowned lion statant guardant on an Imperial crown. It made its first appearance on the Great Seal of Edward III. The crest of Scotland is a lion sejant erect affronté gules, crowned or, holding in the dexter paw a sword, and in the sinister a sceptre, both proper. For Ireland : a tower triple-towered or, from the port a hart springing argent, attired and unguled gold. The supporters have already been dealt with in another chapter.

The Royal mottoes are : " Dieu et mon droit " (in use since the days of Henry VI, if not earlier) and " Honi soit qui mal y pense " placed on the garter encircling the shield.

Merely by way of curiosity the mythic arms of the early British and English kings are given here.

According to Sir William Segar, King Brutus who, it seems, reigned over England 1,000 B.C., bore : " or, a lion passant guardant, gule." but in a collection of banners at the Heralds' College this is quartered with azure, three crowns bendwise or. While the equally nebulous King Arthur is given quarterly, 1st and 4th, vert, a cross argent, and in cantel the figure of Virgin and Child ; 2nd and 3rd, gules, three crowns in pale or. Gerald Leigh, a Herald of the reign of Queen Elizabeth, gives the following as the arms of Egbert the Great, who flourished in the early part of the ninth century: "Azure, a cross patonce, or." Ethelwulf is given the same arms as Egbert. Ethelbold: "Azure, a cross potent fitchy, or." Ethelbert, same as his predecessor. Guillim states that King Ethelred I bore his shield emblazoned: "Azure, a cross potent fitchy, or." Alfred the Great: "Chequy or and purple, on a chief, sable, a lion passant guardant of the first." Other writers, however, say he bore: "Barry of five gule and or, a pile counterchanged." Edward the Elder: "Azure a cross patonce between four martlets, or." Other writers substitute "five crowns" for the martlets. Athelstan: "Per saltire, gule, and azure, on a mound a cross boton, or." Some writers omit the mound, and "Crown" the cross. Edmund: "Azure, three crowns, each transfixed with two arrows saltiswize, or." Edred: "Azure, a cross patée between four martlets." Edwy, same as Edmund. Edgar: "Azure, a cross patonce between four martlets, or." Edward the Martyr: "Azure, a cross patonce. between four crowns, or." Ethelred II, same as Edgar. Edmond Ironside: "Azure, a cross patonce, or." Canute the Great: "Or, a cross gule, in the first and fourth quarters semée of hearts, gule, two lions passant guardant, azure; second and third quarters, a lion rampant, gule, supporting a battleaxe argent: upon an escutcheon of pretence, azure, three crowns, or." Harold Harefoot: "Or, on a cross patée, a lion passant guardant, or." Hardicanute is said to have borne either the same arms as Canute, or "Argent, a raven proper." The arms assigned to Edward the Confessor are: "Azure, a cross patonce between five martlets, or." Harold II is supposed to have borne: "Gule, crusily, two bars between six leopards' faces, all or."

CHAPTER XXV

ARMS OF THE OVERSEAS DOMINIONS AND COLONIES

MOST of the older British Possessions over the seas employed arms or special ensigns on their official seals, and in later times the younger Colonies were assigned particular badges, to be followed in most cases by regular grants of arms.

Among the first of these were the armorial bearings granted to the great trading companies, like the Levant Merchants, the East India Company, the Hudson Bay Company, and other such corporations which were given viceregal powers within specified dominions. But some of our possessions owned armorial coats even more ancient than these sixteenth-century grants; for instance, Malta and Gibraltar. Malta bears: per pale argent and gules, a cross of eight points silver, which is the badge of the Knights Hospitallers of St. John of Jerusalem, otherwise called the Knights of Malta, on a shield of their colours. Gibraltar bears: gules, a castle of three towers argent on a mount vert, from the open port a key pendent from a chain or.

The Commonwealth of Australia bears: quarterly of six: 1st, argent, a cross gules charged with a lion passant guardant between, on each limb an estoille of eight points or; 2nd, azure, five estoilles, one of eight, two of seven, one of six and one of five points (representing the Constellation of the Southern Cross), ensigned with a royal crown; 3rd, of first, a Maltese cross of the fourth surmounted by the Imperial crown; 4th, of the third, on a perch wreathed vert and gules an

Australian piping shrike displayed proper (black and white) ;
5th, gold, a swan naiant to the sinister sable ; 6th, of the first,
a lion passant of the second ; the whole within a border ermine.
For crest, a seven-pointed star or. Supporters, dexter, a
kangaroo ; sinister, an emu. The whole composition surrounded by branches of the wattle tree (mimosa) vert fleuri or.

The States within the Commonwealth have their individual
arms or badges. New South Wales : azure, a cross argent,
voied gules (otherwise a cross gules fimbriated argent, which
is the Cross of St. George of England) and on each limb a
star of eight points or ; in the 1st and 4th quarters a
fleece of the last banded by the second ; 3rd and 4th, a
garb or. Crest, a rising demi sun or, each ray tagged
with a flame gules. Supporters, dexter, a lion rampant or ;
sinister, a kangaroo or. Formerly New South Wales had an
unofficial coat, quarterly, 1st, gules, a fleece or ; 2nd, vert, a
sailing ship on the waves proper ; 3rd, vert, a barrel and
ingots or ; 4th, azure, a garb, gold. Victoria : azure, five
stars argent, as the Constellation of the Southern Cross.
Crest, a demi kangaroo proper, holding in its paws an Imperial
crown or. Supporters, dexter, a female figure of Peace,
vested argent, cloaked azure, wreathed round the temples
with a chaplet of laurels and holding in her hand a branch
of olive proper ; sinister, a female figure of Prosperity, vested
argent, cloaked azure, wreathed round the temple with a
chaplet of corn, or, supporting a cornucopia of fruit and
cereals. Queensland : per fess, the chief or, the base per
pale sable and gules, in chief a bull's head caboshed in profile
muzzled, and a merino ram's head respecting each other argent ;
in dexter base a garb gold, in sinister on a mount vert, a pile
of quartz argent, issuant therefrom a pyramid of gold, in
front of mount a spade surmounted by a pick saltirewise
proper. Crest, on a mount vert a Maltese cross azure surmounted by an Imperial crown proper, between two sugar
canes vert. South Australia uses a pictorial coat by way of
badge, showing cliffs by the sea with a naked aborigine armed
with a spear, seated, and Britannia leaning on a shield of the
United Kingdom, advancing towards him. Western Australia :

or, a swan naiant to sinister, sable. Tasmania: or, a lion passant guardant gules. Fiji: argent, a cross gules, between three sugar canes couped, a cocoa-nut palm couped, a dove volant holding an olive branch in its beak, and a bunch of bananas, all proper; on a chief of the second a lion passant guardant crowned or, holding between the paws a cocoanut pod. Crest, a Fijian canoe with outrigger and sail. Supporters, dexter, a Fijian native affronté, round his waist a tapa sulu (kilt of mulberry tree bark cloth), or and sable, holding a barbed spear, all proper; sinister, a like native holding a pineapple club.

The Dominion of New Zealand: quarterly, azure and gules, on a pale argent three lymphads sable, in the first quarter four stars in cross of silver, each surmounted by a star of the second (disposed to represent the Constellation of the Southern Cross); 2nd, a fleece; 3rd, a garb; 4th, two mining hammers in saltire, all or. Crest, a demi lion rampant guardant, or, supporting a flagstaff with the Union flag. Supporters, dexter, a female figure proper, vested argent, supporting a staff with the flag of the Dominion of New Zealand; sinister, a Maori Rangatire (chieftain) vested proper, holding a taiahia (native halbert) all proper. (He is vested in a kilt of bark cloth, barry argent and sable, with a cloak about his left shoulder, and two white plumes in his hair.)

BRITISH COLUMBIA.

For the Dominion of Canada, the arms of Ontario, Quebec, Nova Scotia and New Brunswick are borne quarterly on one shield. The arms of the Provinces are: Ontario: vert, a sprig of three leaves of maple leaf or, veined gules; a chief of St. George (argent, a cross gules). Crest, a bear passant sable. Supporters, dexter, a moose; sinister a deer.
Quebec: or, on a fess gules, a lion passant guardant gold, be-

tween two fleurs-de-lis azure, and a maple leaf vert. Nova
Scotia : or, on a fess wavy azure a salmon naiant argent, between three thistles proper. New Brunswick : or, a lymphad
with oars in action proper, with sail set and flag flying gules, on
a sea in base azure ; on a chief gules a lion passant guardant
or. Manitoba : vert, a bison passant on a mount in base proper ;
a chief of St. George. Before this official grant was made,
Manitoba bore : vert, three garbs in fess or ; a chief per pale,
dexter the Union Badge of 1707 (a combination of the crosses

| ONTARIO. | QUEBEC. | NOVA SCOTIA. | NEW BRUNSWICK. |

| MANITOBA. | PRINCE EDWARD'S ISLAND. | ALBERTA. | SASKATCHEWAN. |

of St. George and St. Andrew), and azure, three fleurs-de-lis
or. Prince Edward's Island : argent, two trees on an island
vert ; on a chief gules a lion passant guardant or. British
Columbia : argent, three bars wavy azure ; over all from
base point a demi sun in splendour or ; in chief the Union
Badge (or Union Jack) with an ancient crown in the centre
or. Alberta : azure, in front of a range of snow mountains
proper, a range of hills vert, in base a wheat field surrounded
by a prairie proper ; a chief of St. George. Saskatchewan :
vert, three garbs in fess or ; on a chief or, a lion passant
guardant gules.

UNION OF SOUTH AFRICA.

CAPE TOWN AND COLONY.

RHODESIA.

The Union of South Africa, quarterly: gules, a female figure of Hope resting the dexter arm upon a rock and supporting with the sinister hand an anchor argent; 2nd, or, two black wildebeesten in full course at random proper; 3rd, or, upon an island an orange tree vert, fructed proper; 4th, vert, a trek waggon argent. Crest, a lion passant guardant gules, supporting with the dexter paw four staves erect, alternately argent and azure, banded or. Supporters, dexter, a springbok; sinister, an oryx (gemsbok), both proper. The Cape of Good Hope: gules, a lion rampant between three annulets or; on a chief argent as many hurts, each charged with a fleur-de-lis gold. Crest, the figure of Hope, vested azure, her dexter hand on a rock, and her sinister hand supporting an anchor sable, cabled proper. Supporters, dexter, a gnu; sinister, an oryx, both proper. Natal: azure, in front of mountains, on a plain two black wildebeesten in full course at random, all proper. Orange River Colony: argent, on a mount a springbok; on a chief azure, the Imperial crown, all proper. Transvaal in the old Colonial days bore: per pale, azure a cross gules, fimbriated argent, and per pale vert, and tiercy per fess gules, argent and azure. Cyprus has been given as badge a white disc with two lions passant guardant gules; but the arms of the old Kingdom were: argent, a lion double queued rampant gules, crinned or; and of the ancient See, quarterly, 1st and 2nd argent, a cross botony gules, and 3rd and 4th gules, three suns in splendour, or.

Jamaica: argent, a cross gules, thereon five pineapples or. Crest, a crocodile on a log, proper. Supporters, dexter, a West Indian native woman proper, crined or, girt about the waist with feathers alternately gules and argent, holding a basket of fruit, the head wreathed with a band azure rising therefrom a feather gold; sinister, a West Indian native man proper, girt about the waist with the feathers, holding in his hand a bow or, the head wreathed with a band azure, rising therefrom a circlet of feathers alternately gules and argent.

Mauritius: quarterly, azure and or; in 1st quarter a lymphad gold, oars in action, the sails furled; 2nd, three palm trees eradicated vert; 3rd, a key in pale, wards downwards, gules; 4th, a pile rising from the base and in chief a star argent. Supporters, dexter, a dodo per bend sinister embattled gules and argent; sinister, a sambar deer per bend embattled argent and gules; each support a sugar cane erect, proper.

Ceylon: argent, on a mount vert between a grove of eight coconut palms and mountains in perspective, an elephant affronté, all proper.

British Honduras: tiercy, per pale and per chevron; 1st, argent, a squaring axe, in bend sinister, surmounted by a paddle in bend sable; 2nd, a beating axe in bend surmounted by a sword in bend sinister argent; 3rd, azure, on a sea in base proper, a three-masted ship with sails silver and flags gules; in a canton the Union Badge. Crest, a mahogany tree proper. Supporters, two negroes proper, breeches argent, the dexter with an axe over his shoulder, the sinister with a paddle.

Exceedingly unheraldic grants have also been made to the Leeward Islands, Bermudas and St. Vincent.

CHAPTER XXVI

STANDARDS, BANNERS AND FLAGS

FLAGS and banners of all kinds owed their origin to the standards, which were essentially martial in character. The earliest form of standards of which records have come down to us are those of Egypt, where every territorial district had its particular standard, used both as a rallying-point for its military levies, and as a veritable cognisance indicating the district in all hieroglyphic inscriptions. These standards were long staves with cross-bars at their top, supporting a number of badges, including the totem-like animal, local gods and conventional figures. Assyrian standards were constructed much on the same lines. We are told that the oldest Roman standard was a bundle of hay tied to a pole, suggestive enough of the necessity for preparing war chargers, and thus linking us up with the Scythian and Arab horse-tail standards, still retained by the Turkish Pashas. The more formal Roman standards were also of the Egyptian type, long poles, with short cross-bar, supporting a series of discs and rings, with figures of animals, almost invariably the open right hand (the sword hand held up in sign of command), and later portraits. Some of these had pendent badges, also the cross-bar was flattened and used as a cartouche for inscriptions. Pliny tells us that Gracius Marius, Consul, first ordained the use of eagle standards for legions, though they had been carried by some long before his time. For cavalry the vexillum was used, and this was a veritable banner, being a square piece of cloth, suitably decorated, and supported by cords from a cross piece at right angles from the pole, in the style of that gonfanon. Later came the labarum, or

Imperial standard, of purple silk, bearing badges and fringed with gold. It was flown both like the gonfanon and also like our flags. Constantine placed the monogram of Christ at the top of his Imperial standard pole, and thus gave rise to a long list of cross and crucifix standards. Those in Italy were substantial constructions, carried to battle in a special chariot, the carroccio, just as the Saracens placed their red banners on an ox-waggon.

Constantine's labarum naturally found a resting-place in the church when not required, and this gave rise to gonfanons set up by every parish church and ecclesiastical establishment. The famous Oriflamme of France carried by Clovis in 507 against Alaric, and by Charlemagne against the Saracens was reputed to be the cloak which St. Martin, the Roman warrior martyr, divided with a naked beggar, and was kept first at the Abbey of Marmoutiers and then at the Abbey of St. Denis. So far was this church banner practice adopted that we find Charles the Bald in his capitularies of 855 directing his lieutenants in the provinces to see to it that each bishop, each abbot and abbess should cause their armed retainers to march under their banners to reinforce the royal army. Again, in 1110 Louis le Gros ordered all towns to levy armed forces, to march to war with their parish priest under the church banners.

William of Normandy gathered his forces for the invasion of England under a white consecrated banner sent to him by the Pope. We do not see this on the Bayeux tapestry, but many flags of divers sizes and shapes are shown. Some are small squares, usually ending in three or four short spikes, and charged with coloured bars, roundels and other figures. Others are triangular, and some are streamers. At this period large square banners, with or without streamers from the lower end, and also those ending in swallow-tails, were in use.

DRAGON STANDARD FROM BAYEUX TAPESTRY.

At our Battle of the Standard, fought at Northallerton in 1138, the Scots were attacked by the English, who rallied round a carriage whereon was an altar, over which floated consecrated banners.   Later our national banners were those of St. George—white with a red cross ; and of St. Edmund— blue with three golden crowns ; St. Edward the Confessor— blue, with a cross flory between five martlets of gold ; and a red flag bearing the triangle of the Holy Trinity.   It is not until the battle of Agincourt that we hear of the great banner with the royal arms.   But certainly armorial banners were flown earlier than that.   It was about 1250 that knights banneret and the nobility fought under large square flags, under which they gathered their followers and vassals.   In feudal language they held " fiefs en bannières," commanding lesser knights who gathered a few armed squires and vassals from smaller fiefs and fought under pennons.   Menestrier tells us that a knight bachelor having won his spurs before the enemy, and having possession of sufficient land to maintain a given number of horse or foot men-at-arms, gathered his following and went to war with his pennon.   On the field of battle he declared to the king, prince or royal lieutenant in command his ability to rally the required number of men. Thereupon the commander of the forces, having found sponsors ready to vouch for the volunteer, took his pennon and, cutting off the tails, returned it to the owner as a square banner, under which he was told to lead his men loyally.   Froissart gives an account of how the Black Prince elevated Sir John Chandos to a knight banneretship at the battle of Navarette. The number of armed men to be provided by a " fief en ban- nière " varied.   It was over sixty in France, somewhat less in England, and only twenty-five in Flanders.   Some of the great noble houses of the Continent, especially in France, still blazon their arms on square " banner shields."

A banner was large, square, or nearly so, and blazoned with the arms.   It is an error to talk as one does of the Royal Standard.   For the standard was square near the staff, long, tapering slightly with split, rounded ends.   With us it bore the banner of St. George near the staff, then was parti-coloured, " the colours " of the owner blazoned with the " beasts," badges, charges from his arms or others showing alliances, and his motto. The gonfanon was square, but pendent by a cross-bar and cords at right angles from the staff, and was usually of an ecclesiastical nature. The guidon, or more properly guidehomme, was a small standard with one point. The ancient, a small guidon. The pennon was half the size of the guidon, decorated with the badge and motto only, and had two or more tails or points. The pendant or pennant was the ship's guidehomme. The pennoncelle, or pencil, a small pennon on a lance decorated with heraldic devices, was not split. They were used at funerals and other ceremonies for heraldic display. The pavon was a triangle, horizontal on its lower side. The banderolle, a long narrow flag, usually bearing the St. George's cross at the upper end, flown beneath the armorial banner. A vane was a small flag.

The King's standard to be set before his tent was to be eleven yards long ; that to be borne in battle eight or nine yards. A duke's, seven yards. A marquis's and an earl's, six yards long. A viscount's and a baron's, five yards, A knight's, four yards. Every standard and guidehomme was to have " in chiefe the Crosse of St. George, the beast or crest with his devyse and word, and to be slitt at the end."

They were quite gorgeous affairs and were displayed with great lavishness, not only in warfare and at tournaments, but at all pageants, ceremonials and funerals ; for they conveyed not only the status and family alliances, but even the personal idiosyncrasies of the owners.

Mention has been made of religious banners. In England of modern days the ecclesiastical flag is formed of the banner of St. George next the staff, impaled with the arms of the diocese in the fly.

We already have a Flag of Mercy in the red cross of Geneva on a white ground (identical with the banner of St. George) used by both military and civilian ambulances. But we still await a Peace Flag ; yet one was actually designed by the Kaiser Wilhelm. It came about in this way. At the Peace Congress held at Monaco in 1902 a proposal for a World's

Peace Flag was raised, but not settled. This the Prince of Monaco told the Kaiser at a dinner party on board the *Hohenzollern* at Kiel. Thereupon the Emperor drew a device consisting of a white cross on a red background. In the middle of the cross was a great star. The top left hand section of the flag was intended to take the flag of each different country, while the other three sections were to be filled with white stars on the red ground. Through some misunderstanding the design was not adopted.

CHAPTER XXVII

BRITISH FLAGS

A S pointed out in the preceding chapter, for long centuries there was no definitely settled national flag. The red cross of St. George and the heraldic devices assigned to St. Edmund and St. Edward the Confessor were borne side by side, and then shared honours with the Royal armorial banner.

This Royal Banner, or Standard as we now wrongly call it, was borne at least as early as the battle of Agincourt, as a red flag emblazoned with the three golden lions passant guardant. But the Royal Banner naturally followed all the changes introduced in the armorial shield, for the blazoning is the same in both cases, only the banner is rectangular and should measure 15 feet by 7½ feet. The undifferenced Royal Banner is the personal flag of the King, and should, properly speaking, only be flown when he is present. Other members of the Royal Family either have the banner differenced with their labels (and the children and grandchildren of Queen Victoria with the arms of Saxony in a shield of pretence), or within a border of ermine.

The Royal Standard is flown, undifferenced by Viceroys and Colonial Governors, only on Imperial public holidays.

Among our national flags, it has been seen, was one with the red cross of St. George (symbol of martyrdom) on a white ground. Tradition says that this was a signum given to an English king by Joseph of Arimathea, who is supposed to have come over to convert the natives of this island in A.D. 72. But as a matter of fact we do not hear anything of this flag until the return of Richard the Lion-Hearted from the Crusades. Now, St. George, the martyred Roman centurion, was venerated by both Christians and Moslems in the Near East; for he was regarded as the preux Chevalier par excellence, a man of pious deeds, of exalted aspirations, of proved valour in arms. We find him regarded as a patron saint of places so far apart as Genoa and Moscow, Geneva and London. It was Richard who fell under the spell of the warrior saint, and after the conquest of Cyprus adopted him as his patron. Devotion to St. George grew apace, for he was proclaimed patron and protector of England by Edward III, who in 1354 dedicated the Royal Chapel at Windsor to him, and placed the Order of the Garter, instituted in 1350, under his guardianship. Thenceforward the national flag of England was the white banner with red cross. It was borne side by side with the royal banner, and marshalled with the armorial insignia of prince, noble and knight as their standards. And so it remained until

UNION FLAG OF 1707.

1604, when came the political union of England and Scotland under James I. It was found necessary to mark this union of two neighbouring kingdoms by the blending of the two national flags, which had so often been the rallying signs of opposing English and Scots on many a gory field. The Scottish patron saint was St. Andrew, and his banner was blue with a white diagonal cross (azure, a saltire argent), for tradition said the Apostle suffered death on such a cross. The method of blending adopted was according to well-known heraldic laws; the cross of St. George was placed " over all." So that we had a blue field with a white saltire, surmounted by a red cross, fimbriated with a thin border argent.

This was the first Union flag and was used for the two kingdoms when acting together, each, however, retaining its own ensign; but in 1707 it was proclaimed as the " ensign armorial of the United Kingdom of Great Britain." It was often called the Union Jack, and it was supposed to be in allusion to King James, whose name, in its French form Jacques, was assumed to be connected with the heraldic description. As a matter of fact, the term Jack is at least as old as the first years of Edward III's reign, and is connected with the French term for jacket. At that time, and for as long as the arrow and cutlass were the chief weapons of attack, sailors wore padded shields on their chests and backs, somewhat in the shape of shields. For England these were emblazoned with heraldic devices or with the cross of St. George. These "jacks" when not in use were hung up near the ship's bulwarks, like lifebelts are nowadays. They appear to have been retained for ornamental purposes long after they had ceased to have had any practical value.

This first Union flag lasted until 1801, when, on the union with Ireland, a new marshalling was adopted, the banner of St. Patrick, a white field with red saltire, being added. This was done by uniting the two saltires on the blue field, but to adjust matters as far as possible the red saltire, with its narrow fimbriation of white, was counterchanged with the white saltire, the white being given precedence. As a result we have in the upper quarter a compound limb of the saltire composed of a narrow edging of white, a broad band of red, and a band of white equal to the red and white beneath it, and this arrangement is reversed in each succeeding quarter. It is a somewhat dislocated saltire, but surmounted by the red cross of St. George with its white border, looks quite well.

UNION FLAG OF 1801.

Our ensigns are composed of the Union banner and a coloured field, the Union, or Jack, forming the upper quarter. Before 1864 Admirals of the Red, commanding the "Red," or first squadron, placed the Union on a red flag. This is now used for merchant shipping and pleasure craft. Admirals of the "White," or second squadron, had the Union on a white ensign. This is now replaced by the Union on an ensign of St. George, and forms the flag of the Royal Navy and the Royal Naval Yacht Squadron. Finally, Admirals of the " Blue," or third squadron, placed the Union on a blue ensign, which has now become the flag of the Royal Naval Reserve, of various Government Departments, and of all yacht clubs enjoying the privilege of the title " Royal."

Governors of Colonies are entitled to use the Union flag, with the badge of the Colony placed at the intersection of the crosses, surrounded by laurel leaves, except in the case of Canada, where maple leaves are used, and New Zealand, where ferns replace the laurels.

The Government of each colony use the blue ensign, and merchant vessels the red ensign with the Colonial badge in the fly, though with Australia the arrangement is somewhat different. For the Canadian Dominion the quartered coats of Ontario, Quebec, Nova Scotia and New Brunswick is the badge. Each province uses its own armorial shield. The Governor-General of Australia has for badge

FLAG OF THE AUSTRALIAN
COMMONWEALTH.

a golden star of seven points, ensigned by an Imperial crown, within a wreath of laurels. The Commonwealth flag has the Constellation of the Southern Cross in the fly, represented by four white stars of seven points and one of five, while a larger star of seven points is placed below the Union quarter. Queensland's badge is a blue Maltese cross surmounted by an Imperial crown. New South Wales has a red cross with a lion passant guardant between four stars of eight points, all gold; Victoria, a blue circle with the Constellation of the Southern Cross (five stars) ensigned by an Imperial crown; South Australia, a yellow circle with an Australian black and white piping shrike perched and wings elevated; Western

Australia, a black swan on a yellow circle ; Tasmania, a red lion passant.

In practice the dimensions observed in designing a Union flag are as follows : the St. George's cross, red part, one-fifth the width of the flag, or 1 foot 6 inches ; the white border, one-fifteenth the width, or one-third of the red part, that is 6 inches ; St. Andrew and St. Patrick crosses : the red of St. Patrick one-fifteenth the width of the flag, or one-third the red of St. George, that is 6 inches ; the narrow white border one-thirtieth of the width of the flag, or one-sixth of the red of St. George, that is 3 inches ; the broad white of St. Andrew's cross one-tenth the width of the flag, or half the red of St. George (equal to the red of St. Patrick's cross together with one of its narrow white borders), that is 9 inches. As regards the Ensigns, the Union should be one-half the length of the flag and one-half its breadth. The Union part of an ensign should be always uppermost and against the staff or hallyard. To fly it otherwise is a sign of distress. In the Army, the Artillery and Royal Engineers have no flags. Cavalry regiments have small square standards, the colour of its facings emblazoned with its badges and mottoes. The Household Brigade of Life and Horse Guards have crimson standards, emblazoned with the royal cypher and their regimental honours. Each infantry battalion, with the exception of the Rifle Corps, has two flags—the King's colours, which are simply the " Union Jack," and the regimental colours, in which the field is of the colour of the regimental facings, with the " Union Jack " in the upper corner. They are emblazoned with the titles, badges, and names of the various battles in which the regiments have distinguished themselves. With the Guards it is different ; the King's colours are crimson, with the Royal cypher and crown ; the regimental colours are the " Union Jack."

When Lord Ampthill was in office in India he suggested a " national " flag for the whole Viceroyalty ; but nothing came of it. Thereupon " Nondescript," in the pages of an Anglo-Indian weekly, put forward the following design : " Draw a rectangle 8 inches by 5 inches, and give it a red border $\frac{1}{4}$

of an inch wide, the enclosed rectangle measuring $7\frac{1}{2}$ inches by $4\frac{1}{2}$ inches. Draw a vertical line at the staff end 1 inch from the border, leaving $6\frac{1}{2}$ inches by $4\frac{1}{2}$ inches. Divide the depth of $4\frac{1}{2}$ inches into three horizontal bands, each $6\frac{1}{2}$ inches long and $1\frac{1}{2}$ inches deep, coloured respectively, from the top, dark blue, green, and light blue. The vertical band, $4\frac{1}{2}$ inches by 1 inch to contain the Constellation of Orion, a familiar sight in the Eastern sky, set upright, silver stars on a purple background. United India would be represented by the stars of the Constellation (the number being modified to suit the United Provinces and States); the " Foreign " element, which has welded India into a whole, and which keeps it united, by the red border; the deep blue band would stand for Hindus and Buddhists; the green for the Mahomedans; and the light or sky-blue band for the Indian Christians." Moreover, he thought that the " Orion " vertical band should have a compartment or space, about $\frac{3}{4}$ inch deep, reserved at top, for provincial or State ensigns or (in case of flags floating over Government Imperial buildings, forts and ships) the royal arms.

In a like spirit Mr. Joseph S. Dunn in 1897 put forward a proposal for a further addition to the Union Jack in order to symbolise Imperial unity. For this purpose he suggested a golden ring to surmount the intersections of all three crosses, representing the earth girdling Empire " on which the sun never sets."

CHAPTER XXVIII

FLAGS OF VARIOUS NATIONS

LIKE our Union Jack the American "Stars and Stripes" is a thing of slow growth; taking its origin in the distant past, even yet it is not definite. Much poetical nonsense has been penned about the American "red, white and blue." We have been told that the red represents blood shed in defence of the nation, that the white stands for liberty, and the blue for hope in the future. As a matter of fact, the colours are a sentimental tribute to the past, a proud claim to kinship.

In the early colonial days the flag used was the St. George's ensign, sometimes adorned with a royal crown and monogram. Then came the first British Union flag, a combination, as we have seen, of the English red and white and the Scottish blue and white. The local element was represented by a green pine tree or a globe displaying the Western Hemisphere. Hence the colonials derived their colours. When the unfortunate family tiff over tea chests and principles began, the local troops gathered round a variety of flags. Sometimes the flag was red, sometimes white, sometimes blue. As a rule, however, the cross of St. George was retained; though not always, for one popular banner represented a rattlesnake on a red ground, with the motto, "Don't tread on me!"

Then George Washington, somewhat exercised at the laxity, or want of uniformity, brought forward a new proposal. He suggested a white flag, decorated with a green fir tree, and the motto, "An Appeal to Heaven." These colours were flown by the local navy. Still, much doubt was shown,

Colonel Moultrie's blue flag with a golden crescent proving rather attractive. Nevertheless, it was felt that it was too great a departure from time-honoured devices, and under

RED ENSIGN OF ST. GEORGE
WITH AMERICAN PINE.

UNION JACK WITH STRIPES
OF THE STATES.

the auspices of Washington a committee evolved a fine device, based on the Union Jack and the East India Company's flag.

It was decided that the ground of the flag should be divided into thirteen horizontal stripes, alternately red and white, thirteen being the number of the States acting in concert; while the Union Jack, which told flattering tales, was reinstated. After this there were a few divergencies, but not many, the chief one, perhaps, being the white flag with crossed sword and staff, the latter crowned with a cap of liberty, and the words " Liberty or Death," which was seen at the battle of White Plains, October 1776.

FIRST STARS AND STRIPES.

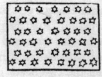

PRESENT DAY AMERICAN JACK.

In June 1777 came a decided rupture. It was " That the flag of the thirteen United States be thirteen stripes, alternately red and white, and that the Union be blue with thirteen white stars of five rays, representing a new constellation." Even here, nevertheless, the historical continuity was not completely abandoned. The form of the flag was based on the British, the colours were the same. It should, however, be mentioned that George Washington's arms were : argent, two bars and in chief three stars gules, as this may have had some influence in the design.

Later on it was decreed that every State admitted to the Union should be represented by a star ; but the stripes remain to recall the original thirteen component parts of the new nation.

Some divergence was shown in the display of the stars. Originally there was a crown of twelve round a central star. In 1818 these were beautifully arranged to form one big star of five points ; but on the same date the Navy Department said they should be placed in four rows of five, arranged alternately. In 1819, there were four rows of five stars placed in exact alignment. To-day there are six rows of eight stars.

Abyssinia has an Imperial banner tiercy in fess red, yellow and green, while the national flag consists of three long wedges, or pointed pennons red, yellow and green respectively.

Argentine Republic has a flag tierced per fess, light sky blue, white, and light sky blue ; on the white a sun (with human face) in glory. President's banner : light sky blue, an oval per fess blue and argent, in base two hands clasped proper, in front of a staff ensigned with red Phrygian cap, the oval surrounded by a wreath of laurel and ensigned with a rising sun in glory gold ; in the four corners of the flag a silver star of five points.

Austria-Hungary : Imperial banner, orange, charged with the arms of Austria-Hungary on the breast of the black double-headed crowned eagle displayed, the wings and tail charged with eleven armorial escutcheons, an Imperial crown between the two heads of the eagle, three Imperial crowns on the dexter and three on the sinister side, and one in base, the whole within a border pily counter pily argent, gules, orange and sable. The banner of the Empress has only four Imperial crowns, one in each corner. Those of the Archdukes and Archduchesses are without the Imperial crowns. Naval ensign, tierced per fess red, white and red ; on the white an escutcheon tierced per fess red, white and red, within a border gold, ensigned with a crown encroaching on the red. Admirals have the same flag, but within a border pily counter pily orange and sable, with stars to denote rank. Merchant flag, horizontal band of red, another of same width white, and third (lower) band, per pale red and green; on the white an escutcheon, crowned, of Austria as above, and in fly an escutcheon per pale, dexter barry of nine gules and argent, sinister gules, on the summit of three hills vert, a patriarchal cross argent, issuing from a crown palisade or, the whole within a border gold, ensigned with the crown of St. Stephen (for Hungary). Military flag as the naval, but with a canton in dexter chief tiercy per fess sable, yellow and sable. Badges for Field Marshals, three double-headed black eagles with arms of the Empire placed two in fess, one in base; for generals, three gold stars.

Belgium : Royal banner, tierced per pale, black, gold and red ; on the yellow band the arms of Belgium ; sable, a lion rampant or, supporters two lions rampant guardant or, the shield ensigned by a royal crown. The national ensign is the tricolour without the arms.

Bolivia : tierced per fess, red, yellow, green.

Brazil : green, thereon a large yellow diamond charged with a celestial blue sphere with the southern constellations in white, and a white band inscribed " Ordem e Progresso." Naval flag, blue with a cross of twenty-one five-pointed white stars ; admirals place star badges of different kinds in the upper quarter.

Bulgaria : Royal banner : red, with a yellow crowned lion rampant, surmounted by an escutcheon of Saxony, within a border pily counter pily yellow, black and white. Crown Prince's banner : white, a green saltire surmounted by a blood red cross, the whole surmounted by the Royal banner as above. Naval flag, tierced per fess white, green and blood-red, in upper quarter a red canton with crowned yellow lion rampant. National flag as above without the red canton.

Chile : per fess white and red, a black canton charged with a white star of five points. For the President of the Republic the flag is charged with the national arms : per fess

sable and gules, a star of five points, argent ; crest, a plume
of three ostrich feathers, gules, argent and sable respectively ;
a condor and a deer, both crowned and gold.

China. Under the late Imperial Government the flags were
as follows : yellow with aerial, wingless dragon in blue, white
and green, its feelers nearly encircling a small red disc. The
dynastic flag was a yellow pointed pennon, with a scalloped red border. The Chinese Republican flag is composed
of six horizontal bands, red, yellow, blue, white, and black.
Military and naval flag, red, on a blue canton a white sun
in splendour.

Colombia : tiercy per fess, a broad band of yellow, bands of
blue and red, the two last equalling in breadth the yellow
band. Broaching on the blue and yellow, a blue oval charged
with a silver star, the whole within a red border. This badge
is replaced by a white oval charged with the national arms,
for the President's flag. It is to be noted that the same
tricolour, with slight modifications, is also borne by Ecuador
and Venezuela, which at first formed with Colombia the
Republic of New Granada, and then of Gran Colombia.

Congo : blue, with a large yellow star of five points.

Costa Rica : five horizontal bands : blue, white, red (equal
in breadth to the blue and white together), white and blue.

Crete : blue with a white cross, the first quarter (upper
left-hand corner) red with a white star of five points.

Cuba : five horizontal stripes, blue, white, blue white and
blue, from the staff a triangle of red charged with a white
star of five points.

Denmark : Royal banner, white charged with the royal
arms and supporters. Another type is, red, a white cross
quadrate charged with the royal arms. Ensign, red with
white cross, the fly forked.

Dominican Republic : quarterly blue and red, with a
white cross over all.

Ecuador : same flag and arrangement as Colombia, but
the blue, pale sky tint ; the national flag plain ; the Presi-
dential banner charged with the arms of the Republic (azure,
two mountains vert, in chief three stars argent).

Egypt : Khedive's banner, red with three groups of crescent and star, two near the staff and one in the fly.

Federated Malay States : per fess, white, red, yellow and black ; broaching on the yellow and red, a white oval with a tiger courant. The State of Perak has a flag tierced in fess white, yellow and black. Selangor, quarterly red and yellow, in upper quarter a crescent and star yellow. Negri-Sembilan, yellow upper quarter, per bend, red and black. Pahang, per fess, white and black.

France : Mention has already been made of the Oriflamme, the celebrated sacred banner of the French kings. The early type is supposed to have been red, though some say blue ; the second also red with yellow flames. This second Oriflamme, preserved at the Abbey of St. Denis, had first three then five streamers. It was last raised at Agincourt. Charles VII of France used a banner of his arms for flag, that is a blue field powdered with golden fleurs-de-lis. To this he added the white cross of Armagnac, a device which became the flag of Garde Royale, and persisted among the infantry down to 1789. But side by side with this were the Colonel's colours, white, which first appeared towards the end of the sixteenth century, and was adopted as a general army flag in 1638, the King then being Colonel-General of the whole forces. It was through this that Louis XIV adopted the white flag with three golden fleurs-de-lis as the royal banner and ensign. Then in 1798 a tricolour was adopted by the National Assembly. It was really a fraternal emblem, for it associated the white of the Royal Guards with the blue and red of the national guard, who were dressed in the colours of the City of Paris. This flag was continued by Napoleon and by Louis Philippe, but Louis XVIII and Charles X during their short occupancy of the throne re-introduced the white flag with golden lilies. The Imperial

NAPOLEONIC
EAGLE
STANDARD.

banner was the tricolour powdered with golden Imperial bees, the central white stripe also bearing the crowned

Imperial eagle. During the Bourbon period the flagstaff was surmounted by a fleur-de-lis, during the Reign of Terror by a red Phrygian cap, under the Republic by a simple spear-head, and under Louis Philippe by the ancient fighting cock of the Gauls.

Germany : Imperial banner, orange, charged with a black cross patée, edged with white and encircled with the words " Gott Mit Uns. 1870 " distributed on the four limbs ; the cross surmounted by a gold escutcheon charged with the black eagle, on its chest an escutcheon with a black eagle displayed, surmounted by a shield quarterly sable and argent, the whole surrounded by a collar of the Order of the Black Eagle, and ensigned with the crown of Charlemagne. In the angles of the cross, four Imperial crowns and twelve eagles displayed. The Ensign and Naval flag is argent, a cross cotised sable, on the centre a round shield bearing the arms of Germany ; and in

PRUSSIAN EAGLE.

the upper quarter, tierced per fess, sable argent and gules, on centre band a representation of the Iron Cross (*i.e.* a black cross patée, edged silver). The mercantile flag is per fess black, white and red. The banner of the Duke of Saxe-Coburg and Gotha is barry of or and sable, a crancelin in bend vert and in a canton the royal arms of England, differenced with a silver label of five points. The Waldeck and Pyrmont tricolour is tierced per fess black, red and yellow. All the other German States have their own royal or princely banners.

Greece : In the Greek War of Independence a red flag with a white cross was used, but on the election of Otto of Bavaria as king, the colour of the flag was altered to the light blue characteristic of the Royal banners of the Bavarian family and of the Bavarian military uniforms. The Royal banner is a blue flag with white cross, charged with a mantled escutcheon of the Greek arms. The ensign and national flag has five light blue and four white horizontal stripes, and in the upper corner a blue canton with white cross.

Guatemala : per pale light sky blue, white and light sky blue, the white on the ensign charged with the national badge.

Hayti : per fess blue and red, in the middle a large white rectangular cartouche.

Honduras : tierced per fess, blue, white and blue ; on the white five yellow stars in saltire.

Italy has a tricolour per pale green (for Sardinia), white (Florence) and red (Savoy), adopted to honour those States which have worked for a " redeemed and united Italy." On the white is an escutcheon of Savoy, or of Savoy-Carignan : *i.e.* gules, a cross argent ; and, for the differencing Savoy-Carignan, within a border azure. These arms are traditionally said to have been granted in 1315 to Amadeus, Duke of Savoy, by the Knights of St. John of Jerasalem in reward for the part he took in the defence of Rhodes. The naval and military ensigns have the coat-of-arms ensigned with a royal crown. The Royal Standard is of blue, thereon the arms of Savoy placed on the chest of a sable eagle displayed, ensigned with a royal crown, surrounded by a collar of the royal order, and in the four corners, royal crowns.

Japan : Imperial banner, red, a gold chrysanthemum of sixteen petals. For the Empress the fly to the banner is split. For the Imperial princes, the badge is placed within a white border. Ensign, white, with a red disc and radiating therefrom sixteen wedge-shaped red rays, the disc placed about one-third distance from the staff.

Liberia : six red and five white horizontal stripes, at the upper corner a canton of blue charged with a silver star of five points. It will be seen that this flag is based on the Stars and Stripes of the United States of America.

Mexico : a tricolour, green, white and red, the white

charged with a Mexican eagle, holding a green snake in its beak, rising from cactus leaves and surrounded by laurel wreaths.

MEXICAN EAGLE.

Monaco : Prince's banner, white, charged with royal arms (fusily argent and gules), supporters, royal crown and mantling of the arms, lined ermine. Flag, per fess red and white.

Montenegro : Royal banner, red, charged with a double-headed white eagle, displayed, sceptre and mound in talons, ensigned with royal crown, surmounted by an escutcheon with the initials H. I. ; beneath the eagle a yellow lion passant, the whole within a white border. National flag, tiercy per fess red, blue and white, the blue charged with a crown and the initials H. I.

Morocco : the old Saracenic flag, plain red.

Netherlands : Royal banner, orange, a blue cross, charged with the arms of Nassau (azure, billity or, a lion rampant crowned, holding in its dexter paw a bundle of silver arrows, in sinister a sword, or) surmounting the ribbon of the family Order of Knighthood, the badge pendent ; in four quarters, blue hunting horns, stringed red. The banner of the Prince Consort is light blue, with an orange cross, the cross charged with the arms of Nassau ensigned with a royal crown, in the upper and lower outer corners a yellow griffin rampant. National flag, tiercy per fess, red, white and blue. These colours were derived from the French, and date from the days of the Batavian Rupublic.

Nicaragua : tiercy per fess, light sky blue, white and light sky blue, charged on the white with the national badge for the ensign, and with a blue fouled anchor for the merchant flag.

Norway : Royal banner, red charged with a crowned yellow lion rampant, holding in his paw an axe, the blade white. Merchant flag, red, with a white cross surmounted by a blue cross.

Panama : quarterly, white charged with a blue star, red, blue, and white with a red star.

Paraguay : tiercy per fess, red, white and blue, with a circular badge on the white near the staff.

Persia : Imperial banner, blue grey, charged with a white circular disc, thereon a yellow lion passant, holding in his dexter paw a scimitar, a demi sun rising at his back, in chief a Persian crown, in base branches of green laurel. In the upper corner a canton tiercy per fess, green, white and pink. National flag, tiercy per fess, green, white and pink. Before the abdication of the late Shah, the flags were white, with an inner border of green and an outer one of red, the border round the top, bottom and fly only. This flag was charged with the respective heraldic devices above described to form the Royal banner and the Ensign.

Peru : tiercy per pale, red, white and red.

Portugal : per pale green and red, the outer strip of red twice the length of the green ; broaching on the two colours the arms of Portugal (argent, five escutcheons azure, in cross, each charged with five bezants in saltire, with a border gules charged with seven castles triple-towered gold), placed on a yellow armillary sphere. Previously to this the President's banner was green, with the above device on it. Earlier still the flag was per pale red and green, thereon a blue disc with a white band bearing the inscription "Patria e Liberdade." During the Monarchy the Royal banner was red, with the national arms ensigned with a royal crown ; and the national flag, per pale blue and white, charged with the crowned shield of Portugal.

Roumania : Royal banner, yellow, with a narrow blue band near the staff, and a narrow red band in the fly, the yellow charged with the arms of the kingdom (quarterly, 1st, azure, an eagle displayed and crowned or, looking towards the sun ; 2nd, gules, the head of an ox caboshed, a star over the head, a crescent to the sinister ; 3rd, gules, a crowned lion rampant, holding between his paws a star ; 4th, azure, two dolphins in pale counter embowed, all or ; over all, a shield of pretence, quarterly, argent and sable) ensigned with a royal crown; supporters, two lions or, the whole placed on a robe of state gules, lined ermine, ensigned with a royal crown; in the four quarters of the flag, royal crowns. Princes use the same banner, but without the four crowns. National flag, per pale blue, yellow and red, with the royal arms with mantling on the yellow for the war flag.

Russia: Imperial banner, yellow, with the black double-headed eagle displayed, carrying in talons the sceptre and orb, each head crowned, and a crown between the heads, the chest surmounted by an escutcheon gules, St. George on horseback, with cloak azure, slaying the dragon, argent, within a border or, the whole surrounded by the collar of the Order of St. Andrew; the wings charged with eight escutcheons of dominion. The Czarevich's

RUSSIAN EAGLE.

banner is red, with a blue saltire edged with white, surmounted by a white cross, the whole surmounted by the Imperial banner. Grand Dukes bear the same banner as the Heir Apparent, but with the Imperial banner arranged on a circular disc. War flag, white, with a blue saltire. Merchant flag, tiercy per fess, white, blue and red.

Salvador: five blue and four white horizontal stripes, the jack (resting on the top of the third blue stripe) red, charged with fourteen five-pointed white stars, placed 5, 4 and 5.

Samos. The first flag was blue, with a white triangle charged with a red cross couped. This has been replaced by a flag per fess red and blue, near the staff, impinging on the two columns a white cross couped.

Sarawak: yellow, with a cross per pale black and red, a crown being placed on the cross for the Rajah's flag.

Servia: Royal banner, tiercy per fess, red, blue and white, within a border pily counter pily white, blue and red, the whole charged with the royal arms. Merchant flag, tiercy per fess, red, blue and white.

Siam : Ensign, red, with a white elephant on a golden stand, with trappings of gold, green and red. War flag, white, with a blue saltire. Merchant flag, red, with the white elephant without trappings.

Spain : Purple, with an oval shield of the royal arms, ensigned with a royal crown and surrounded by the collar of the Order of the Golden Fleece. Ensign, per fess, a yellow band between two red bands, the yellow twice the width of the red. On the yellow an oval escutcheon, per pale, gules, a castle triple towered gold, and argent, a lion rampant gules, ensigned by a royal crown. Merchant flag, per fess, yellow and red ; a yellow band equal in width to both the above ; then red and yellow, these bands together equal in width to the centre yellow band.

Sweden : Royal banner, pale sky blue with a yellow cross, the fly split into three tails. On the centre of the arms a white square charged with the royal arms within the mantling. National flag, light sky blue, with a yellow cross, the outer limb longer than the others.

Switzerland : red, a white cross couped.

Tunis : red with a large white circle charged with a decrescent and a star, both red.

Turkey : The supreme religious flag is green, and is said to be the bed curtain of Mahomet's favourite wife, Fatima. It is always kept in a mosque, except when a Holy War is declared, and the staff is surmounted by a clenched fist, holding a manuscript roll of the Koran. The Imperial banner is maroon, with the " tougra " or Imperial sign manual, encircled by an oval glory of gold rays. The Ensign and national flag is red, a decrescent and a five-pointed star, both white. The Khedive of Egypt has a similar flag for banner and ensign, but with three groups of decrescents and stars, two placed in pale near the staff and the third just in front of them.

Venezuela : tiercy per fess, yellow, sky blue and red ; on the blue a crown of seven five-pointed stars. Formerly a central star was surrounded by a ring of six others.

CHAPTER XXIX

HERALDS' COLLEGE

HERALDS came long before the art of armory was developed, for the office is an extremely ancient one, partaking both of the military and diplomatic character. They were confidential officers of rulers, who conveyed messages of war or peace. By a natural transition they controlled the ceremonials of courts, and from messengers conveying offers of marriage or tidings of births and deaths, soon became family historians or recorders. So when armory assumed definite shape and grew to some importance, it naturally fell to the lot of the heralds to act as the prince's deputies in regulating the assumption, bearing and transmission of arms. Hence heraldry is an art embracing all that appertains to armory, genealogy, precedence and ceremonial generally.

We hear of heralds and their novitiates, the pursuivants, acting as armorists and genealogists early in the thirteenth century. They were incorporated by Richard III in 1483, and granted extended privileges by Edward VI. It is this body which to the present day constitutes the heraldic authority in England, and is known as the College of Arms or Heralds' College. It consists, under the direction of the Earl Marshal, an office hereditarily attached to the Dukedom of Norfolk, of thirteen members, of whom three are Kings of Arms, six Heralds and four Pursuivants. Before the reign of Henry IV the principal officer was known as the King of Heralds; afterwards the title was changed to King of Arms. The office of Garter, Principal King of Arms, dates from 1417, when we find him taking charge not only of the ceremonial duties connected with the Noble Order of the Garter, but exercising a general supervision. His arms are: argent, a St. George's cross; on a chief azure, a ducal coronet encircled with a garter, between a lion of England ducally crowned on the dexter side, and a fleur-de-lis on the sinister, all or. Before 1559 there was also a dove in the first quarter. Then comes Clarenceux (formerly known as Surroy), also instituted by Henry V, his jurisdiction extending over the whole of England south of the river Trent. His arms are: argent, a cross of St. George; on a chief gules, a lion of England ducally crowned or. Up to 1595 a fleur-de-lis was placed in the first quarter. Norroy, whose office dates back to the reign of Edward II, if not before that, has jurisdiction over all England north of the Trent. His arms are: argent, a cross of St. George; on a chief per pale azure and gules, a lion of England ducally crowned, between a fleur-de-lis on the dexter side and a key wards in chief on the sinister, all or.

All three kings are entitled to coronets, consisting of circlets heightened with sixteen oak leaves. They also wear gold collars or chains of S.S. They wear tabards, blazoned back and front and on the wing sleeves, with the royal arms, and carry short wands of office, topped by a crown.

The Heralds are: Chester, instituted by Edward III; Lancaster, instituted by Edward III, whose official badge is a crowned red rose; Richmond, instituted by Edward IV, official badge: a white and red rose en soleil dimidiated and crowned; Somerset, instituted by Henry VII; Windsor, instituted by Edward III, official badge a sun-burst; York, official badge a white rose en soleil.

The Pursuivants are: Rouge Croix; Blue Mantle, instituted by Edward III, as assistant to Garter King, official badge a blue mantle, lined argent and tied with gold cords; Rouge Dragon, instituted by Henry VII, official badge a red dragon; and Portcullis, instituted by Henry VII, official badge a portcullis.

Both Heralds and Pursuivants wear tabards of the royal arms.

Bath King of Arms was instituted in 1725, as herald and registrar of the Order of the Bath. He has jurisdiction in Wales. He is not a member of the College.

Many other Heralds and Pursuivants were formerly appointed; most of the monarchs from the later Plantagenets to the last of the Tudors instituted such officers, often bearing names of their favourite badges, such as Falcon, Antelope, and so on. Extraordinary heralds have also been created. Edmondson, the well-known heraldic author, was Mowbray Herald Extraordinary. Most of the great noble houses also had their pursuivants, to act as their genealogists and masters of ceremonies.

In Scotland heraldic authority rests with the Lyon Office and Register, presided over by the Lord Lyon King of Arms, instituted early in the fifteenth century. His official arms are: argent, a lion sejeant affronté gules, holding in his dexter paw a thistle proper and in his sinister an escutcheon of the second; on a chief azure a saltire silver. The Heralds are Rothesay, Ross and Albany; the Pursuivants, Unicorn, March and Carrick.

In Ireland, the chief herald is Ulster King of Arms, instituted by Edward VI in 1551. He appears to have succeeded Ireland King of Arms, who was instituted by Richard II. Ulster King's arms are: or, a cross gules; upon a chief of the last, a lion passant guardant between a harp in the dexter and a portcullis in sinister, all gold. There are two Heralds, Dublin and Cork, and one Pursuivant, Athlone.

The duties of these three authorities is to grant arms, within their jurisdictions, subject to the sanction of the Crown; to register matriculations of arms after claimants have proved their rights to bear such arms; to grant and register badges to persons entitled to bear coat armour; to grant supporters or augmentations subject to the approval of the Crown; and under circumstances to act as directors of court ceremonial; to proclaim the death of a monarch; the succession of a monarch to the throne; his election and

crowning; and perform other kindred duties. Their offices
being repositories of pedigrees, rolls of arms and MSS records
of visitations, registers of matriculation and other documents,
the officials are able to render valuable services in tracing
genealogies.

CHAPTER XXX

HERALDRY IN THE APPLIED ARTS

HERALDRY, boldly yet judiciously applied, can lend great dignity and charm to the decorative arts. Not only are the forms of shields with their charges and externals immensely varied, but they are sufficiently conventionalised to blend with any other decorative motif, while the pomp introduced by vivid contrasts of delightful harmonies of pure colours, impart just those " jewelled " effects which give life to a whole composition. While appealing to the eye through arresting outlines and bright tinctures, the imagination is also quickened by the symbolism. In order to appreciate this we have merely to visit such national storehouses as Westminster Abbey, Canterbury Cathedral or York Minster, or study such domestic examples as the splendid *cheminée armoiriée* of the Palais de Justice at Bruges, those other chimneypieces fom Tattershall Castle (casts of which are to be seen at the Victoria and Albert Museum), or the fine plaster and other ceilings, such as we find at Hampton Court Palace, the Chapel Royal, St. James's, and in many old mansions.

To the builders of the Gothic period heraldry was a thing of instant, everyday import, and this is reflected in the best work of the time, whether ecclesiastical or domestic. Heraldry became an integral part of the design, structural in value as well as purely decorative, for it springs out of the design and appears essential to it. This secret of good design also characterises much of the Renaissance work of the early and middle periods ; and it was possessed to quite a remark-

1628· ·EX LIBRIS· 1910

MURRAY OF BLACKBARONY.

able degree by our own masters of carving and plastering craftmanship.

In early heraldic work, whether seen in carving or illumination, there is a boldness of touch in design, an elasticity in the treatment of detail which makes for diversity and artistic effectiveness. At one unfortunate period of armorial evolution this conventionalisation was regarded as an error, and an attempt was made "to return to nature," while conforming to cast iron rules of the seventeenth century heralds. This fallacy of the nineteenth century is well illustrated by the underlying sarcasm in the story that once upon a time an old country coach-painter visiting London was taken to see the lions at the Tower, and promptly regarded the tawny brutes as frauds. "Those lions!" he cried. "No, no, I've been painting lions in all kinds of positions in the coats-of-arms of the nobility on coaches and hatchments for fifty years and more, and I ought to know what a lion is like!" Now undoubtedly the heraldic lion is unlike any beast in creation; but it conveys the idea of the proud "King of beasts," which prevails in ancient tradition. Moreover, it is to be observed that the more the painter conventionalises the lion, the better the decorative effect. Whenever an attempt is made to draw a symbolical or heraldic lion true to nature failure results. It is quite impossible to do justice to the real animal in the limited space and under the restricted conditions imposed upon the artist in heraldry, and consequently strong conventionalising is necessary. Look at the ancient sculptures of Assyria and Egypt; how bold the queer lions are, in spite of their acrobatic positions and plaited manes. Early herald painters displayed the same happy freedom, and evolved a prancing lion, ragged of outline, of attenuated body, huge head and grinning jaws. He is far superior to the fat, smirking heraldic lion of the eighteenth and nineteenth centuries. Heraldry is essentially conventional, and so it should be treated sturdily, preserving freedom within the rules, but without any attempt to copy nature. That this need not lead to dead uniformity is clearly shown by old examples and the work of the best artists during the past thirty years. While herald painters of the feudal days recognised certain broad distinctions as regards outlines and attitudes of beasts, they yet knew how to keep their own individuality, though never losing sight of the central idea to be conveyed by the picture. Thus we may admire a wonderful succession of lions "of England" on the monuments in our ancient churches, on seals, in illuminations, not only for the fidelity in the main ideal, but for the endless variety introduced. On each of these shields of England six lions are given, they are fundamentally identical, yet excellently diverse, the elevation of the paws, the cock and curl of the tail, the lolling of tongue and rolling of eye, give individuality and life. This leads to one of the most satisfactory tricks of early practice, the drawing of charges so as to fill spaces. These six lions " of England " on the quartered shield are not of uniform pattern or size, as is the case in later work. If the shield was of the kite or spade pattern, the lions in the fourth quarter were of diminishing stature, so as to cover the field, which again lent diversity to the composition. This desire to cover the field is also conspicuous in the early treatment of such recurring forms as the fleur-de-lis or cross, which were depicted as truly " powdered," so that at the edges we often see only half of the charge.

While it is true that, exceptionally, great value was placed on shields of a single tincture, or of a combination of tinctures, or with a single uncharged ordinary, the artistic tendency was to treat the field as a mere background for the charges. Yet this did not mean overcrowding with detail. Simplicity was aimed at. Thus the charge was brought out with great distinctness, and, if it could not be made to fill the available space, then the aid of diapering was sought. This diapering consists of covering the plain spaces of field or the larger ordinaries with a small pattern of squares or lozenges enclosing diminutive ornaments, or else using a running geometrical or floral design. But diapering being mere ornamentation, without heraldic or symbolical meaning, this beautifying must be kept distinctly subordinate to the charges themselves. This is done by making the design small in detail, very light in outline and subdued in tincture. Thus the diapering is usually carried out in a tint either lighter or darker than the field, in silver on gold, gold on silver, or sometimes in a different tincture to the field. Very beautiful examples of this kind of work are to be seen on the tombs of William de Valence, Earl of Pembroke, and of Ralph. Earl of Stafford, in Westminster Abbey. Other instances as appearing on the Great Seals of England have already been mentioned.

With what happy decorative effect heraldry can be used both our public and domestic buildings attest. Writing of the South Porch of Canterbury Cathedral, Willement says:

" The ceiling is ornamented by intersecting ribs, handsomely disposed, and at each intersection is placed a shield of arms, sculptured in stone, but not painted." And then, speaking of the Cloisters, he adds: " This portion of the Cathedral presents an heraldic assemblage unparelleled in any other church. In some compartments of the ceiling the bosses are composed of those beautiful varieties of foliage common in pointed architecture at an early period; but generally each intersection of the ribs that compose its elaborate vaulting is covered by a sculptured shield of arms. These were undoubtedly emblazoned in their proper metals and colours, for considerable indications are yet visible, and the whole, in its original perfection, must have given that extraordinary splendour of effect which is peculiar to the rich colour and judicious contrast of heraldic combinations. On the ribs of the vaulting immediately connected with each shield was written the name of the person to whom the coat belonged." Two of the bosses so well described are shown in this volume. Of domestic plaster work ceilings many examples are happily still extant, and a photograph of one is given here.

In the examples of carving shown, it is well to observe how naturally the shields appear in their places. They are truly part of the design, not merely shields stuck on. With the chimney-pieces illustrated, the case is somewhat different, for there we have obviously a representation of actual shields hung up on the wall, as was, indeed, done in feudal times. These chimneypieces are, therefore, treated as heraldic galleries.

Beautiful work is also to be seen in metal, apart from engraving, embossing and enamelling. Some of the Italian, German, Flemish and English iron strapwork is excellent, the heraldic character being preserved while conforming to the natural characteristics of the material used. Our own native craftsmen showed great taste in the ornamentation of purely domestic pieces of leadwork, such as the magnificent cistern shown here, the rain-water gutter heads to be seen at Warwick Castle and elsewhere.

There should be a revival in this direction, as there has been in painted glass work.

CHAPTER XXXI

GLOSSARY

Abased (from the French *abaissé*). A term applied to an ordinary borne in a lower position than usual. In contradistinction to "enhanced." If placed quite low, it is termed "in base."

Abatement, or Rebatement. Marks of dishonour invented by certain writers and intended to be used in debruising coats by arms. As a matter of fact the only abatements ever adopted were those relating to illegitimacy of birth (see Chapter XIII, "Differencing and Marks of Cadency"). The abatements were : (1) Delf tenné, assigned to one revoking or receding from his own challenge (see **Delf**). (2) Inescutcheon reversed sanguine in fess point, assigned for dishonourable conduct to a woman, or flying from the banner of his prince. (3) A point dexter tenné, assigned to a vainglorious boaster. (4) A point in point sanguine, for cowardice. (5) A plain sanguine, for lying to prince or commander. (6) A point champagne tenné, for slaying a prisoner after demanding quarter. (7) A gore sinister tenné, for behaving in a cowardly way towards an enemy. (8) A gusset sanguine, borne on the right for adultery, on the sinister for drunkenness. (9) The whole armorial shield reversed, for treason. All these eight first-named abatements are coloured sanguine or tenné. This is important to remember, for the charges themselves, when of other tinctures, are quite honourable. For a description of their outlines, see under the respective names.

Accolée. Placed side by side. Usually applied to two shields bearing respectively the arms of husband and wife, or paternal arms and official insignia, grouped as a pair, as an alternative to impaling.

Accosted. (1) A principal charge placed between others. (2) Two animated creatures placed side by side.

Achievement. A complete grouping of armorial devices. Often applied to hatchment (*q.v.*).

Acorned. Adorned with acorns.

Addorsed, or Endorsed. Placed back to back.

Adumbration. The shadow of a charge, usually shown as a "transparency," the figure being painted of a darker shade of the field.

Affronté. Animated creatures placed full-face.

Alaisé, or Alesé. A charge not extending to the side of the shield is said to be "alaisé." In English the term "couped" is more general, and a cross is often said to be "humetty."

Alerion. An eaglet, usually depicted without beak or feet, and with points of wings downwards.

Alerons, Ailettes, Alettes. Small armorial shields worn on the shoulders of knights in pageants and on like occasions, and shown on sepulchral brasses. They were sometimes circular, and also square for knights banneret. Also termed emerasses.

Allocamelus, or Ass-Camel. An ass with neck and head of a camel. It was the crest of the East Land Company (granted 1579).

Ambulant. Walking.

Anchored, Ancred, Ancré. Terminating with outward curved projections, like the flukes of an anchor.

Animé. A term applied to an animal with its eyes of a different tincture to that of its body.

Annulet. This represents the ring hung from a cross-beam at a tournament or joust, which had to be carried off on the tip of a knight's lance as he rode by at full tilt. As a mark of cadency it denotes the fifth son and his house.

Annulety, or **Annuleted.** Ending in annulets.

Appaumy. An open hand, showing the palm.

Apre. A bull with the tail of a bear.

Argent. Silver.

Arm. The "dexter" arm is called in French heraldry "dextrochere"; the "sinister," a "senestrochere."

Armed. Beasts and birds when their teeth, tusks, horns, claws and talons are of a different tincture to that of their bodies, are said to be "armed" of the special tincture. Stags and antelopes, banners, are said to be "attired."

Ashen Keys. The drooping bunch of fruit of the ash-tree.

At Gaze. A term applied to stags and kindred animals when standing.

Attire. The horn or horns of a stag. When the horns of a stag, antelope or goat are of a different tincture to its body, it is said to be "attired" of the special tincture.

Augmentation. Charges added to a shield-of-arms as a mark of distinction granted by a reigning prince.

Aulned, Awned, Bearded. Said of corn in ear when the spikelets are of a different tincture to the grain.

Avellane. Filbert nuts, or in the shape of filbert nuts in their cups or involucres.

Azure. Blue.

Badge. A cognisance or device, personal or hereditary. Not worn on the helm, as a crest, or placed on a wreath, but intended to be borne on clothing and affixed to property. Badges also appeared on armorial standards.

Bagwyn. An heraldic antelope, but with long horns curved over the ears, and the tail of a horse.

Banded. When a bale, or a collection of objects, is bound together by a band of a different tincture, it is said to be "banded" of that tincture.

Banner. A rectangular flag charged with armorial bearings. Properly the banner itself should be treated as a shield, but in modern heraldry the flag is often charged with an armorial shield, or even a complete achievement.

Bar. A horizontal band across the shield, occupying one-fifth of the field. It is a diminutive of the fess.

Barbed. (1) An arrow with the head of a different tincture to the shaft is said to be " barbed " of the tincture. (2) An object with barbed terminations.

Barded. A caparisoned horse.

Barnacle. A Solan goose.

Barnacles, or Breys. An instrument used to curb horses.

Barrulet. The diminutive of the bar.

Barry, Baruly. A shield divided by an even number of horizontal lines. As a rule the number of divisions should be specified. A shield divided by horizontal and vertical lines is sometimes called a field " barry paly," though the proper term is " checky." " Barry bendy " is a field divided by horizontal and diagonal lines from dexter chief to sinister base. " Barry bendy sinister " is the same as the last, but with the diagonal lines from sinister chief to dexter base. Such shields are also called " barry bendy lozengy." " Barry indented " are divided by horizontal and by diagonal lines from both right and left. In " barry pily " the horizontal lines are drawn at alternating slopes, so as to produce a number of horizontal piles or wedges.

Baton. The diminutive of the barrulet sinister, and is the most commonly used mark of bastardy. It is generally borne couped.

Beaver. That section of a helmet which opens to show the lower part of the face.

Belled. A hawk, or other charge, having bells affixed.

Bend. A broad band, occupying one-third of the field, drawn diagonally from dexter chief to sinister base. A bend sinister has its position reversed.

Bendlet. A diminutive of the bend, one-half its width.

Bendy. A shield divided by diagonal lines in the shape of the bend. A shield may also be " bendy sinister." " Bendy barry " is the same as " barry bendy " (*q.v.*).

"Bendy dexter sinister" produces a field checky of diamonds. "Bendy pily" is divided by piles in bend, For "bendy paly," see "Paly."

Bezants. Circular gold discs,

Bezanty. A shield or charge powdered with gold discs.

Billet. A small oblong figure.

Billetty. A field or charge powdered with billets.

Birdbolt. A blunt-headed arrow.

Blue Bottle. The cornflower.

Boar. The wild boar.

Border, or Bordure. A band round the edge of the field. It is one of the sub-ordinaries and should occupy a fifth of the field.

Boterol. The metal end-piece of a sword scabbard.

Botony, or Botonné. Adorned with three round buds.

Breys. See **Barnacles.**

Brisures. A French term applied to differencing, such as marks of cadency, augmentations, etc.

Brocket. A young stag.

Cabled. A charge twisted round by a rope. An anchor with a cable attached is said to be "cabled," but if the rope is twined round the shaft it is called a "fould anchor."

Caboshed, or Cabossed. The head of a beast borne full-faced without the neck showing. The head of a lion or leopard so borne is generally called a "mask."

Cadency, or Difference, Marks of. These are badges borne on the upper part of a shield, on crests and supporters, to distinguish various members and branches of a family. Strictly speaking only the head of a family, or house, is entitled to use the arms or crest without a "difference." In the early days of heraldry various branches often made a distinction by changing the colours of the field and charges, and making some alterations. But as the hereditary principle became more firmly established marks of cadency were adopted. The mark for the eldest son is the label, for the second the crescent,

for the third the mullet, the fourth a martlet, the fifth
the annulet, the sixth the fleur-de-lis, the seventh the
rose, the eighth the cross moline, the ninth the double
quatrefoil, or octofoil. The sons of the second son
should all bear a crescent charged with the marks as
above given ; the sons of the third son should have a
mullet, also differenced as above, and so on. The
practice with our Royal Family is for all the sons and
daughters to use the label, but in each case differenced
with a special badge determined by patent issued by
the reigning sovereign.

Camelopardel. A giraffe.

Canton. A diminutive of the quarter.

Cantoned, or **Cantonné.** A cross or saltire between four
charges.

Caparisons, or **Housings.** The ornamental coverings or
clothing of a horse.

Capricorn. A goat with a fish's tail.

Carltrap, or **Calthrop.** A four-spiked object thrown on the
ground to impede cavalry attack.

Champagne, or **Champaine.** The lower part of the shield cut
off by a horizontal line. Much used in Continental marshalling of arms.

Chape. The metal end-piece of a sword scabbard. Also
called " boterol."

Charge. Anything borne on an armorial shield. A charge
itself may be " charged " with another figure.

Chequy, or **Checky.** A field or charge divided into squares
of horizontal and vertical lines. The squares are alternately of metal and colour.

Chevalier. A man in complete armour.

Chevron. Bands rising from the dexter and sinister sides
of the shield and meeting in an acute point in the middle.
It is an ordinary, and should occupy one-third of the
field.

Chevronel. A diminutive of the chevron, one-half its
width.

Chevronny. A field divided by chevron lines.

Chief. The upper third of the shield cut off by a horizontal line.

Cinquefoil, or Quintefoil. A five-lobed flower shown in plane.

Clarion. See **Rest.**

Climant, or Clymant. Applied to the goat when "saliant."

Closet. A diminutive of the bar, one-half its width.

Cockatrice. A wyvern, or two-legged dragon, with the head of a cock, having a forked tongue.

Combatant. Two wild beasts rampant and counter rampant, facing each other.

Confrontant, or Confronting. Two animated creatures, other than wild beasts when rampant, fronting each other.

Contourné. Charges facing towards the sinister side.

Cornish Chough. A bluish black bird of the crow family with red legs and beak.

Coronel. The head of a jousting lance, somewhat like an ancient crown of four radiant points.

Cotices, or Cotises. Diminutives of the bendlet, and generally borne in pairs, one on each side of a bend. In such a case the bend is said to be " cotticed."

Couchant. Lying down.

Counterchanged. When a shield is divided and is half of a metal and half of a colour, and the charge impinging on both halves, or a group of small charges are of the same tinctures but reversed from that of the field, the composition is said to be "counterchanged."

Couped. Cut off by a straight line. A cross or other ordinary which does not touch the edges of the shield.

Couple-Close. A diminutive of the chevron, one-fourth its width. They are always borne in pairs, and often one on each side of the chevron, which is then said to be " couple-closed."

Courant, or Current. Running.

Coward. A beast with its tail between its hind legs.

Crampet. The metal end-piece of a sword scabbard. Also called "boterol" and "chape."

Crancelin. A crown of rue in bend. (See **Crowns.**)

Crenelated, or **Crenelly.** Embattled; decorated with an outline of alternate depressions and square projections.

Crescent, is a half-moon, frequently used in heraldry. If the horns point upwards it is called a crescent; if the horns point to the left it is said to be increscent; if pointing to the right, decrescent. The crescent is the mark of difference used by the second son and his house.

Cresset. A fire beacon; usually shown as a tripod supporting a circular iron basket.

Crest. A figure placed on a helmet; and in later practice on a crest-wreath.

Crined. Hair when of a different tincture to the head.

Crosier, or **Crozier.** The crook of an archbishop, bishop or abbot.

Cross. An ordinary, composed of an amalgamation of the fess and the pale. Should occupy one-third of the field. See Chapter III.

Crusily. A field or charge powdered with crosses.

Cubit Arm. An arm cut off between the wrist and the elbow.

Dancette, Dancetty. A zigzag line of partition.

Debruised. An animal or other charge surmounted by an ordinary. The term "surmounted by" is more usual.

Decrescent. See **Crescent.**

Deer. Includes buck, hart and stag. The hind (or female) has no attires, or horns. Various special deer have been introduced into heraldry from the colonies, such as the moose and reindeer from Canada, the wildebeesten and oryx from South Africa.

Defamed. A beast deprived of its tail.

Defence. The tusk of a wild boar or an elephant.

Delf, or **Delph.** Variously represented as a spadeful of earth of irregular shape (very rare), or as a billet, or oblong, with its thickness shown in perspective. If of tenné it is said to be an "abatement" (*q.v.*).

Demi. Half.

Demi Vol. A single wing.

Dexter. The dexter or right-handed side of an armorial shield is that on the left of the spectator, for the shield is assumed to be worn by its owner.

Dextrochere. See **Arm.**

Differences, Marks of. See **Cadency.**

Dimidiated. Two coats-of-arms cut in halves, and the halves impaled; the same process may be applied to charges, *e.g.*, the rose and thistle badge. Little practised since the seventeenth century.

Dormant. Sleeping.

Dorsed. The back of a hand, the contrary to "appaumy."

Dragon. A fabulous monster, represented in two forms: (1) A four-footed beast, having the build of a lion, with scaly body, large bat wings, forked tongue and tail. (2) A long, worm-like scaly monster, with short legs and long wings. The first type is a symbol of vigilance; the second represents some form of evil and is generally shown as trampled upon or transfixed, as in the badge of St. George, patron of England.

Eagles. See Chapter V.

Effets. Lizards.

Embattled. See **Crenelated.**

Emblazon. To describe armorials.

Emblazoned. A shield or banner bearing heraldic charges.

Embowed. Bent.

Embrued. Dropping with blood.

Emerasces. See **Ailettes.**

Endorse. A diminutive of the pale, one-fourth its width.

Endorsed, or Addorsed. Placed back to back.

Enfiled. A charge surrounded by a coronet, chaplet or motto-scroll is said to be "enfiled."

Englanté. The same as **Acorned.**

Engrailed. A pitted line of division.

Enhanced. A term applied to an ordinary when placed in a higher position than usual.

Ensigned. A term applied to a charge with a crown, coronet, cap, helmet or cross placed above, but touching it.

Eradicated. A tree torn out by its roots.

Erased. Torn off, with a rough edge showing.

Ermine. A fur, argent with sable spots.

Esquire, or **Equire.** A shield or chief with corners gyronny.

Estoille. A star, usually with points, or alternate points, wavy.

Eyrant. Birds in their nests are said to be "eyrant" or "ayrant."

Fer de Moulin. See **Millrine.**

Fess. A band carried horizontally across the shield, occupying one-third of the space. One of the ordinaries.

File. See **Label.**

Fillet. A diminutive of the chief.

Fimbriated. An ordinary with a very thin border of another tincture.

Fitchy. Crosses with spikes on the lower limb, or at the ends of all limbs, is said to be "fitchy."

Flasque. A diminutive of the flaunche, always borne in pairs.

Flaunches or **Flanches.** The sides of the shield cut off by incurving lines, this giving an hour-glass appearance to the middle of the shield.

Flory, or **Floretty.** Adorned with fleurs-de-lis.

Fountain. A roundel, or disc, of argent, crossed by wavy bands of azure.

Fourchée. Forked. See **Queue Fourchée.**

Fret, Fretty. (1) See Chapter II, "Sub-Ordinaries." (2) A field covered with fret-work.

Fret. Narrow bendlets in saltire, interlaced with a mascle.

Fretty. A field or charge crossed by bendlets from dexter and sinister.

Fructed. Bearing fruit or seeds.

Fusil, Fusilly. (1) Elongated lozenge. (2) Field covered with fusils ; or charges composed of fusils.

Fylfot. A cramponed cross. See Chapter III, "Crosses."

Gad. An oblong figure, like a billet, but with its thickness shown in perspective, the tinctures being either or, argent, gules, azure or sable. It is supposed to represent an ingot of metal.

Gamb, or Jamb. The leg of a beast.

Garb. A wheatsheaf.

Gimmel-Ring. Two rings interlaced.

Gobony, or Compony. An ordinary composed of one row of small squares of alternate tinctures is termed "gobony."

Golpe. A roundel, or disc, when of purpure.

Gore. A portion of the shield cut off by a curved line as with the flaunches, but ending in a point. When placed on the sinister side is one of the fanciful abatements (*q.v.*).

Gorged. A beast or bird having a coronet, collar or wreath round its neck is said to be gorged.

Goutes. Pear-shaped drops or tears, having different names according to their tinctures.

Gouty. Powdered with tear drops.

Grey. A badger.

Grice. A young wild boar.

Griffin, or Gryphon. A fabulous beast, with the body of a lion, the beak and forepaws of an eagle, and wings which may be either feathered or of the bat type. It has sharp pointed ears, is generally represented rampant, and is a symbol of vigilance.

Guardant. Said of a beast walking with its dexter forepaw elevated, and its face turned to the spectator.

Gules. Red.

Gunstone. A roundel or disc of sable.

Gurges, or Whirlpools. One of the sub-ordinaries. See Chapter II.

Gusset. A section of the shield cut off by a slanting line from the chief to the honour point, and then a vertical line to the base. They are usually borne in pairs. If of sanguine, they come within the list of fanciful abatements (*q.v.*).

Gyronny. A field divided per cross and per saltire, the tinctures alternating.

Habited. Clothed.

Hame, or Heame. Horse collar.

Harpy. Vulture with breast and head of a woman.

Hart. A male deer.

Hatchment. Diamond-shaped frames on which complete armorials are placed for affixing to the houses of deceased persons, or the churches where the funeral service is held. Now rarely used. A reigning sovereign has the complete composition on a black ground. Bachelors, widowers and widows follow the same rule. Officials having right to official arms, bear their paternal arms impaled with their insignia, the latter in the dexter side ; then the background is divided vertically into halves, one white and the other black. The official insignia is placed over the white section. A husband having lost his wife impales her arms and has the black section of the frame under her arms. A wife having lost her husband also impales his arms, and places the black on the dexter side under his arms.

Hauriant. A fish borne in pale, the head upward.

Herse. Old French term for portcullis.

Hind. A female deer.

Hoofed, or Unguled. A term applied when the hoofs of an animal are of a different tincture to that of its body.

Humetty. See **Couped.**

Hurst. A clump of trees on a hill.

Hurt. A roundel, or disc, of azure.

Impaled. Two coats-of-arms borne side by side on one shield or banner.

Incensed. Said of wild creatures with fire issuing from their eyes and mouth.

Increscent. See **Crescent.**

Indented. A chevrony line of division.

Insignia. A term often applied to official arms and badges.

Invected. A pitted and curved line of division.

Issuant. Arising from, or out of.

Jamb, or **Gamb.**   The leg of an animal.

Jessant.   Shooting forth.

Label, or **File,** is the mark of cadency for the eldest son and his house, and members of the Royal Family.   It consists of a horizontal bar with three (or more) pendent points, usually in the form of wedges.

Lambeaux.   Same as **Label.**

Lambrequin.   Mantling placed behind a coat-of-arms.

Langued.   A beast having its tongue of a different tincture to its body is said to be "langued" of that tincture.

Lozengy.   A field or charge divided by diagonal lines at an angle to form pointed diamonds.

Lucy.   A fish : the pike.

Lure.   A hawk's lure is composed of two wings tied together by a tasselled cord.

Lymphad.   An ancient ship or galley.

Mantling.   The ragged scarf behind the helmet or crest, and the robe of estate placed behind a shield.

Marined.   Said of any animal with a fish's tail.

Martlet is the swallow or martin, and is depicted as having a very short beak, long wings, thighs, but no legs or claws.   It is used as a charge and also as the mark of difference for the fourth son and his house.

Mascle.   A lozenge voided, represented as a link from chain armour.

Masculy.   Field divided by a meshwork of mascles.

Masoned.   The lines formed by the different courses of stones or bricks in a building, picked out in a distinctive tincture.

Maunch.   Ancient sleeve with long pendent cuff.

Millrine, or **Fer de Moulin,** is a charge much in the form of a cross, but with each limb split into two and the ends curved outwards, resembling the iron ties sometimes used in building.

Mound.   A globe surmounted by a cross.   It is one of the emblems of sovereignty.

Mount. Small hill, usually green, placed in base of shield. In French styled a " terrasse."

Mullet. This is a star of five points, pierced in the centre, and represents a spur rowel. It is a common charge, originally of a military character, and also the mark of difference used by the third son and his house.

Mural Crown. A coronet formed of battlements and turrets. See chapter on **Crowns.**

Murrey, or **Sanguine.** Blood red.

Naissant, or **Nascent.** Growing out of the middle of an ordinary.

Nebuly. An undulating division line.

Nowed. Twisted into a knot.

Ogress. A roundel, or disc, of sable.

Opinicus. A lion with short tail, fore part and wings of a dragon and head of a griffin.

Oppressed. The same as **Debruised.**

Or. Gold.

Orb. See **Mound.**

Orle. An ordinary. It is a border, but detached from the edge of the shield. Charges are frequently borne placed in the position of an orle.

Over All, or **Surtout.** A term employed to describe a charge placed over several others ; or a small shield-of-arms placed in pretence, that is, in the middle of another armorial shield.

Pairle. Charges borne in the form of the upper part of a saltire and the lower of a pale, are said to be " in pairle."

Pale. A vertical band occupying one third of the middle. One of the ordinaries.

Paly. A field or charge divided by vertical lines.

Paly Bendy is a field divided by vertical and diagonal lines.

Pall. A charge representing the ecclesiastical pallium, somewhat in the shape of a Y.

Panache. A plume of feathers, usually of different tinctures.

Passant. A beast walking past, its dexter paw elevated.

Pegasus. A winged horse.

Pellet. A roundel, or disc, of sable.

Pheon. The head of a dart, having an outer cutting edge, and barbed on the inner sides.

Phœnix. An eagle rising from flames.

Pile. A wedged shaped charge pendent from the top of the shield.

Pily. A shield divided by lines to form a series of piles.

Plates. Roundels, or discs, of silver.

Pomeis, or Pomey. A roundel, or disc, of vert.

Pomel. A cross. Also called **Pommelly, Pomy, Pomelty, Pommettee** and **Bourdonnée.**

Potent. A fur, represented by crutch-shaped figures.

Powdered. A field or charge sprinkled with small charges. Also termed **Semée.**

Proper. A term applied to show that the charge is of its natural colour, or natural shape.

Purpure. Purple.

Quarter. The dexter fourth of the shield, cut off by horizontal and vertical lines. One of the ordinaries.

Quartered. A shield divided into partitions to receive different coats-of-arms is said to be "quartered," whatever the number of divisions, if four or more. If divided into three, the shield is said to be "tiercy."

Quatrefoil. A four-lobed flower, drawn in plane.

Queue Fourché. Forked or double-tailed.

Queued. An animal having a tail of a different tincture to that of its body is said to be " queued " of that tincture.

Raguly. An ordinary, or the limb of a tree, having projecting pieces, placed alternately on each side and couped, is said to be "raguly."

Rampant. An animal rearing on its hind legs.

Recercelé. A term applied to an ordinary, usually the cross or saltire, with outwardly curving ends, rather more pronounced than in the moline.

Reflexed. Carried backwards, as with tail curved over back, or chain from collar.

Regardant. An animal looking backwards.

Respectant. Two animals borne face to face when not rampant. In the latter case they are said to be combatant.

Rest. A curious charge, like a mouth-organ with a curved handle.

Roundels. Round discs, now given different names according to their tinctures. If of or the roundel is called a bezant; argent, a plate; gules, a torteaux; azure, a hurt; vert, a pommeis; purpure, a golpe or wound; sable, either pellet, ogress or gunstone; sanguine, a guze; tenné, an orange. A plate crossed by horizontal wavy blue lines is called a fountain.

Rustre. Lozenge pierced with a circular opening, thus differencing from the mascle, which is an outlined lozenge.

Sable. Black.

Saliant. A wild beast leaping forward.

Saltire. A diagonal or St. Andrew's cross. Charges of all kinds may be arranged "in saltire" or "salterwise." See Chapter III, "The Cross."

Sanguine, or Murrey. Blood red.

Segréant. A term applied to a rampant griffin.

Sejant. An animal sitting.

Semée. Sprinkled with small charges.

Senestrochere. See **Arm.**

Shafted. An arrow with its shaft of a different tincture than the head and feather is said to be "shafted" of the special tincture.

Sinister. The left-hand side of an armorial shield is that on the right hand of a spectator.

Slip, Slipped. A small branch. The stalks of flowers.

Sovereign. Obsolete term for the chief.

Stars have five or more points. Often the alternate rays are shown as wavy, to represent the twinkling effect of light. They differ from the mullet in not being pierced.

Statant. Standing. But a stag in this position is said to be " at gaze."

Supporters. Figures or inanimate objects placed on the sides of, or behind, shields to sustain them. In Scotland they were formerly called " bearers." The French distinguish angelic and human figures and all creatures having a resemblance to man, as " tenants," animals as " supports," and inanimate objects as " soutiens."

Suppressed. Occasionally used instead of " surmounted."

Surmounted. An ordinary or other charge borne over a charge.

Surtout. A shield of pretence.

Surtout. See **Over All.**

Swastika. A cramponed cross. See Chapter III, "The Cross."

Tau, or **St. Antony's Cross,** in the shape of the Greek T. See Chapter III, " The Cross."

Tenné, or **Tauney.** Orange colour.

Throughout. Extending right across the field.

Tierced, or **Tiercy.** Divided into thirds.

Tinctures. The metals and colours used in heraldry.

Toison d'Or. The Golden Fleece.

Torse. French term for crest wreath.

Torteaux. A roundel, or disc, of gules.

Trangle. A term for the closet ; little used.

Transfixed. A sword, lance, arrow, etc., thrust right through an animal or object ; as distinct from pierced when the weapon is merely buried in the animal or object.

Transposed. Borne in the reverse order.

Trefoil. A three-lobed leaf.

Tressure. A diminutive of the orle ; often borne double, as in the arms of Scotland, which is also flory-counter-flory.

Trick. Outline sketch of a coat of arms, the tinctures being represented by letters, and the number of objects by numerals.

Truncated, Trunked. A tree with the trunk of a different tincture to the branches.

Trussing. An eagle, falcon or hawk preying on something.

Tufted. Bunches of hair on thet ail or other parts of an animal.

Undy. A wavy line of division.

Unguled. A term applied to animals having hoofs of a particular tincture.

Unicorn. A horse with a pointed horn springing from its forehead, and tufts of hair under its chin, on its hind legs and its tail. It represents knightly honour. The right-hand side supporter of the British Royal Arms is a silver unicorn rampant, with horn, hoofs, mane and tail of gold, a golden coronet (with fleur-de-lis and cross paté on the fillet) round the neck, a chain attached thereto and reflexed over the back. This is the supporter of the Scottish Royal Arms, and was first used in England by James I.

Urchin. Alternative term for hedgehog.

Urdée. Pointed or serrated.

Urinant. A fish borne hauriant reversed, or diving.

Vair. A fur represented by cup-shaped figures.

Vallary, or **Palisade Crown.** A coronet of palisades. See Chapter XXI, " Crowns, Coronets and Caps."

Vambraced. Arm encased in armour.

Vannet, Vannot. Escallop shell without its ears.

Verdured, or **Verdoyed.** A charge adorned with leaves ; trees or flowers are said to be " leaved."

Vert. Green.

Vervels, also **Varvals.** Small rings.

Vested, or **Habited.** Clothed.

Visor, or **Vizor.** The upper movable part of a helmet, provided with bars or eye-holes.

Voided. Charges, especially ordinaries and sub-ordinaries, with the middle part removed.

Voiders. A diminutive of the flaunche, always borne in pairs.

Vol. Two wings borne conjoined.

Vorant. An animal in the act of devouring.

Vulned. An animal with bleeding wound.

Wallet. A pilgrim's pouch, like a handbag.

Wreath, Wreathed. (1) A crest wreath, composed of twisted silk, on which the crest rests. (2) Decorated with a wreath, chaplet or garland, as a figure wreathed about the loins and temples, that is having a garland of leaves below the waist, and a chaplet of leaves or flowers round the head.

Wood. See Hurst.

Wyvern. This is a dragon (*q.v.*), but with fore legs only and a forked tail. It is the typical dragon of Continental heraldry.

INDEX

*** Figures printed in *italics* refer to illustrations in the text.

A

Abased, 322
Abatement, 322
Abbeville-Bourbers-Tunc, 152
Aberdeen See, arms of, 80
Abyssinian flag, 302
Accolée, *141*, 323
Accosted, 323
Achievement, 323
Acorned, 121, 323 ; cross, *26*
Acre, Sir Edmond de, 126
Adamoli, 80
Addorsed, 37, 323
Adelaide of Louvain, 274
Adelaide of Saxe-Meiningen, 279
Admiralty badge, 110, 111
Adossé, 37
Adumbration, 323
Affronté, 36, 323
Agulon arms, 176
Aikenhead, 121
Ailesbury supporters, 237
Ailettes, 323
Alaisé, 323
Aland, 43
Alberta Province, *285*
Alder, 125, 328
Alderberry, 125
Alerons, 323
Alerion, 50, 323
Alesé, 323
Alettes, 323
Alexandra of Denmark, 279
Alleyne, 184
Allocamelus, 323
Allusive arms, 159
Almonds, 124
Alten, 190
Altenburg, 279
Amants, 86

Ambulant, 323
Amherst, Earls, supporters, 258
Anchor, 110
Anchored, 323 ; cross, *25*
Ancré, 323
Ancred, 323
Androuet, Jacques, 163
Angels, 79, 244, 250
Angoulême, 270
Anhalt, 279
Animé, 73, 323
Anjou, Counts of, 100, 275
Anne of Bohemia, 274
Anne Boleyn, 186, 276
Anne of Cleves, 276
Anne of Denmark, 276
Anne Nevil, 274
Anne, Queen, 273
Annulets, 15, 102, 147, 163, *186*, 323
Annulety, 323
Antelope, 42, 71
Antelope, white, badge of Henry IV, 225
Antrobus supporters, 257
Ants, 63
Antwerp, city arms, 87
Apollo, 80
Appaumy, 324
Apples, 123
Appleton, 123, 161
Apre, 324
Arabin, 123
Arches, 107
Argent, ix, 324
Argentine flag, 302
Argus, 83
Ark, 109
Armed, 45
Armes à enquirire, xix
Armes parlantes, 159

Armillary sphere, 249
Arms, 89 ; of dominion, 143
Arragon, 271
Arrows, 102, *182*
Arthur, King, fabulous arms, 280
Arundel of Wardour, 52
Ash, Mountain, 229
Ashen keys, 126, 324
Ashford arms, 126
Ashton, 125
Askew, 43
Aspe, 63
Ass-Camel, 323
Assil, 43
Astley, 180
At gaze, 44, 342
Athenore, 38
Atlas, 80
Atsea, 161
At speed, 44
Attires, 44, 324
Aubry, John de, 99
Audele label, 137
Augmentation, 144, 324
Aulned, 324
Australia, badge of, 227 ; Com-
    monwealth arms, 96, 282 ;
    flag, 297
Austria-Hungary, arms, 271 ;
    flags, 302
Austrian crown, 234 ; eagle, 248
Avellance cross, 23
Avellanes, 124, 324
Awned, 324
Ayrant, 330
Azalea, trailing, 229
Azure, xi, 324

B

Bacchus, 80
Badger, 44
Badges, 81, 85, 88, 92, 103, 105,
    107, 112, 124, 126, 128, 129,
    181, 186, 199, 221, 324
Bagwyn, 324
Banbury borough, 92
Banded, 127, 324
Banner, 105, 324 ; armorial carried
    by supporters, 257
Bannerman, 163
Banner shield, 207
Bar, 4, 324
" Bar sinister," 153
Bar, county and duchy, 61, 275

Barbed, 325 ; arrows, 102 ; cross,
    24
Barbel, 61
Barbs, 181
Barded, 325
Bardoulf, 180
Barking Abbey, 177
Barnacle, 325
Barnacles, 103, 325
Barnes, Bishop of Carlisle, 81
Baronets' badge, 88
Barons' coronets, 237
Barragan, 82
Barrels, *117*
Barrulet, 4, 325
Barry, 325
Baruly, 325
Basset, 149, 220
Bastardy, Marks of, 4, 153
Bath city, 106
Baton, 4, 152, 325 ; " perri en
    bar," 152
Batoon, 4
Battenberg, 151
Battuli, 117
Bayeux tapestry, 19, 77, 205, *290*
Bayford, 125
Bay leaves, 125, 232
Baynes, 30
Beacon in flames badge, 225
Beaked, 55
Bean cods, 127
Beane, 127
Bear and tree, 225
Bears, 40 ; of Berri, 246
Bearded, 127, 324
Beauchamp of Hacche, 276
Beauforts, 153
Beaumont, Earls of Leicester, 180
Beaux, 92, 275
Beaver, 42, 325
Becheron, 101
Beckington, 164, 240
Bedford town, *48*
Bees, 63, 126, 211
Beheim, 108
Belgian flag, 303
Belled, 50, 323
Bend, 3, *4*, 152, 325 ; sinister,
    4, *8*
Bendlet, 3, 325 ; enhanced, *8* ;
    sinister, 153
Bendlice, 189
Bendy, 7, 325
Benoit, 87

Berengaria of Navarre, 274
Berkeley arms, 6, 152; livery, 265

Berri, Duke of, seal, 246
Bertie, 107
Bessell, 134
Best, 84
Bewdley town, 103
Bezantée, 139, 326
Bezants, 14, 325
Bightine, 6
Bilberry, 228
Billets, 15, 326
Billety, 326
Bilson, 123
" Binding Flower," 130
Birche, 128
Birch twigs, 128
Bird bolts, 102, 326
Birds, fleurs-de-lis, 170, 171, 175, 176
Birtles, 128
Bishops, 79
Blackberry, 229, 240
Black cockade of Neckar, 259; of Hanover, 261
Blacker, 82

Blankenberg, 279
Blazing Star, 97
Bleue celeste. xi
Blondeville, 127
Blue-bottle, 132
Boar, 42, 248
Bog myrtle, 228

Bohemia, crown of, 234; John, King of, crest, 199
Bohun white swan, 51, 225, 226, 246

" Boke of Saint-Albans," 113
Boleyn, Anne, 186
Bolivian flag, 303
Bones, 86
Bones-Combas, 89
Book-plates, 243
Books, 117
Border, 12, 138, 150, 326
Bordure, 12, 326
Boterole, 101, 326
Bothell, 132
Botonné, 326
Botony cross, 18, 326
Bottles, 116
Bourbers-Abbeville-Tunc, 152
Bourbonée cross, 18

Bourbons, 153, 173; crown, 236
Bourchier knot, 223
Bourdonée, 18
Bowen knot, 223
Bowgets. See Water-bowgets
Bows, 102
Box-wood, 228
Boys, 81
Brabant, John, Duke of, 198, 199, 216, 248, 271
Bracken, 229
Bradway, 123
Brambles, 229, 240
Bramwell, 31
Brandenburg, 277
Bray, 103
Brayne, 121
Brazilian flag, 303
Bream, 61
Brehna, 279
Bretland, 125
Brewers' Guild, 117
Breys, 325
Bridges, 106
Bridport, 115, 116
Brisures, 326
British Columbia, 284, 285
— crowns, 234, 235
— Honduras, 287
Brittany, 139, 140
Brock, 44
Brocket, 326
Broken, 8
Broom, 128, 225, 228
Broome, 128
Brotherton, 276
Bruce, 33
Bruckhausen, 278
Brugière, 128
Brunswick arms, 273; crest, 215
Brutus, King, legendary arms, 280
Buccleuch, Duke of, supporters, 258
Buchanan, badge, 228, ; tartan, 268
Buckles, 103
Buffalo, 41, 152
Bugles, 118
Bulgarian flag, 303
Bulls, 41
Bulrush, 229, 232
Burgh, de, 275
Burgundy arms, 271; cross, 33
Burnet, 125
Bury town, 114

Butcher's broom, 229
Butler, 276
Byzantine crescent, 94 ; crowns, 234

C

Cabbage, 127
Cabled, 110, 326
Caboshed, 44, 44, 326
Cabossed, 326
Cadency, 326
Cæsars, 188
Calote, 207
Calthrop, 102, 327
Calvary cross, 17
Cambis, 121
Cambridge, Duke of, 279
Cambridge city, 105
Camel, 42
Camelopardel, 327
Cameron badge, 228 ; tartan, 268
Camin, 278
Campbell badge, 228 ; tartan, 268
Canada, arms, 142, 284 ; badge, 126, 227 ; flag, 297
Cannon badge of Edward VI, 227
Canterbury, archbishopric arms, 33
Canterbury city arms, 52
Canton, 5, 7, 152, 327
Cantoned, 327
Cantonnée, 29, 327
Caparisons, 43, 327
Capeline, 209, 219
Capricorn, 327
Cape of Good Hope, 286
Cap of Dignity, 238
Cardillac, 38
Cardinal's hat, 239
Carlten, John, 99
Carltrap, 327
Carnation, xi
Carnegie cross, 98
Carnwath arms and supporters, 81
Caroline of Brandenburg-Anspach, 272
Caroline of Brunswick-Luneburg, 278
Carp, Golden, of Oudhe, 145
Castanea, 124
Castile, 271

Castle, 48, 78, 105, 115, 246 ; badge of Edward II, 225
Cassuben, 278
Cathcart, 95
Catherine of Arragon, arms, 275 ; badges, 182, 186, 187, 188
Catherine of Braganza, 277
Catherine Howard, 276
Catherine Parr, arms, 276 ; badge, 85
Cauldron, 104
Celestial crown, 233
Centaur, 73
Ceylon, 287
Chains in saltire, 33
Champagne, 142, 327
Champagne, arms of, 274
Champaine, 327
Chape, 7, 10, 327
Chaperonné, 7
Chaplets, 134, 189, 231
Charge, 327
Charged, 29
Charlemagne, crown, 233, 273
Charlotte Sophia of Mecklenburg-Strelitz, 278
Charlton, 139
Charnwood, Lord, supporters, 257
Chatillon, 275
Chaussé, 7
Checky, 327
Chequy, 11, 13, 327
Cherries, 124
Cherubs, 79
Chess rooks, 113
Chester feudal arms (facing title-page), 127
Chestnuts, 124
Chevalier, 327
Chevron, 4, 5, 123, 152, 327, per chevron, 154 : reversed, 5
Chevronée (chevronny), 5, 98, 327
Chevronel, 5, 327
Chichester, Bishopric of, 79
Chief, 2, 8, 41, 327
Chilean flag, 303
Chimera, 74
Chinese dragons, 65 ; flags, 304 ; lion, 71 ; phœnix, 73 ; unicorn, 71
Chisholm arms, 82 ; badge, 228 ; tartan, 268
Christ, 79

Chrysanthemums, 130, *131*
Cinquefoils, 180, 327 ; Japanese, 132, *133*
Civic crown, 238
Clair-voies, 11
Clare, 6, 137
Clarence, John de, 154
Clarendon, Roger de (facing title-page), 153
Claret, 97
Clarion, 118
Claved, double, cross, *30*
Clechée cross, 23, 24
Cleland hare, 44
Clerk, Sir John, 144
Clerkenwell, Borough of, *104*
Cleves, 100, 276
Clifford, Bishop of Bath and Wells, 240
Clifford, Robert de, 138
Climant, 327
Clive, 134
Close, 47
Closet, 4, 327
Cloudberry, 228
Cloudburst, 92, 225
Clouds, 97
Cloves, 134
Club-moss badge, 228
Clymant, 327
Cobham, 150
Cock, 53, *54*, 162 ; marine, 76 ; snake, *54*
Cockatrice, 70, 328
Cœur, Jacques, 86
Coffee shrub, 125
Cointice, 212, 218
Colleoni, 86
Colquhoun, 228
Columboll, 53
Columbian flag, 304
Columbine, 132
Columbus, Christopher, 143
Comares, 82
Combatant, 328
Combs, 114
Comet, 97
Commonwealth arms, 272
Componée cross, 28
Compony, 331
Concha-Chaves, *104*, 108
Condor, 56
Confrontant, 328
Confronting, 328
Conger eels, 59

Congo flag, 304
Conie, 44
Conjoined, 103
Conjunct, 103
Conti, 96
Contourné, 37, 144, 328
Cooks' Guild, 134
Cooper, 31
Coquerelles, 124
Corbet, 52
Corbie, 51, *52*
Corded cross, *113*
Cordilière, *140*, 211
Corke, 39
Cormorant, 56
Cornflower, 132
Cornish chough, 55, *52*
Cornished cross, 25
Cornucopias, 134, *135*
Cornwall, duchy and county (facing title-page), 139
Cornwall, Richard and Geoffrey de, 139
Coronets, heralds', 313
Coronets, princes', *202*
Corsica, 83
Costa Rican flag, 304
Coté femme, 153
Cotice (cotise), 3, *152*, 328
Cotised, 3 ; cross, 25
Cotton sedge, 229
Cotton trees and slips, 126
Couchant, 36, 44, 328
Couché, 208
Counterchanged, xviii, 328
Counter potent, *xvi*, xxviii
Counter vair, *xvi*, xxvii
Coupé, 5
Couped, 4, 328
Couple-close, 5, 328
Courant, 40, 328
Courtney, 139
Coventry, 132
Cow, dun, badge of Henry VII, 226
Coward, 328
Cowpen, 163
Crab-apple tree, 228
Crampet, 101, 328
Cramponée cross, *17*, 91
Cranberry, 228
Crancellin, 232, 273
Crane, 53
Crehall, 81
Crenelated, 105, 107, 328

Crenelly, 325
Crequier, 124
Crescent, 93, *94*, 147, 328 ; and star, 225
Crespin, 89
Cresset, 329
Crest, 68, 70, 73, *75*, 76, 85, 141, *199*, *213*, *216*, *217*, etc., 329; coronet, 238 ; on livery buttons, 267
Crested, 55 .
Cretan flag, 304
Cri de guerre, 212
Crined, 45, 329
Crocodiles, 63
Cromwell, Nicholas de, 103
Cromwell, Oliver and Richard, 143
Crosen, 278
Crosier (Crozier), 329
Cross, 6, 17, etc. ; cross crosslet, 21, *21*
Crossed keys, 30
Crosswise, 30
Crowns, 231
Croyland Abbey, 117
Crucifix, 17, 31, *185*
Crusily, 29, 329
Crux commissa, decussata, and immissa, 17
Cuban flag, *304*
Cubit arm, 89, 329
Cubitt, 107
Cumin plant, 228
Cumming badge, 228 ; tartan, 268
Cups, *116*
Current, 328
Cyprus, 287

D

Dacre arms, 153 ; badge, 223
Daisie, 130
Daissies, 129
Dalzell, 81 ; of Bins, 249
Dammant, 127
Dancetté (dancetty), 329
Dannebrog cross, 277
Dantzic city, 80
Darcy, 181
Dasilva, 240
Daubeny, 221
Dauphin's arms, 58
D'Aussez, 3

Davidson, 228
Davies, 82
Debased, 9
De Blacas, 97
De Brebier, 122
De Briez, 3
De Brue, 181
Debruised, 2, 153, 329
De Burbentane-Puget, 96
De Castellane, 106
De Chateaubriand, 121, 175
De Chauvelin, 127
De Clermont Tonnerre, 108
Decrescent, 93, 328
Deer, 44, 329
Defamed, 45, 329
Defence, 329
De Ganey, 50
Degraded cross, 25
Degreed cross, 25
Delahay, 92
De la Motte, 122
De Lara, 104
De la Rochefoucauld, 6
De la Tour d'Auvergne, 106
De la Zouche, 150
Delf, 329 ; tenné, 322
Delmenhorst, 277
De Meyronnet, 112
Demi vol, 198
Denmark arms, 277 ; flag, 304
De Pins, 121
Derby borough, 208
De Salis, 125
D'Espaynet, 130
De Vere, 118
De Villeneuve, 11
De Villiers, 12
Dexter, vii, 329
Dextrochére, 324
Deyville, 176
Diane de Poitiers, 93
Diapering, xix. 173, 319
Diepholz, 279
Differencing, 326
Dijon town, 123
Dimidiation, *140*, *182*, 185, *189*, 329
Diminutives, 2
Displayed, 47
Ditmarschen, 277
Divisional lines, *xiv*
Division of shield, *xiii*
Dodo supporters (Mauritius), 287
Dogberry hazel, 228

Dogs, 43
Dolben, 221
Dolphin, 57, *166*, 252
Dominican flag, 304
Dormant, 36, 330
Dorsed, 330
Double parted cross, 24
Douglas, 86
Dove, 53
Dragon, *65*, 67, 68, 330 ; badge, 226 ; crest, *217* ; supporters, *65, 202, 203, 250, 251*
Drake, Sir Francis, 96
Drapers' Guild, 97, 240
Drayton, Michael, 73
Dreux, John de, 138 ; Robert de, 139
Drummond, arms, 81 ; badge, 228
Dublin city, 105
Du Cerceau, 163
Dudley liveries, 265
Duffield, 134
Dukes' coronets, 237
Duncan, Admiral, 145
Dunstable Priory, 101
Dymock, 101

E

Eagles, 47 ; Apostolic, 144 ; Imperial, England, 139 ; Mexican, *308* ; Prussia, *306* ; Russian, *310* ; standard of Napoleon I, *305* ; on crown, 236 ; supporter, *48* ; Roman, *48* ; double headed Hittite, *49*
Earle, 240
Earls' coronets, 237
Eastern crown, *232*
Eberstein, 278
Ecclesiastical flag, 292 ; symbols, 239
Ecuadoran flag, 304
Ecu complet, 143
Edinburgh city, 105
Edmond of Cornwall, King of the Romans, 248
Ednowain ap Bradwen, 63
Edward the Confessor, 144, 271
Edward I, 225 ; II, 225 ; III, 225, 249, 271 ; IV, 226, 249 ; VI, 227, 249
Eels, 62, *104*, 160

Effaré, 43
Effets, 330
Eglesfield, 162
Egyptian standards, 289 ; flag, 305
Eisenberg, 279
Eleanor of Aquitaine, 274
Eleanor of Castile, 274
Electoral cap, 238
Elephant, 42, 247
" Elephant's trunk," 204
Elizabeth of York, 275 ; queen, arms, 272 ; badge, 188 ; supporters, 249, *251*
Elizabeth Widville, 275
Ely, See of, 240
Embattled, *xv*, 105, 107, 330
Embowed, 57, 89, 330
Emerasces, 330
Emblazon, 330
Endorse, 3
Endorsed, 323
Enfant, 85
Enfiled, *201, 202*, 330
Englanté, 121, 330
Engrailed, *xv*, 330
England, badges, 227 ; crowns, 234, *235, 236* ; flags, 291, 294
Engoulé, 9, 29
Enguiché, 113
Enhanced, 9, 330
En pairle, 8, 143
Ensigned, 330
Enté en point, 142
Entrailed cross, 24
Epanoui, 172
Equipollé cross, 28
Equire, 330
Eradicated, 330
Erased, 44, 330
Ermine, *x*, xi, *115, 140, 199* ; cross, 30
Ermines, *xvi*, xvii
Erminetes, xvii
Erminois, xvii
Erne, 50
Escallop shells, 62, *104*, 160
Escarbuncle, *100*
Escutcheon of pretence, 143
Esquire, 330
Este of Modena, 277
Estoille, 118, 330
Estover, 124
Esturmi, 276

Estwire, 123
Eton College, 177
Eucalyptus, 126
Everest, 197
Evreux, 275
Exeter city, 105
Eyes, 86
Eyrant, 330

F

Faisant, 55
Falcon, 163 ; badge of Edward
    III, 225
False inescutcheon, 12
— roundel, 15
Farquharson badge, 228 ; tartan,
    268
Fauntleroy, 85
Favenc, 124
Feather crowns and badges, 231 ;
    badge of Scottish chiefs, 230
Fer de moline, 100, 331
Ferguson badge, 228
Ferrara, Duchy of, 277
Fess, 4, 154, 331 ; river in fess,
    debased, 100
Fetterlock, 103
Feudal arms, 139, 141
Field, xii
Fig-trees and leaves, 124
Figuerra, 124
Fiji, 284
File, 331
Fillet, 3, 331
Fimbriated, 29, 295, 331
Findelstein, 60
Fir, Scotch, 228
Fish baskets, 117
Fitchy, 331 ; crosses, 19, 27
Fitz Ercald, 44
Fitz, Hugh, 6, 276
Fitzroy, Duke of Richmond, 71,
    153, 188
Fitzroy, Duke of Monmouth, 153
Fitzwalter, 6
Fitzwilliam, 189
Flames, 15
Flanders, 271
Flasques, 13, 331
Flaunches, 13, 331
Fleece, 41
Fleuri, 125

Fleurs-de-lis, 147, 165, 166, 168,
    174, 176, etc. ; cross, 18 ;
    Florentine, 172, 170 ; Lille,
    169, 172
Flighted arrows, 102
Floretty, 331
Florio, 130
Flory, 12, 321 ; cross, 18
Flowered, 125
Foi, 89
Foljambe, 164
Foot, winged, 90
Forbes, badge, 228
Forcené, 43
Forest, 121
Formée, cross, 19, 165
Fortune, 81
Foul anchor, 110
Foulis, 125
Fountain, 14, 331
Fourchée (tail), 37 ; cross, 25
Fourchette cross, 25
Foxes, 40, 41
Foxglove, 228
France, arms : ancient, 141, 166 ;
    modern, 140, 141 ; flags, 305 ;
    supporters, 252
Fraser, 161, 181, 228
Frases, 161
Fret, 11, 243
Fretty, 11, 331
Fructed, 120, 331
Furriers' Guild, 115
Furs, x
Fusil, 13, 14, 331
Fusily, 14, 331
Fylfot, 91, 331

G

Gad, 72, 331
Gamb, 38, 331
Garb, 126, 331
Garden lilies, 135
Garter, 3
Gates, 162
Gaveston, Pierre de, 171
Gellibrand, 101
Gemsbok, 44, 286
George I, 273
German eagles, 144, 306 ; flags,
    306
Gibraltar, 107, 282
Giglio, 172
Gilliflower, 134
Gimmel-ring, 331

Girl, 44
Gladstone, 83
Glasgow city, *59*
Glendening, 29
Gliding, 62

Goats, *115*
Gobony, 331 ; cross, 28
Gonfanon, 105
Goldman, 130
Goldsmiths' Guild, *116*
Golpes, 14, 331
Goodall, 240
Gordon badge, 228 ; tartan, 268
Gore, 331 ; sinister tenné, 322
Gorge, 10
Gorged, *45*, 67, 332
Gorse, 228
Gothland, 277
Goutes, 118, 332
Gouty, 332
Graded, 18
Gradiant, 45
Graham badge, 228

Graminy, wreath of, 240
Granada, 122, 271
Grand quarter, 142
Grant arms, 208 ; badge, 228 ;
    Duke of Seafield, 240 ; Sir
    Alexander's supporters, 257

Grasshopper, 63
Gray, 44
Greece, flag, 306
Greek cross, 17
Green, 276
Gresham, Sir Thomas, 63
Greves, 124

Greyhound, silver badge, 226 ;
    supporters, 213, *250*, 251 ; of
    Earls of Panmure, 257

Grey, 332
Grice, 42, 332
Griffin, 67, 68, *69*, 332
Griffith, Prince of Cardigan, 39
Grimsditch, 82
Gringollée cross, 26
Grocers' Guild, 134
Gryphon, 332
Guardant, 332
Guatemala flag, 367
Guige, 208, *319*
Guilbert, 222
Guildford town, 106
Guivrée cross, 26

Gules, xv
Gunn badge, 228
Gunstone, 14, 332
Gurge, 10, 14, 332
Gusset, 322, 332
Guyenne, 276
Gyron, 10
Gyronny, 332

H

Habited, 89, 332
Hachement, 209
Halberstads, 278
Hales, 102
Halifax, 80
Hames, 103, 164, 332
Hamilton, 66
Hands, 87
Hanover arms, 273 ; cockade,
    261
Hansarde, 96
Harcourt-Deke, 140
Hares, 44
Harp, 191, *192*, *195*, *197*, 227
Harpendene, 119
Harpfield, 197
Harpman, 197
Harpy, 67, 70, 332
Hart, 44, 332 ; white, badge of
    Richard II, 225, 226
Hastings arms, 113 ; liveries, 265
Hatchment, 332
Hatte, 38
Hauriant, 57, 333
Hawk, 50
Hawk-headed Horus, 69, *94*
Hawke, Lord, 145
Hawthorn, 125, 228 ; bush, 226
Hays, 12
Haytian flag, 307
Hazel nuts, 124
Hazelrigg, 124
Heads, 83, *90*
Heame, 332
Hearts, 86, *186*
Heater shield, 206
Heath, bell and common, 128,
    228 ; Menzies', 229 ; five-
    leaved, 229
Heathcote supporters, 257
Hedgehog, 44
Heights, 199
Heliotrope, 129

Helmets, 102, *213*, 216, 217, *221* ; of gentleman, *225* ; knight, *224* ; peer, *224* ; sovereign, *223*
Heneage knot, 223
Henneberg, 279
Henrietta Maria of France, 277
Henry II,, arms, 270 ; III, 225 ; IV, arms, 271 ; badge, 225 ; supporters, 249 ; V, 225, 249 ; VI, 226, 249 ; VII, 226, 249 ; VIII, 227, 249
Heralds, instituted, xii ; visitations, xii
Herrings, 61
Herrison, 44
Herse, 107, 333
Hertford, Marquis of, supporters, 258
Hilted, 101
Hind, 44, 333 ; white, badge, 225
Hippopotamus, 42
Hirato mons, *131*
Holbeame, 6
Hopwell, 44
Hohenstein, 278
Hohenzollern, 278
Hoja, 278
Holland, 274
Holland, flag, 308
Holly, 125, 228
Holstein, 277
Holworth, 241
Holy Roman Empire, 274
Homburg, 278
Honduras flag, 307
Honourable ordinaries. *See* Ordinaries
Hood, Viscounts, *243*
Hoofed, 45, 333
Hope supporters, 258
Horse, 43 ; supporters, 257 ; winged, 73
Horns, 109, 203
Houpes, 239
Housings, 327
Howard arms, 276 ; badge, 39 ; liveries, 264
Hudson Bay Company, 42
Huddersfield city, 126
Hughe, 222
Humetté (Humetty), 29, 333
Hungary, arms, 275 ; crown, *234*
Hungerford, 112
Huntingdon, 78

Hunting horns, 112
Hurst, 333
Hurts, 14, 120, 333
Hydra, 68
Hythe town, 110

I

Iceland, 62
Icicle, 118
Illegitimacy, marks of, 153
Impaled, 333
Impaling, 140, 271, 273
In bend, 3
Incensed, 333
Increscent, 93, 328
In cross, 30
Indented, vii, 333
India, badge, 227 ; flag, 298
Indorsed, 3
Inescutcheon, 11 ; reversed, 322
Infant, 85
In pale, 7
In point, 6
Insignia, 333
" In true love," 125
Invected, *xv*, 333
Ireland, arms, 272 ; badge, 227
Iron Cross of Valour, 144
Ironmongers' Guild, 72
Irvine, 125
Isabel of Angoulême, 274
Isabel of France, 275
Islands, 112
Isles, See of, 79
Islip, 164
Issuant, 333
Italy, arms, 307 ; flag, 307
Ivy, 128, 232 ; rock (badge), 228

J

Jambs, 38, 333
Jamaica, 287
James I, arms, 272 ; supporters, 256
Jane Seymour, 276
Janer, 85
Japanese dragons, 65 ; family badges, 15, *131*, *133* ; heraldry, 130, 132 ; flags, 307 ; lion, 71 ; unicorn, 71
Jay, 85
Jelloped, 55
Jerusalem, xiii, 275 ; cross, 20, *29*

Jessant-de-lis, 39, *40*, 172, 333
Jessed, 50
Joan of Navarre, 275
John Lackland, Count of Montaigne, 270
John, King, 225
John of Gaunt, *246*
John the Bastard of Orleans, 4
Johnson badge, 228
Jollie, 134
Jordan, 124
Juliet, 276
Juniper, 228, 229

K

Kangaroo, 227
Katherine of France, 275
Kempenfelt, Admiral, 82
Kendrig, 84
Kensington borough, 240
Keys, *104*, 107 ; in cross, 30
Kiku-mon, Japanese Imperial device, 130, *131*
Kings of Cologne, 82
King's Lynn, 59
Kiri-mon, *131*, 132
Klettenberg, 278
Kingston-on-Thames, 61
Knots, 118, 211, 222
Konigsteîn, 4

L

Labarum, 289
Label, 137, 138, 147, 155, 333 ; of British Royal Family, 280
Lacy lion, 39 ; knot, 223
Lagrené, 5
Lake, Baron, 145
Lambeaux, 333 ; cross. 26
Lambrequins, 208, 333
Lamont badge, 228
Lancastrian ~badges, 225 ; rose, 182
Lances, 101
Landsberg, 279
Landscape shields, 111
Langued, 333
La Poer, 31
Lathom, 247
Latimer, 176
Latin cross, 17
Lauenberg, 279

Laurel, 125, 231 ; spurge, 228
Lauterberg, 278
Leaved and slipped, 181
Leeds city, *41*
Leek badge, 227
Leeson, 97
Legion of Honour, cross of the, 144
Legs, 89, 91
Leicester borough, 180
Leipold, 41
Lenden, 240
Leon, 271
Leopard, 39 ; face, 39,
Leslie-Melville, 128
Les Lilas, 129
Leven, 128
Leveson, 126
Leverers, 44
Levincz, 123
Liberian flag, 307
Lichfield, 79
Liedlow, 108
Lilac, *129*
Lilies, 135
Limburg, 275
Linlithgow, Marquis of, supporters, 258
Lioncels, 39
Lions, 35, 318 ; fish, *61* ; of England, 270 ; of St. Mark, 164
Liveries, origin of, 263
Liverpool city, 56
Livingston, 122, 134
Llama, 135
Lloyd of Plymog, 84
Lodged, 45
Logan badge, 228
Lombardy, iron crown of, 233
London, City, 65 ; See, 102
Long cross raguly and trunked, 23
Longespée, William, 137
Lorne, Lordship of, 109
Lorraine, 50, 275 ; cross, 21
Lotus, 166, 177, 227
Lozenge, 13
Lozengy, 14, 333
Lucies, 160
Lucy, 334
Luneberg, 273
Lupus, 123
Lure, 51, 334
Luther, Martin, *186*
Lutterell, 42
Luxemburg, 275

Lylde, Bishop of Ely, 82
Lymphad, 108, *109*, 334
Lynx, 40
Lyon Office of Scotland, 314
Lyre, *51*, 118
Lys, brothers of Joañ of Arc, 175

M

MacAllister badge, 228 ; tartan, 268
MacAlpine badge, 228
MacArthur badge, 228
MacAulay badge, 228
MacBean badge, 228
MacBride, MacKenzie, on Scottish clan badges, 229
MacCall badge, 228
MacDonald badge, 228 ; tartan, 268
MacDougal badge, 228
MacDuff badge, 228
MacFarlane badge, 228
MacFie badge, 228
MacGillivray badge, 228
MacGregor arms, 121 ; badge, 228 ; tartan, 269
MacInnes badge, 228
MacIntosh badge, 228
MacIntyre badge, 229
MacIver badge, 229
MacKae badge, 229
MacKenzie badge, 229
Mackerel, 160
MacKinnon badge, 229
MacLachlan badge, 229
MacLaren badge, 229
MacLean badge, 229 ; tartan, 268
MacLeman badge, 229
MacLeod badge, 229 ; tartan, 269
MacMillan badge, 229 ; tartan, 269
MacNab badge, 229
MacNaughton badge, 229
MacNeil badge, 229
MacPherson badge, 229 ; tartan, 269
MacQuarrie badge, 229
MacQueen badge, 229
MacWilliam arms, 276
Madeston, 85
Madgeburg, 277
Madonna lily, 167, 177
Magdalen College, 177
Magi, 82

Maitland, 37
Malay States flag, 305
Malherbe, 128
Mallerby, 128
Malmaine, 88
Mal ordonée, 173
Malta, 282
Maltese cross, 20, *21*
Man, 81 ; naked, chained beneath shield, 257
Man, Bishop Henry, 85
Man, Isle of, 90
Manched, 89
Manitoba, *285*
Manners, Earls and Dukes of Rutland, 145
Mansard, 107
Mantelé, xiii
Manticora, 74
Mantling, 208, 334
Maple leaves, 126, *142*, 227, 229
Marck, 276
Margaret of Anjou, 275 ; supporters, 251
Margaret of France, 274
Margeurie, 130
Marigold, 129
Marine cock, 76
Marined, 74, 332
Markham, 163
Marlborough, Duke of, 145
Marlborough town, 43
Marmion, 249, 276
Marquises' coronets, 237
Mars, 80
Marshall, 241
Martlet, 52, 147, 334
Mary, Queen of England, 81, *182*, 188, 249, 271 ; of Este, 277 ; of Teck, 279
Mascle, 14, 334
Masculy, 334
Masculy-pometty cross, 24
Masculyn, 85
Masoned, 106, 334
Matilda of Boulogne, 274
Matilda of Flanders, 274
Matilda of Scotland, 274
Mauleverer, 44
Maunch, 113, 334
Mauritius, 107, 287
Mayere, 112
Maynard, 88
Meaux, 240
Mecklenburg, 278

Medici, 15, *141*, 175
Meissen, 279
Melosine, 75
Membered, 55
Menzies badge, 229 ; tartan, 269
Mercers' Guild, 84
Merchants' marks, *99*, 207
Mermaid, 74, *75*, *243*
Mermen, 74
Metals, xv
Mexican flag, 307
Midas's head, 85
Middleton, 117
Milan, 62
Milford, 121
Millrine cross, 25
Millrines, 100, 334
Mimosa, 227
Minden, 278
Mirrors, 62, 114
Mirtle, 124
Mitres, 238, 240
Moeles, 118
Mohun, 113
Moline cross, *25*, *29*, 147
Molyneux, 100
Monaco, 305
Monad, Eastern, *14*
" Monstreu," 68
Montenegro flag, 308
Moons, 92, *94*
Moors' heads, 83
More, 53
Morians, 124
Moroccan flag, 308
Morpeth, 105
Mortimer arms, 275 ; crest, 199
Motto, 212 ; Royal British, 280
Mound, 334
Mount, 334
Mount Stephen, Baron, 126
Mountain ash, 229
Mountains, 111
Mountbourchier, 104
Moussue cross, 24
Mowbray arms, 145 ; badge, 124
Mulberries, 124
Mulgrave, 127
Müller, Baron, 126
Mullet, 15, 118, 147, 149, 334
Mundham, Adam de, 99
Munro badge, 229
Mural crown, 278, 334
Murrey, xvii
Murray badge, 229

Murray mark of bastardy, 4
Murray of Ochtertyre, 30
Musicians' Guild, *51*
Myerton, 241
Myrtle, bog, 228 ; wreaths, 232

N

Naiant, 57
Nairnes, 189
Naissant, 334
Naples, 275
Napoleon's crown, *236* ; eagle, *305*
Nascent, 334
Nassau, 272
Natal, 286
Naval crown, *238*, 240
Nebuly, *xiv*, 334
Negri-Sembilan flag, 305
Nelson, 145
Neptune, *56*, 80
Netherlands, flag, 308
Nettles, 128
Neuburg, 2
Neuilly-sur-Seine, 127
Nevil arms, 33, 149
New Brunswick, *285*
Newcastle borough, 105
Newport, 5
New South Wales arms, 283 ;
    flag, 297
Newton, 31, 84
New Zealand, 96, 284
Nicaraguan flag, 308
Nice city, 112
Norway arms, 277 ; flag, 308
Nova Scotia, *285*
Nowed, 37, 51, 62, 63, 334
Nowy cross, 22
Nurnburg, 278

O

Oaks, 121 ; badge, 228, 229 ;
    wreaths, 232
Oars, 111
Ogilvie badge, 229
Ogress, *14*, 334
Oke, 121
O'Kelly, 149
Oldenburg, 277
Oldham, 164
Oliphant badge, 229
Olive branches, 122, 232

Olivier arms, 122
Ondoyant, 62
O'Neil, 87, 193
Ontario, 284, *285*
Opinicus, 335
Oppressed, 335
Or, xv
Orange, xvii
Orange River Colony, 287
Oranges, 14, 122
Orb, 335
Ordinaries, 1 ; sub-ordinaries, 10
Oriflamme, 290, 305
Orle, 12, 240, 335
Osier wands, 125
Ostrich, 52, 200 ; feathers, 199
    201, 202, 203, 225, *246*
Oswald, 81
Otter, 42
Overall, 335
Owain, Sir James ap, 222
Owen, 125
Owls, *41*
Oxen, 41
Oxenbridge, 164
Oxney, 164

P

Pahang flag, 305
Pairle, 8, *37*, 335
Pale, 3, 335
Palet, 3
Pall, 13, 33, 335
Palisade crown, *233*
Palms, 121, 232
Paly, *7*, 335
Panache, 198, 215, 335
Panama flag, 309
Pandal cross, 25
Panmure, Earls of, supporters, 257
Pansy, 86
Panther, 226
Paraguayan flag, 309
Paris, City, 110, 176 ; University,
    92
Parks, 112
Parr, Catherine, badge, *187*
Parsley, 232
Parrots, 55
Parted and fretted cross, 114
Partridge, 55
Party per, 8
Paschal lamb, 42

Pasquier, 130
Passant, 35, *36*, 335 ; guardant,
    35, *36* ; regardant, 35, *36*
Passion cross, 17
Pastoral staff, 114
Patée cross, 17, *19* ; fleury, *19* ;
    concave, *19* ; invected, *19* ;
    fitchy at each point, *19*
Patonce cross, *18* ; acorned, *26*
Patriarchal cross, 21
Patyn (Waynflete), 177
Paulet livery, 265
Pawne, 161
Peaches, 163
Peacock, 52, 55, *56*, 161 ; feathers,
    x, 200, 210
Pean, *xvi,* xvii
Pears, 123, 161
Peché, Sir John, 164
Pegasus, 73, 335
Pelham buckles, 103
Pelican, 53
Pellen, 240
Pellets, 14, 335
Penché, 208
Pendragon, 66
Penn, 15
Pens, 163
Pentney Priory, 117
Pep, John, 114
Perak flag, 305
Per cross, 7
Percy badge, *39* ; liveries, 265
Periton, 123, 161
Pershore Abbey, 63
Persian flag, 309
Peru arms, *135* ; flag, 309
Peverel garb, 224
Pfuhl, 97
Pheon, 102, 335
Philippa of Hainault, 116, 274
Phœnix, 72, 335
Pied nourri, 173
Pierced, 8
Pignatelli, 104
Pigs, 42, 246
Pike, 61
Pile, 6
Pillars of Hercules, 249
Pineapple, 124
Pines, 120
Pinks, 134
Pipe, 162
Pisan cross, 24
Plantagenet badge, 128

Plates, 14, 335
Pleissen, 279
Point dexter tenné, 322
Pointed cross, 22
Point in point, 322
Points of the shield, *vii*
Poitou, 139
Pomegranate, 122, 227
Pomeis, 14, 335
Pomel cross, 22
Pomey, 335
Pommern, 278
Pommes, 14
Pont, 97
Popinjay, 55
Porcini, 246
Porhoet, Comte de, *200*
Port, 105
Portant cross, 23
Portcullis, 105, 107
Portrate cross, 34
Portugal arms, 277 ; flag, 309
Potatoes, 127
Potent cross, 20 ; quadrate, 20 ; *21* ; double fitchy and rebated, *21* ; fleurs-de-lis, *21*
Pount, 106
Powdered, 335
Powdering, 152, 210
Powney, 150
Primrose, 130
Prince Edward's Island, *285*
Prince of Wales' arms and badges, 199
Proper, 135, 336
Proude, 42
Prussia, arms, 277 ; eagle, 248
Pryce, 101
Purefoy, 89
Purpure, xi
Pyne, 121

Q

Quadrate cross, 22
Quarter, 7, 336
Quartered, 336
Quartering, *141, 142*, etc.
Quarterly pierced, 8
Quatrefoil, 180, 336 ; double, 145
Quebec, 284, *285*
Queens, 8⊖ ; heads, 84
Queensland arms, 283 ; flag, 297
Queue fourché, 336

Queued, 336
Quilled, 56
Quills, 163
Quintefoil, *see* Cinquefoils

R

Rabbit, 44
Rabot, 97
Radiated crown, *232*
Raguly, 336 ; cross, 23 ; cross tau raguly, *34*
Ramridge, Abbot of St. Albans, 161, 163
Rain, 97
Rainbows, 97
Rampant, 35, *36*, 336 ; guardant, 35, *36* ; regardant, 35, *36* ; combatant, 36 ; adossé, 37
Ratzeburg, 278
Raven, 82
Ravensberg, 279
Ravisant, 40
Rayonnant, 91 ; cross, *30*
Reading, 84, 90
Rebatement, 322
Rebus, 164
Recercelée cross, 20, 336
Reflexed, 336
Regalien, 278
Regardant, 35, 336
Regenstein, 279
Reinach, 38
Respectant, 336
Respecting, 45
Rest, 118, 336
Reversed shield, 322
Rhinoceros, 42
Rhodesia, *286*
Ribbon, 3
Ribs, 86
Richard I, 225, 270 ; II, 225, 246, 249, 271 ; III, 249
Rising, 56
Roaches, 160
Robe of estate, 210
Robertson badge, 229 ; supporters, 257
Rochead, 84
Rochfort, 276
Rodes, 248
Rogers, 240
Roman eagles, 47, *48* ; standards, 289 ; symbols, vii
Rompu, 8 ; en pointe, 5

Throgmorton, 2
Throughout, 337
Thunderbolt, 98 ; cross, 25
Thuringia, 279
Tiara, 239
Tierced, 7, 338
Tigers, 40
Tilers' nails, 162
Timbré, 214
Tinctures, xii, xv ; variations of, 148, 152
Tokugawa Shoguns' mon, *131*
Tomyris, 98
Torse, 218
Torteaux, 14, 338
Totness town, 107
Toulouse cross, 24
Tourney arms, 6
Towers, 105
Trade symbols, 113
Tramail, 89
Transposed, 6, 338
Transvaal, 287
Trees, 120
Trefoil, 126, 338
Treille, 11
Trenowith, 2
Tressure, 12, 338
Tricolour cockade, 260 ; flag of France, 305
Tricorpate lion, 37
Triparted symbols, 167 ; cross, 24
Trippant, 44
Tritons, 56, 74, *243*
Tron ornée cross, 23
Trout, 61
Troutbeck, 61
Trusbuts, 104, 161
Trussed, 56
Tubal Cains, 254
Tudman, 190
Tudor, Owen and Jasper, 140
Tudor dragons, 67, 202 ; roses, 181, *182*, *187*, 188, 227, *250*
Tunisian flag, 311
Tuns, 99, *117*, 125
Turbots, 160
Turkey, flags, 311
Turks' heads, 83
Turnip, 127
Tusked, 45
Twitchers, 103
Tyler, Bishop of Llandaff, 162
Tyrol arms, 271
Tyne, 44

U

Ulster Office of Arms, 314
Umfreville, Earls of Angus, 180
Undy, xiv, 338
Unguled, 45, 333
Unicorn, 67, 70, 250, 338
Union Jack, 29, 145, *295*, *296* ; badge, 227
United States of America, arms, 97 ; flags, 300, *301*
Urdée cross, 22, 23
Urinant, 57, 338
Urquhart badge, 229
Ursins, des, 275
Urso d'Abitot badge, 40

V

Vair, xvi, xvii ; cross, 24
Vairy cuppy, xviii
Vallary crown, *232*
Vambraced, 89, 338
Vandalia, 277
Vane, 102
Vanhatton, 122
Van Noort, Admiral, 211
Vans, 117
Varvels (vervels), 338
Varvelled, 50
Vaughan, 85
Vault, 122
Venetian lion, 39
Venezuelan flag, 311
Verdured, 126, 338
Verdoyed, 126, 338
Vermandois, 139
Vert, xi
Vexillum, 289
Victoria State arms, 97, 283 ; flag, 297
Victoria, Queen, 273
Vidames' coronets, 237
Vincent, 180
Vines, 232, *123*
Vipont, Robert de, 138
Virgin Mary, 84
Viseleben, 6
Viscounts' coronets, 237
Visigoths, crowns of the, 233
Visor, 338
Voided, 338 ; cross, *28*
Voiders, 13, 338
Voiding, 7
Volant, 47

Vorant, 40, 338
Vulcan, 80
Vulned, 45, 339
Vulture, 162 ; Egyptian, 50

W

Wake knot, 223
Walbert, 128
Walden, 123
Wales, arms, 272 ; badges, 227 ; arms of the princes, 39 ; Prince's crown, 236
Wallflower, 229
Walsingham, 113
War cry, 212
Warden, 161
Warnchampe, 82
Warren, 276
Warriors, 82
Warwick bear and ragged staff, 40
Warwick, the Countess of, 137
Water-bowgets, 104, 161
Waterford, See of, 31
Water symbols, 5, 10, 14, 75, 98, 100, 115
Wattle badge, 227
Waves of sea badge, 227
Waynflete, William, 177
Weavers' Guild, 115
Wellington, Duke of, 145
Weimar, 279
Wenden, 278
Western Australia, arms, 283 ; flag, 297
Westphalia, 273
Whale, 58
Whalley Abbey, 59
Wheathampstead, 127, 164
Wheatsheaves, 127
Whips, 118
Whirlpool, 332
White cockade : Bourbon, 259, 260 ; Jacobite, 261

Whortleberry, 228
Widville, 275
Wild boar. *See* Boar.
Wild men as supporters, 244
William I, 270
William and Mary, 272
Williams, 31, 125
Willoughby arms, 85, 100 ; de Eresby supporters, 257
Willows, 125
Winchester College, 177 ; city, 105
Winged foot, 90 ; hands, 87, 88 ; solar disc, 91 ; spurs, 102, 103
Winnowing baskets, 117
Without number, 173
Wolf's head, 45
Wolves, 40, 162
Women's heads, 84
Wood of Balbigno, 108
Woolpacks, 114
Worthing town, 135
Worthington, 240
Worcester town, 123
Wounds, 14
Wreath, 134, 212, 218, 219, 231, 339
Wreathed, 339
Wrede, Counts of, 240
Wyvern, 68, 339

Y

Yale, 71
Yarmouth borough, 61, 62
Yate, 162
Yeates, 162
Yew, 228
York rose, 182
Yorkist badges, 226

Z

Zouche, 150